P  *share* **CH**

"I fell in love with the characters in *The Timeshare* and was immediately hooked. I laughed with them, cried with them and found myself celebrating victories with them. If you're looking for a compelling story of family and healing that reminds us that all of our inner selves deserve to be loved and celebrated, this is a great book for you. Once you start reading, you won't want to put it down."

—Mim Chapman, PhD, author, coach and polyamory mentor

"*The Timeshare* was a revelation for me. Through it, I have come to better understand my spouse–learning that she was coping with trauma that I had not been aware existed. It was healing to understand that I could trigger her desperation but not necessarily be the root cause. *The Timeshare* helped me better understand that I'm not alone in dealing with these issues and experiences, and it filled me with compassion by seeing things through her eyes. The book is wonderfully enlightening and a fun thriller to read!"

—Rick M

"*The Timeshare* is a powerfully written page turner. You will find yourself lost in the rich and delicious story and in the wonderful depth of each character. As a licensed counselor who has been working with clients for 40 years, I have never read a book that so beautifully demystifies what D.I.D. is and brings a wellspring of insight and understanding. *The Timeshare* is a testament to the strength, deter- mination and resilience of the human spirit. You will find yourself laughing, crying and gasping throughout the story. It has instantly become one of my favorites—a book that I believe will revolutionize the way people perceive and understand the warriors of spirit that many have misunderstood. I give this treasure my highest recommendation."

—Brad Simkins, MA

"*The Timeshare* is an important book that humanizes and compassionately deals with common issues that are rarely discussed. By removing the stigma around mental illness, diversity in human sexuality and relationship orientation, the author helps us all confront and even heal from the belief that different is wrong. This is a timely book for people living with differences as well as their partners and caregivers. *The Timeshare* will also be interesting and eye-opening for anyone who wants a deeper understanding of the multiple ways that the mind and love can be expressed."

—Jessica Fern Cooley, MS

THE
TIMESHARE

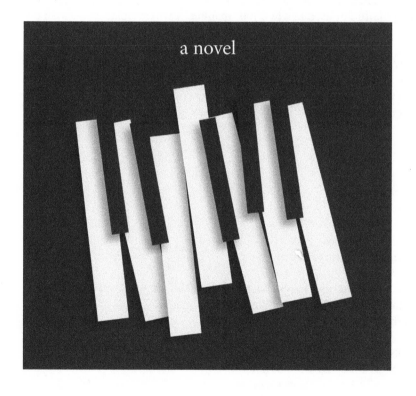

a novel

ARI SHAFFER

The Timeshare
by Ari Shaffer

Published by

Woman in the Moon Productions

aricialafrance@gmail.com

Cover and Interior Design: Nick Zelinger, NZGraphics.com
Editors: Barbara Munson, munsonbarb@aol.com
Author photo: Misha McGinley

ISBN: 978-1-7326702-0-4 (print)
ISBN: 978-1-7326702-2-8 (eBook)
ISBN: 978-1-7326702-1-1 (audio)
Library of Congress Control Number: 2018909451

First Edition

Printed in the United States of America

Note from the Author

As a therapist, I'm consistently impressed with the character of people living with diversity on the mental health and sexuality spectrums. Invariably, those I've met tend to be braver and more tenacious than anyone understands—and perhaps fully appreciates.

I'm equally impressed with partners, children, friends, and family who provide support as their loved ones work towards maximizing their gifts, fighting stigma and living true to themselves.

I've had deep and honest discussions with countless people on the spectrums and their partners to learn about their feelings, their reactions, and their struggles. As they've read through chapters from this book, they've told me it was like reading their own story—they felt heard and understood.

My hope for readers of this book is that it will encourage people on the spectrums to feel seen and respected, support partners in feeling appreciated, and reach the general public as they seek to understand. I hope as well that empathy, peace of mind, and answers will meet you as you read.

Please know that I tried to present a candid story of dissociative identity disorder and related issues, and that some of the information may be triggering to individuals, so keep yourself safe and reach out as needed.

Finally, for all, be proud of what you have survived, recognize your strength and resilience, and know that my wish for you is to find hope for what is yet to come.

To the Muse —
You are the reason so many creations that otherwise
would have remained dormant are blooming into life.
You inspire us and provide an example and attitude to aspire to.
Never doubt that the world is a better place because you are in it.
Thank you. – Ari

Character Map:

Steve - Sophie's husband
Kevin - Steve's friend from high school
David and Rebecca - Steve's siblings

Sophie - Steve's wife, diagnosed with multiple personalities
Todd and Becky - Sophie's biological parents
Liz and Laura - Sophie's friends from college
Chuck - Liz's husband
Carla - Laura's partner

Music can enhance our experiences. If you'd like to listen
to the songs that inspired me as I wrote,
please visit *www.booksbyari.com*

Hi, I'm Jamie. I'm kinda best friends of the kids. I love to cook. I'm kind of a guardian of the kids, so I can get directive. I wear a black tank and bandana usually - oh, and an earring sometimes too.

I'm Richard. Protector. I study Krav Maga. From NYC. I smoke. Sorry ahead of time for any bar fights.

Hello I'm Ellya. I do a lot of activist work. I have softer blue eyes and need glasses. I'm usually studying something. I love tea and I enjoy debating. I'm 21.

ELIZABETH. I'M 12 and keep the house tidy.

Seki - I'm 19 and do all the artwork you see around the house. I do modeling for work. You'll be seeing a lot of me.

Anna - I also do a lot of work at the agency. Love you.

Chelsea - I'm kind of like Anna but the junior edition. Hi! ♡

haha not much to know. I'm vegan though.

April 5, 2016

Once again, my workday has darted past me too quickly. As afternoon tips into evening, I feel an unsettling mix of curiosity and dread fighting for my attention. I find myself staring at the simply framed photos of me and my wife Sophie on my desk: sitting on a California beach smiling, enjoying a snow day at our cabin in the Colorado mountains, a summer fishing trip to Minnesota. They capture a different time.

The April sun fools me into believing it's earlier than it really is, but the buzz of my co-workers as they wrap things up to head home for their weekends tells me it's late. The noise crescendos and falls off as people leave. Suddenly, the ticking of my wall clock is audible.

As a Senior Curriculum Developer, I appreciate that my work is fairly predictable, compared to my personal life anyway. I used to try to get a handle on my home life—to anticipate, to plan. But at some point, you have to relinquish control, leave, or lose your mind.

Six o'clock and I'm alone. I shuffle a few papers, but finally concede that I have to leave my orderly and certain haven. I start down the hall and catch my reflection in a glass door. That's not me, I think, and am briefly startled. In college, I had been an athlete and loved running, playing handball, and doing anything physical, but a knee injury had sidelined me. It's long healed now, but I'm out of the habit and it shows.

My Scandinavian heritage is still apparent in my wavy blonde hair, which is just starting to recede and is cut shorter than I like. My entire family has ice blue eyes, but mine are more gray. People say it softens my appearance—makes me easy to talk to. I had hoped to hit 6' as my older brother David had. At 5'8", I was always going to be the little brother and David loved to rub that in. I wanted to age like Brad Pitt, but even at 38, I was starting to look more like my father. Not a bad-looking guy, but pretty generic. I could see the lines starting to show on my face and the weight was gradually creeping up.

As I often do, I take my time getting home, imagining a romantic evening with my wife. I'd love to cook dinner together tonight, research vacation spots over drinks and enjoy a relaxed weekend.

Then I chastise myself. I know not to do this. In our situation, we don't get to decide how we'll spend our time and we don't count on keeping any plans.

I hear our therapist Dr. Newman's voice in my head. "Stay in the moment. Expectations mean disappointment. Focus on the good stuff."

On the way home, I wash the car and run a few errands that I don't need to do. I pull into the driveway and sit there in my Land Rover for a bit. I bought this thing for road trips that Sophie and I both pretended would happen. There are a million things to see in Colorado, but Sophie feels safer at home.

I turn up the music until it crowds out my thoughts, closing my eyes and promising myself I'll go in as soon as this song ends. But I sit through another and then one more. I take a deep breath and try to relax, but the muscles across my shoulders have turned to knots. Neighbors are pulling into their driveways. They know what to expect when they open their front doors and I envy them. Tonight, they'll go out for a movie or find some live music somewhere. Tomorrow, they'll BBQ with their family, see a play, or hit the slopes for some spring skiing. Their time is their own.

My weekend will be dictated by my wife's condition. It's what fills our calendar and every second of free time. My wife has Dissociative Identity Disorder (DID).

The way this disorder translates into my weekend reality is that, tonight, I may be comforting a distressed 6 year old named Rachel, having an intense discussion with a brilliant activist personality named

Ellyn, or baking pies with Jamie, the companion and guardian angel of the child alters. These are just some of the others sharing my wife's body. Trauma at a young age had brought on DID and shattered her personality.

Bracing myself, I turn my key and open the front door. My senses suddenly sharpen—an instinctual response of self-preservation. If I can anticipate who's home, the night will go more smoothly. I don't hear the TV, so Sophie isn't running the show. I don't smell dinner cooking, so Jamie isn't out. No toys, no Rachel.

As I walk up the steps to the living room, a familiar cologne begins to envelop me. It smells expensive. I catch tones of leather and dark, spicy saffron and hope the seductive alter Anna is around. Then I smell a hint of cigarette smoke hanging in the air. It's not Anna. This is either Seb or Richard.

My hopes for a romantic evening dissolve. My arms suddenly feel heavy and the couch looks inviting. I hang my jacket on the back of a dining room chair, kick off my shoes and flop down, hoping whoever is out just wants to watch a movie and eat pizza. I'm disappointed, but I learned a long time ago that rolling with this thing made it less painful for both of us.

I flip the TV on and take a deep breath, finally recognizing the cologne as Seb's. Though the scent is comforting and seductive, I feel defensive at the thought of seeing him. Seb had really hurt me, and even though we've worked it out, the bad memories associated with that 19-year-old personality still make me flinch.

I consciously work to relax, forcing myself to shift my thoughts. Look for the positive. I'm grateful the child alters aren't out. I don't have the energy for them tonight. And Richard is so intense, I'm glad I won't have to spar with him. Chelsea's not here right now, so I don't need to be on high alert.

"Breathe," I tell myself.

My beautiful wife of eight years suddenly appears at the top of the steps. She's wearing a black t-shirt and black skinny jeans. The stylish silver belt buckle, too big for her delicate frame, makes her look more boyish than the young man she believes herself to be at this moment. A ratty gray scarf throws off an otherwise polished look.

Her face appears more square when Seb's out. She stands taller with her chest out and wears a confident, easy smile. She's expansive, using more of the space around her. Her long, dark chocolate hair has been swept into a knot. A charm of St Christopher hangs around her neck and the watch she's wearing is Seb's, but it seems to have become a sort of security blanket for her entire system of alter personalities.

Adapting my expectations for the evening, I manage a smile. "Hey, Seb. What's up?"

Sebi smiles back approvingly. After all these years, he still gets a kick out of it when I recognize him.

"What's the plan for tonight?" I ask. "I'm wiped. Mind staying in? I can order pizza."

Seb painlessly clips down the steps and as he blows past me, he says, "We can stay in. I need to go through the shelves and label my stuff for that sale at the art center anyway. It's coming up fast! But no pizza. I knew you'd be tired so I ordered stuff from The Grill." Motioning to the shed, he asks, "Wanna help or do you need a nap, old man?"

"I'll be out in a minute," I say, promptly falling asleep on the couch. Twenty minutes later, a loud commercial wakes me. Seb is busy in the shed and I feel like I've got my second wind. Switching off the TV, I change into jeans and my Stanford sweatshirt.

"Hey, do you need coffee?" I ask Seb, poking my head out the back door.

"That'd be great. Thanks," drifts back.

I snag myself a beer and make a latte for him with our new espresso machine. It's an extravagance, but it saves us from hitting Starbuck's ten times a day. Tonight it's cool out, so I grab a sweater for him. Once Seb gets rolling on something, he won't stop, even if he's cold, hungry, or exhausted.

The ash from a recent pottery firing hits my nose as soon as I step out of the house. As I get closer to the shed, the scent shifts to the earthiness of clay. I breathe it in. This is one of the first really nice evenings we've had—snow season is coming to an end and the intense heat of summer isn't here yet.

Seb sees me and smirks, "No nap needed, huh?"

"Well, a quick one."

I hand him his coffee and he rolls his eyes at the sweater I brought out.

"Hey, it's getting chilly. Put it on," I direct.

"Okay, Mom!" he says, grabbing it and pulling it over his t-shirt. He winces, favoring his left side, and I wonder what's going on. Then he shivers and admits, "It is starting to get cold out here. I hadn't noticed."

A sip of latte later, he asks, "You wanna help?"

"Sure. What can I do?"

He doesn't answer and looks a little dazed. I wonder if my time with him is over. Another alternate personality may be coming forward.

He blinks, glances at me like the captain to the quarterback before a game they both know they'll win, and I can see from his eyes that Sebi is still here. I catch a passing wink and a crooked smile. He grabs a clipboard and pen, spinning it absentmindedly as he checks through the list, comparing it to the finished pieces, so he'll know how much to charge.

I admire his discipline and the perfect order he keeps in the shed. Spotless sculpting tools in well-organized baskets, carefully labeled bags of clay grouped together by type, and a progression of projects in various stages of completion. I've always aspired to that level of neatness, but I don't want to put in the time.

"We need to get everything priced that came out of the kiln a couple weeks ago," he says. "And I have some older stuff I'm ready to let go of, too." His records show the details of each piece as well as any notes that might interest appreciative patrons.

I'm pulled from my thoughts as Sebi points to the corner and directs, "Um. Would you mind setting up a table? Thanks."

He flips a switch and alternative rock music blares. I make a face he doesn't look up to see, and say, "Really, dude?"

He doesn't answer. This is his favorite band. I'm more of a folk and jazz guy myself.

As I set up the table for him, he examines a small statue of a fox with its eyes slyly looking to the side, a porcelain cigarette dangling from its mouth. It wears a purple and orange paisley jacket.

"I like him. I think he'll be the first in a series. What do you think, Steve?"

"I think $175."

Seb smiles at the compliment and puts a sticker on the back, handing it to me to put on the table. He picks up another—a dog with one ear folded over as its head cocks sideways. Winking, it has a playful smirk on its face and a rose in its mouth. It's glazed black with honey brown eyes.

"I think people would love this one. Or we could put him in the hall bath? What do you think? I'm kind of attached to him. I think I'll call him Skippy."

He continues, "Skippy...hmmm, I hope dinner gets here soon. I'm starving. How long has it been?" He grabs a jar of peanut butter he keeps in the shed and digs in with a spoon. He eats it like an ice cream cone and as he finishes the first spoonful, a look of consternation crosses his face.

"Oh shit!" he laughs out loud. "Were we supposed to pick up the food?"

I shake my head and join in on the laughter. "How the hell am I supposed to know? I just got here!"

Sebi puts the peanut butter back on the shelf, scratches his head and pulls out his phone. He calls The Grill and they tell him that dinner is on the way. We've learned to laugh at times like these. Memory loss is a side effect of both multiplicity and the PTSD meds used to suppress flashbacks. When there's nothing you can do about a situation, humor makes it easier to tolerate.

Seb squints and takes a sip of coffee as he's staring into the face of his creation. I can't help but wonder if this playful, gregarious personality is who Sophie would be if she hadn't been split apart. I get tangled up in my own thoughts, remembering the healthy, vibrant, fun Sophie I'd known in college. You couldn't help but fall in love with her. But chronic pain and anxiety had taken her away from me years ago and I rarely saw that happy-go-lucky girl anymore.

"Steve?"

I'm suddenly aware that Sebi is staring at me. "Dude. You with me?" he says lightly, pulling up the sleeves on his lime green cardigan and tucking a stray lock of hair behind his ear.

I don't want to hurt Sebi or dampen the mood of our evening, so I keep my thoughts to myself. "Sorry. I just enjoy seeing your stuff."

A smile of pride spreads over his face. He squeezes my shoulder as he gives me an enthusiastic "Thanks!"

"So, what do you think?" he asks, waving towards the dog sculpture. "Skippy?"

"I love it. I wouldn't mind seeing him every day. Are we adopting him or will some lucky art lover snag him at the sale?"

Seb chuckles. "I say we adopt him for now. We can always share him with the world later. Hall bath?"

I nod. Then, out of the corner of my eye, I notice what looks like a thin red ribbon encircling Sebi's wrist. I look closer and see that it's a series of fresh, deep scratches—and some cuts—that are just starting to heal. I instinctively grab his arm for a closer look. "Seb, what's this from?"

His eyes widen as he stutters and pulls away from me, the flow of our evening disrupted. He gives his wrist a quick rub before pulling the sleeve of his sweater back down to cover it.

"Oh, my God. Umm, yeah. Do you...do you remember that twine that I got to make bracelets? It's crap! I wore the bracelet around for a few days and now my wrist is all rashy and cut up."

"It doesn't look like it was caused by twine, Seb." He's looking panicked now and I'm compelled to ask, "Do you remember what happened?"

Defensive, his mood darkens and he sounds like a teen being mothered too much. "Jesus, Steve. Would you quit with the worrying? I'm sure it's not a big deal."

I know not to push at this point, but I make a mental note to follow up. I need to know what this is about. He's not lying. He's desperately trying to fill in a blank spot and I'm concerned.

The doorbell rings and saves us from the awkward moment. I grab the beer while Seb gets the food, tipping the driver generously. He nods at the back door. "Wanna eat outside? It's so gorgeous!"

I follow him out to the deck. He's ordered our favorites—shrimp salad for me and salmon with lemon asparagus for him. He sets the food out between us so we can share, and then sees they've thrown in a baguette. He holds it up and says, "I love these guys!"

He runs into the house and grabs a plate, olive oil, and herbs. Wiping off his hands, he settles into his spot at the table, then tears off a huge piece of the crusty bread. He drizzles olive oil onto the plate and, with a wave, sprinkles it generously with oregano and rosemary. Finally he dunks the bread in. His eyes are laughing as oil drips down the side of his mouth.

"Oh, dear God, that's amazing! Seriously, no offense, dude, but better than sex." Then he slowly smiles and half jokes, "With you anyway."

"Thanks for that," I laugh, remembering a disastrous sexual experiment years ago. That time had started out badly and quickly disintegrated into comedy.

"Any time." He joins me in a laugh as we share the memory.

Seb wipes his mouth with the back of his hand and digs into the salmon. I feel relief washing over me. Chronic pain usually steals Sophie's appetite, but Seb enjoys every bite. He perceives himself as tall, lean, and well-defined. He eats like a teenage boy and exercises like an athlete. Food is a celebration to him, not the enemy.

Halfway through dinner, Sebi raises his eyebrows, holds up his empty beer bottle and waves it. I reach for another beer, flip the lid off, and hand it to him. Our easy flow is restored, but I can feel our earlier conflict hanging between us. The mood is light and fun as long as I don't cross another line.

Seb prefers to stay in the positive and asks, "Did I ever tell you about the family that lived across the street from me as a kid?"

"I don't think so," I say. I've heard the story at least a dozen times, but Seb can't remember. I don't mind hearing it again and it saves him from feeling embarrassed.

"Chiara Moretti," he starts. Just saying the name makes him grin. "She was this totally uninhibited, creative genius. She did these amazing sculptures and her whole house was like an art gallery. I remember one summer she was working on these giant cacti in her garage. It was just wild. They were like eight feet tall with giant spikes sticking out. Not something you routinely see in the Midwest.

"Her son, Jason, had been my best friend and sometimes we got to play in her pottery studio. We'd be down there totally covered in clay with music blasting and she'd bring us rice pudding."

"Sounds like it was a great place."

"It really was. And Jason was such a great friend. He offered to help me run away once. We had it all planned out. He was going to wait for me and I was supposed to sneak out at midnight. He said he'd take me somewhere safe and stay with me." A smile lights up his eyes but there's a sadness there, too. I know he won't get into why, but I can see darker thoughts threatening to flood him.

He pulls himself away from them. "I think that's where pottery became synonymous with freedom for me. I probably should have majored in fine arts at high school, but they say to study to your strength, which put me in theater. I wanted to do pottery, but the pre-req was drawing, so that was a hard no."

"You know, Seb? I always wondered what was up with that. You're so creative, but you have such an aversion to drawing. I mean, it doesn't stop you, but it does not seem like a fun thing for you."

The memory seems to make Seb uneasy and he quickly shifts gears, ignoring my question in favor of asking his own. "Anyway, how's work going? Is the new boss still making you nuts?"

"Yeah, he's a jerk. But, remember what you said about other people's expectations?"

"That they can suck the life out of you?"

"Exactly. I think he's really just trying to make his problems mine. He doesn't know what he's doing, so he sort of pushes that off on everyone else. I decided to just do what I do. He's actually happier with me now than when I was killing myself trying to figure out what the hell he wanted."

"Ironic, right?"

"I can't even tell ya."

As we finish dinner, we share a cigarette and get back to work preparing for the show, our conversation carrying us through the evening. We finish with the first and second racks, but by now it's dark and we're both getting tired.

Pretty soon Sebi yawns. "Hey, let's head in. I'm exhausted. We have another rack to do, but I've got time."

I check my phone. "No wonder we're tired. It's after 11."

"Seriously? I'm tired, but I'm hungry again too," Seb admits.

"Cheesecake?" I ask.

"Oh my God, are you kidding me? Did you stop by the bakery today?"

"Yup. On the way home."

We reward ourselves with the best cheesecake in Denver smothered in blueberries, and then Seb gets Skippy situated in the hall bath before turning in.

———

Our entire house has become a revolving art exhibit. We've even set up the bathroom to display sculptures and prints. A muted yellow over eggshell paint creates the perfect backdrop for the black and white frames. A walled shelf provides space for a parade of sculptures that come and go.

In the long hallway to our bedroom, a small painting of oranges, partially peeled, has a place of honor. It was painted by Seb's childhood art teacher, Constance.

A rough sketch of a wooden shoe filled with candy done by his elementary school art teacher has been matted and framed professionally. He had snagged it from her trash can. It was just a class demo, but he loved it.

And a pastel-colored drawing of a busy art festival from Seb's beloved teacher Pete is just outside his bedroom, so it's the first thing he sees when he opens his door in the morning.

As I'm closing the curtains in my bedroom, I feel arms slipping around my waist from behind and a head nuzzling my neck. "Mind if I crash in here tonight?"

I turn around to try and interpret the intent behind the question and to ascertain who's asking. I'm surprised to see it's still Sebi. He reaches his hand behind my neck and pulls me to him. We share a few kisses, but they feel more friendly than romantic. It's a concession of the hard-fought battle for common ground. After an earlier attempt years ago, we'd agreed that Seb would initiate any intimacy between us, and he never had.

We crawl into bed and he curls himself around my back. As I pull his arms closer, I notice there are matching gashes around his other wrist. Now I'm worried.

As I drift off, the worry over Seb fades into the comfort I feel in the arms of my wife. But as sleep overtakes me, I'm carried back to a time years before I'd met Sophie. There's something familiar about this. I feel accepted and I feel safe, but it's tinged with a bitter shame.

The next morning, we wake up late and eat the leftover cheesecake for breakfast. I want to tell him how much I loved having him in my bed, but I know that would create pressure. I want to ask about his wrists, but that would mean an unproductive fight. Instead, I ask him to finish a thought.

"You never answered me last night, Seb. What's up with the drawing? You're so great at sculpting and I've seen your paintings. You play piano, you act. It seems like the arts are a natural gift for you," I say, leaving the question in the air.

Finally Seb responds, "Okay, first, you know how I feel about natural gifts. That's not a thing. It's about passion and discipline. You have to love something enough to work your ass off. That's all."

I knew discipline was not a natural quality for him. It had been ground into him like glass. He'd told me that, growing up, perfection was not a goal. It was the baseline.

"I have no idea what's up with drawing," he says now. He knits his brow and squints as he reflectively adds, "I loved it as a little kid and then I just hit a block. No idea what happened.

"When I was in 6th grade, I had this amazing art teacher. She was so bizarre and fantastic. She was sarcastic and hyper-verbal and hilarious. A real fashion plate, too.

"Near the end of the year, they announce this drawing contest. We're all going to be doing a portrait of our English teacher, who everyone loves.

"They had to call my name three times before I could believe it. I won first place and I felt like maybe I got the art gene. I had busted my ass on that drawing and it paid off. That was a great day."

I'm puzzled, feeling like I'm not connecting the dots. "So what's up that you feel you're not good at drawing now? Sounds like you were talented from the time you were a kid."

Sebi frowns and shrugs his shoulders. "I don't know. But every time I face a blank page, I get an anxiety attack. If that was it, I could push through it, but my drawings are still just crap even after all these years and all the lessons.

He continues, "I've had a weird thing about drawing for almost as long as I can remember. That's why I decided on an art history major instead of fine arts—so I could avoid the drawing classes. Then I found out I had to take one anyway. I almost dropped out! But I squeaked by with a C- and that teacher was being generous. You were there. Remember? We had to show a drawing at that exhibit—just before Christmas junior year?"

I *had* gone to that show and I'd never forget the piece Sophie displayed. A naked female figure shivering in the snow, pressing her face against a living room window pane to look in at a perfect Christmas scene of a mom, dad, and their baby girl. Pretty stark. It brought me to tears then and I could feel myself tearing up again now.

"Yeah," I say, my voice a whisper. "I remember."

Sophie's mom, Becky, had been a costume designer. Her dad, Todd, an actor. But they were young and her mom had serious postpartum issues when Sophie had been born, so she'd given Sophie to her parents while she recovered. Months stretched into years and Sophie never went home. Then later, they had another girl, who they kept. Sophie never got over feeling abandoned and rejected—replaced. She still relentlessly nourished her creative side, believing any artistic ability would somehow validate the genetics, make her more a part of that family she'd always wanted.

"Well," Seb continues, "that's about the extent of my drawing talent. Anxiety attacks and moderately crude figures. I keep trying, but I'm not sure it'll ever get much better. Pete has been a great teacher, but I think I have some sort of block."

SIX YEARS AGO - *November 18, 2010*

I love the variety travel provides in my job, but I hate being away from Sophie. I generally arrive home from trips in the early evening but, this time, everything fell into place and we were able to get our work finished a day ahead on Friday. That meant I could fly home early and have the weekend—and Monday—with my wife.

Now, as I look out of my hotel window at beautiful San Francisco, I imagine what it would be like if Sophie could travel with me again. We could enjoy the beach, see all the sights, and sit on the Pier, sipping coffee. But travel was nearly impossible for her these days because she had so much anxiety: the claustrophobia of the plane, strangers patting you down and going through your stuff, all the uncertainty. Flying wasn't going to happen and driving took too much time. Our road trips were rare.

We sometimes talked about going to the mountains and dreamed about the places we'd fly once she's better. One year, we'd even made all the plans, but when the day came, Sophie couldn't do it. We tried a few times after that, but it just seemed to make her anxiety worse, so we quit and just settled on enjoying being home as much as possible. The doctors call it agoraphobia.

She's been working with a therapist on her anxiety and had asked me to come with her to her next appointment. I don't like the idea of going, but I do look forward to a time when we'll have a more normal life—once she gets things under control. And I want to help her get there.

In anticipation of better times, I've been looking at trucks that can handle the mountains. I love traveling. Growing up in Iowa, I hadn't really gone all that far from home and I was ready to take in the world.

Now, after my business trip, as the red eye lands in the Denver snow just before sunrise, I imagine burrowing under the covers and into our warm bed. I smile as I think about waking up late, reading together and eventually enjoying a big breakfast.

I inch my way home and trudge through the snow that had accumulated on the driveway to our little urban brick house, leaving my suitcase in the trunk until I can shovel the walk. I shake off my shoes as I open the door and immediately melt into the scent of home—the coffee and cologne, fire and freshly baked bread. The warmth washes over me and I'm hit with a wave of exhaustion as I step into the living room.

Then I notice a collection of empty beer bottles on the antique wood trunk we use as a coffee table and chuckle to myself—remembering Sophie at a frat party years ago. She had been a fun drunk.

I approach the dining room to swing my coat over a chair, but someone else's jacket is already there. Half-burned pillar candles are grouped in the center of the table. Bamboo placemats hold two plates of half eaten lobster mac and two wine glasses with Merlot pooling at the bottom.

I can feel anxiety beginning to creep up on me from behind. I try to avoid jumping to conclusions, but everything slips into slow motion and I'm pulled to explore. A sliver of hope is pushing me to try to find a truth our relationship can survive. Perhaps this was just dinner with our neighbor Carol, or Sophie's friend Kathy, who sometimes stays the night when I'm out of town?

I pull myself upstairs to the bedroom and stand at the door, taking a breath before opening it. I consider if I really want to know, realizing there's no other choice. I steel myself and slowly turn the knob, the fear of knowing everything could change in the next heartbeat holding me back.

As the door opens into the room, I see Sophie—awake and casually reclining in bed. She usually sleeps in sweats, but this morning, she's in a white tank top. She had heard me come in and is smiling hello. I smile back, relieved that it's just Carol or Kathy staying in the guest room.

As she crawls from the bed, I see she's wearing a pair of plaid boxer shorts. Then I hear a moan of complaint from beneath the covers and realize she's not alone.

Shock steals my voice and I'm sputtering.

Sophie admonishes me with a "shhh" while shooting a sideways glance at the bed. She grabs my robe from the closet and pushes me out of the bedroom as she closes the door behind her and follows me down the stairs.

My heart is pounding in my ears. I trip down the steps and grab my coat.

"This is it, Sophie," I hiss. "I have stuck with you through all of your moods, the anxiety, all of the crap you put me through and this is what you do while I'm at work? You screw around on me? I am so done."

Her voice is calm and deep as she unemotionally states, "Steve, you need to calm down. First, there's more to this than you think."

"I hope there's not more, Sophie, because it looks like you're cheating."

"I'm not. I know that doesn't make sense to you right now, but that's not what this is."

"You're in bed with someone else, Sophie. I'm not sure how else this can add up."

Every instinct is telling me to run and I'm thankful I left my suitcase in the car. I can bolt if I have to.

"I think the critical question at this point is why the hell should I stay with you?"

"I can't answer that for you, Steve. I get why you'd want to leave and if you feel like you have to, then leave. But if you want answers, let's keep our appointment with Dr. Newman on Monday. I think everything will make more sense after that." She sounds like a reporter who's just providing information, like she's completely uninvested in our relationship.

I feel the decision ripping me apart. I'm resentful that she's put this on me. When she drank, she was like this. She'd make a mess, show no emotion, and expect me to clean up the wreckage afterwards. Still stunned, I'm barely able to catch my breath. Our marriage is over but Sophie doesn't seem to know that. Or if she does, she doesn't care.

She shakes out a cigarette, puts it in her mouth and mumbles, "You mind?"

"Yes, I mind! What the hell, Sophie?"

She throws the cigarettes on the coffee table and slicks her hair back with both hands. Spreading her knees wide and leaning towards me, she asks, "What do you want to do?"

I desperately need her to understand how upset I am. I grab the wine bottle and wave it. She has always refused to drink with me, telling me it doesn't agree with her any longer. "Are you kidding me with this?" I blast, tossing it into the fireplace. My face is hot and my head is swimming, but Sophie doesn't flinch.

I can't look at her. I stare at the fireplace full of ashes from the previous night and now broken bits of green glass shimmering against the embers.

I hear keys jangling as Sophie's friend comes down the steps and I'm shocked when I turn around to see a woman.

She's wearing a black slip dress, carrying strappy high heels, eyes wide like they've been caught by one of their fathers doing nothing wrong. Even early in the morning, this thirty-something blonde woman is stunning—her appearance, as well as the way she carries herself. I wonder if Sophie met her while modeling.

The woman nods to me with a degree of familiarity I find unsettling, then grabs my wife's hand and pulls her in for a long goodbye kiss before saying, "I'll see you tomorrow, S. My meeting will wrap up about 4. I'm staying at the regular place. I'll leave a key for you at the desk." My wife juts out her chin in agreement and kisses the woman's wrist, smiling up to her. "I'll be there. Love you, Sweetheart."

Everything feels unreal. I'm incredulous that this is unfolding before me. It feels like I'm on the set of some awful reality TV show.

Sophie and this woman have a relationship and they have no problem with me knowing about it. It wasn't a one night thing. My decision is becoming clearer and I'm fighting the urge to take off and not look back.

The blonde tiptoes past me to snag her jacket. "Sorry," she whispers as I glare at her.

Sophie's gaze follows the woman and as the door closes behind her, Sophie's smile fades. I'm expecting a fight. I'm expecting for her to be frustrated—spitting accusations of neglect and boredom at me to try to excuse her unforgivable behavior. Instead, there's just an annoying self-assuredness beneath a thick layer of apathy.

Confusion, fear, and anger are blazing through me. I don't know what to act on first. I want answers but I'm still in shock. At the very moment I need to make quick, accurate decisions, I feel like I'm trying to swim through wet cement. If I leave, am I throwing away my marriage? If I stay, am I a dupe? Of the dozens of scenarios I'd run through my mind when I worried about my wife and our marriage, this one had never even occurred to me.

"I can't do this," is all I can manage as I head for the door.

———

I want to drive forever, but that afternoon settle on a hotel near the house so I can get some sleep. I keep running things through my head. Sophie hasn't been herself. Even a small amount of alcohol makes her sick and I'd never seen her smoke. Normally, if she unexpectedly heard someone in the house early in the morning, she'd be in a panic. She's always cold, so she sleeps in warm clothes—even in summer. And that woman had called her "S." Things aren't adding up.

At the hotel, I try to get some sleep, but am too worried. I finally give up around 4am and read until 7. I want her to wonder where I am—to miss me. So I eat a casual breakfast and read the paper, waiting until check-out time to go home. I'm anxious to have it out with her, but when I get back just after 11, she's not there. Now I'm feeling lost. We always spend weekends together and, without Sophie, I have no idea what to do. I try to read, but can't focus. I can't get motivated to even consider my to-do list. I wind up wasting the day watching movies.

As night falls, my anger is consumed by concern. She's not answering her phone and she doesn't come home that night, nor the next. I consider filing a missing person's report with the police, but given our circumstances, I'm pretty sure they'll blow me off. *We had a fight and my wife took off.* That's not unusual.

I consider calling her friends, asking neighbors—but I don't want to alarm them, and, in all honesty, she'd done this before. I pick up the phone more than once to try Kathy or Carol, but feel too embarrassed. They'd want an explanation and I don't have one.

November 19, 2010

On Monday I wake to a chill in the air. Rolling out of bed to look out the window, I see huge flakes of snow, coming fast. Even though I don't need to go in to work, I want to keep my mind off of things. I wonder if Sophie will make it to our late afternoon appointment with her therapist. I hope so. We have a lot of issues to work out. Besides, I want to meet the man who's been helping her.

I go through the day in a fog—unable to get anything done other than obsessing about where Sophie is, whether or not she'll show up today, and what to say in our session. The day crawls by and finally dusk is closing in and I make my way through the slush to Dr. Newman's office to find Sophie already there.

I stop at the door. I really only came to be sure she's okay. I don't want to sit through a session with her, but curiosity keeps me from leaving.

All of my fear now turns to anger. While I've hardly slept in days, Sophie looks great. She wears a freshly pressed white button-down shirt, thin black tie and black cardigan with skinny jeans. As I get closer, I smell her cologne—spices, pipe tobacco and suede, which is irritatingly soothing.

Another couple sits across from her in the waiting area so I slide into the chair on her left and whisper sternly, "Where the hell were you?"

She rapid-fire whispers back, "I was in Colorado Springs with Liz. We'd already planned to have the weekend together. It's not my fault that you came home early. Didn't you hear what she said? Didn't you hear me tell her that I'd be there?"

The other couple is trying not to stare at us. Normally, I'm a pretty private person but my anger forces me to betray that. "Is that your girlfriend's name? Liz?"

Sophie rolls her eyes and shakes her head at me like I'm being an idiot.

Just then, the door to one of three offices opens into the waiting room and a kind-faced, heavy set, gray-bearded man peers over his black-rimmed glasses at us. His soft blue eyes seem kind, but his voice is firm with a hint of a smile in it. "Sounds like you two are getting started without me. Wanna come in here to talk?"

Sophie doesn't look at me, but I can feel a coldness as she gets up and turns her back to me to walk into his office. To me, she seems like a celebrity wanting to walk that fine line between being adored and maintaining an uncrossable distance.

I prefer to fight uninterrupted. I'm sure her therapist will take her side and Sophie is clearly in the wrong. But I know I have to swallow my pride if I want to find out what's going on. I reluctantly follow her into the office. I'm intensely uncomfortable, silently sitting there waiting for something to happen. Plus, this guy reminds me of the therapist I went to in high school and that was not a fun experience. Why do they all look the same?

As we settle on the well-worn, dark brown leather couch, I look around, trying to acclimate myself to gain some sense of control. Books crowd a tall, generic-looking bookshelf, framed posters of nature are hanging on the walls. The ceiling has water stains and the wood window frames are clearly 1970's. His roll-top desk is stacked with books with numerous tabs hanging out, and files stacked so high they look like they may crash to the floor at any second. Amusingly, little statues of turtles are everywhere.

Sophie crosses her leg and bounces her foot impatiently. Her long, dark hair is pulled back into a Samurai knot and she wears pricey ankle boots with these weird olive green socks with sloths on them. It looks ridiculous and totally cool at the same time.

Dr. Newman seems to know what's going on and it annoys me that he knows more than I do about my wife. Somehow, it feels like one more betrayal.

"I'm glad you came in today, Steve. I'm Dr. Newman and I'm sure you're wondering what's going on."

"That's the only reason I'm here."

"I get that. This has to be really confusing for you. The best way to explain what's happening is to demonstrate."

"Sophie?" he firmly says—looking directly at my wife.

She doesn't respond. She doesn't look at him, nor does she purposely avoid his gaze. She just sits there chewing her gum and waiting for something to happen.

Dr. Newman glances at me briefly and then quietly asks, "Sebi?"

My wife looks up at him, sighs, smiles slightly and responds, "What's up?"

I feel completely confused and anxiety is rising from my stomach to my throat.

"I don't get it." I blurt out. I've been blindsided, but the blow hasn't quite landed yet.

Dr. Newman's voice is calm, "It's okay, Steve. By the time you leave here today, you will have real answers. I'm sorry if that was a jolt, but I needed to get you up to speed quickly."

I think I know what he's getting at, but am fighting against it. "What exactly is going on? So she goes by another name. I don't get why that's a thing. We all have nicknames."

"Sebi isn't a nickname. And he's not your wife. He's another person that lives in the same body. We call these different people alter personalities or alters for short."

"My mind sputters and I feel paralyzed. It feels like my heart stopped beating and my breath is stuck in my lungs. No one speaks until I find my voice. "Like the guy in the movie *Split*?" my pitch is high and I feel sick.

Sophie bristles at being compared to a criminal and Dr. Newman tells me, "They both have multiple personalities but no, movies tend to dramatize mental illness. Multiples are often portrayed in a negative light. In real life, they're far more likely to be the victim of a crime rather than the offender."

I can hardly focus and I'm desperate for a lifeline. "Everyone has different personas," I sputter. "I'm different at work than I am at home. When I hang out with friends, I'm different than when I'm presenting at a conference. Doesn't everybody sort of have multiple personalities?"

Sophie scoffs and shakes her head.

"No, Steve," Dr. Newman explains. "You're talking about wearing different hats. In that case, you are always you, but sometimes you act differently depending on what the situation calls for. Multiplicity is more like housing different souls. They're perceived as completely separate people."

"So, what does this mean exactly?"

Dr. Newman looks to Sophie, "Seb, is it okay if I give Steve an overview? Remember we talked about what I'd say?"

Sophie closes her eyes for a moment. When she opens them, she reluctantly agrees, "Yeah, I remember. Sure."

He turns to me. "Sophie's been working with me on this for the past couple years. She's learning to live with multiple personalities. But before we get into that, this is overwhelming news. How are you doing?"

"I'm shocked. I don't know how to react. I feel totally betrayed on pretty much every level. I've known Sophie for years and didn't know anything about this. She obviously lied to me about why she was getting treatment. I knew something was wrong, but she'd told me it was anxiety. And then a few days ago, I learned she has a girlfriend." I want him to acknowledge what I'm up against. I want him to tell her what she's done is wrong.

Dr. Newman takes in what I said and responds with, "I can see why you feel betrayed."

"I feel like I was tricked into something—not given a choice. And now I'm trapped."

"So, where do you want to go from here?"

"Honestly, I was ready to file for divorce a couple days ago. Since Sophie split and didn't come home, I came today to make sure she's okay. I'm also here because I want an explanation." Dr. Newman is completely avoiding taking sides and it's pissing me off.

"You're trying to decide whether to go or stay."

"I am. I understood we were coming in to work on Sophie's anxiety. Not this. I feel like I'm going crazy. Sometimes I feel like her anxiety is too much to handle. Now I find out she's *Sybil*?"

Sophie looks like she's about to explode—like my words are a sharp stick, jabbing into her ribs.

"The first thing you need to know, Steve, is that anytime you see multiples in the media, it's not accurate. There's a tiny grain of truth surrounded by a whole lot of drama. You've already been living with this and now we're making sense of it—this is going to make life easier for everyone."

"I thought they were just different moods," I say slowly, considering how everything is starting to make horrible sense. I still feel wounded about having been cheated on and wonder if this is just a massive excuse to get out of the blame. I hope it is, but I can feel that it isn't.

"This is a really serious illness, isn't it?" I wasn't asking a question. I knew it was serious.

"I don't see it that way, Steve. Like most of my patients who are multiples, Sophie had a lot of abuse growing up, but the multiplicity itself is a gift. It's a brilliant coping mechanism. Multiples use their brain differently. Therapy isn't about curing a disorder, it's about finding ways to manage life as a multiple. It's about maximizing the ability."

"Making a disorder work? Isn't there a cure for it?"

"I'm going to ask that you refer to this as multiplicity rather than a disorder. Think of it as having a super power that comes along with challenges. The multiplicity was a normal, life-saving reaction to a chaotic environment. When we call it a disorder, we wind up labeling the survivor—making them "wrong" or calling them "crazy." It's inaccurate and in my belief, damaging. Multiples are highly suggestible— it's part of the predisposition that allows them to develop other personalities—so you have to be careful of what you're suggesting. It's a powerful tool but it can also be a dangerous one. Her home life was chaotic. Multiplicity is one way of trying to make sense of it. "

"Chaos is actually a fairly accurate word for what's been going on at home," I reply. "It doesn't seem like a super power." At this point, I can't absorb much more, yet I feel I have to learn as much as I can as fast as I can.

"What would you call a condition that allows you to not only survive brutal torture but creates new brain capacity so you can change your eye color, effortlessly learn new languages, practice in diverse fields of work, and switch off fear at will? It would come with its own set of challenges, but I wouldn't call that a disability, would you? My job is to help people see the gifts and *abilities* inside of their multiplicity. *I want to help them expand their strengths rather than eliminate a problem.*"

He pauses to take in my expression of complete overload. Then he smiles and puts a hand on my knee, "How are you doing?"

"I'm not sure," I say, trying to grab on to anything. "Her eyes change color? I've seen that, but thought it was just what she was wearing or the lighting or something."

Then something else he'd said finally clicks in. "She was tortured? Like, tortured? I knew she was mistreated, but—tortured? You mean, something beyond abuse? Sorry. I'm grasping at straws. Am I supposed to feel like this? Like I'm having an out of body experience?"

"In a situation like this, yes, I think that's normal. I know it's overwhelming. I probably should not have used that word—but it's accurate for what she went through. Abuse is mistreatment and it hurts. Usually, it happens when a parent is angry and they take it out on their child. Torture is a more structured approach with the intention of causing intense pain and confusion—usually in order to force someone to do something."

I have no idea how to cope with my own feelings, let alone help Sophie. I had just met Dr. Newman and didn't know if I could trust him, yet he was the only life raft available.

"So, what do we do now?" I ask.

"What do you feel like you need to do?"

I laugh. "To be honest? Run."

A smile flashes over Dr. Newman's face. I suspect he's heard this before. "That's not a bad idea—to do something physical. You have a lot of adrenalin racing through you. It wouldn't be a bad thing to take a run. I think that's actually a really good idea. What else do you need?"

"I need to have some sort of normal in my life. I need to know what to expect when coming into the house each night."

"Sounds totally reasonable. Seb, how do we do that?"

Sophie rolls her eyes.

"That's enough, Seb." Dr. Newman is firm. "You don't hold the emotion, but Steve can't compartmentalize. He's helped you guys a lot. Now it's time to help him."

Seb tosses out, "He can text before he comes home. Ask what's going on."

"Would that work, Steve?"

"I think it could. We can give it a try." I'm feeling more in control. Having a plan helps.

"I need something else. I need to know—who's Seb? And is that the only one?" I ask, dreading the answer.

Dr. Newman and Seb look to one another. Seb answers, "I'm not sure we should get into this right now."

I read between the lines and feel a little light-headed. "I think I need a minute."

Dr. Newman offers, "We still have time, but do you want to wrap it up for today?"

"No, I'm okay. I just need some air."

Sebi reaches into his bag and pulls out his cigarettes. "Need one of these?"

"Actually, yes." I grab the pack and the lighter he offers. "I'll be back."

I step outside and light up. I don't usually smoke, but I have no other way to calm down. I let the smoke fill my lungs and cough it out, letting the nicotine soak in. I hack my way through the first one and take another. Now I just feel sick.

I think about leaving, but I need to finish this, one way or another.

I slowly head back to the office, but I'd rather be anywhere else right now. That urge to run is coursing through me.

Seb and Dr. Newman stop talking as I open the door to the office.

"Ready for more answers?" Seb asks.

"I think so. First question—who are you? You seem to know me, but I have no idea who you are."

"Oh my God, Steve," Seb laughs kindly. "You so know me. We've had a lot of time together. You just didn't know I was a different person. I don't really know where to start."

"The basics, I guess?" I look to Dr. Newman for his approval or another direction. He's just here to witness and remains expressionless.

"The basics? You know my name. I'm Seb. I'm 19. An artist, and I work at the modeling agency. I'm not sure what else to tell you."

"What am I to you?"

"You're my roommate. I consider you my best friend."

"You said we've had a lot of time together? How do I know it's you?"

"Well, I knew you at college. I laugh a lot, love food with a passion none of the other alters understand. I drink a fair amount. I smoke. And I wear this," he says, taking the St. Christopher's charm out. "I'm sure you've seen that the clothes I wear are different."

"Are you the only other personality?"

Seb takes a deep breath in and lets it out. He looks at Dr. Newman and then to me. He winces apologetically, "No."

I swallow hard and all I can think of is divorce. I'd be justified. My wife is cheating on me. I had always thought those guys who took off when their wife got sick were jerks. Now, standing in their shoes, I totally get it.

"I need to know how many more there are."

Seb looks hesitant to tell me, but I silently hold his gaze until he answers.

"There are seven main personalities."

"What does that mean? Seven *main* personalities?"

Seb nods at Dr. Newman, who tells me, "It means you're unlikely to ever spend much time with more than seven different personalities, so we don't really need to worry about more than that."

"How many are there—total?" I ask, looking to Dr. Newman and Seb, who are looking at each other with concern in their eyes. "I need to know what I'm dealing with."

Dr. Newman steps in to answer, "That's not really how this works. On TV it is, but in real life, these systems are dynamic, with personalities coming and going, fragments being formed and released."

The fact that I don't know the terminology and can't keep up must be apparent on my face because Dr. Newman briefly explains, "Fragments are personalities that aren't fully developed. They may not have a name and may only have a short-term function. We can get into more of that later."

I feel like my entire world has collapsed in the course of an hour. Nothing is the same. Everything feels surreal.

"What else do we need to handle before we start wrapping up for today?"

I'm drowning in new information, but it's not helping me feel any better. I don't want to be sent home alone with Sophie. I feel totally responsible for her and ill-equipped to handle that. I'm still angry about the affair, and instead of getting answers, I'm expected to step up and help Sophie.

"Is there anything I need to know?" I ask, "I mean, in terms of...how to take care of her?"

Seb looks at me, raises his eyebrows and sarcastically asks, "Care and Feeding of Your Multiple? You have a lot of books, Dr. Newman. Where's the manual?"

Dr. Newman shoots a disapproving look at him. "Seb, that's not helping. Steve, you've already been living with this for years. The only thing that's changed is that now you have a label for what's been happening. You and Sophie are the experts on what works. Now we need to fine tune. Let's plan to meet again on Friday and we can talk more. If you have questions between sessions, you can always call. We're going to get you all the support you need, but for right now, just get your bearings."

I was having a hard time believing this was even real. I start babbling, "My plan was to help Sophie through her anxiety—a few sessions so we could get back to our lives. Sounds like we'll never get back to normal."

"It's a lot to take in," Dr. Newman says sympathetically, "When you're ready, there's a lot of help."

"I'm going to need it."

Dr. Newman hesitates and looks like he's evaluating me. "Would it help for me to give you one of my books on the subject?"

"A book might help me get a handle on this."

"Okay," he says, getting up to scan his bookcase. He runs his fingers over the titles until he rests on one. "Let's start with...this one," he offers, handing me a thin book with a cartoon on the cover. *United We Stand*, by Eliana Gil. I absent-mindedly take it and tuck it into my bag, thanking him before heading home with this stranger named Sebi.

We walk out to the waiting room together and, as Dr. Newman's door closes gently behind us, I suddenly feel abandoned. I want to be back in his office. I'm a mix of feeling weary and freaked out, exhausted and keyed up.

"What do we do now?" I ask.

"Coffee?" my wife suggests.

We'd driven separately, so we meet at Starbuck's. Now I start noticing things, like when Sophie is dressed this way, she drinks coffee. The rest of the time, she drinks tea. And when she gets tea, she likes to sit in a private corner. When she gets coffee, she sits at the window to people-watch.

Seb, as Dr. Newman had called her, gets a latte and leads the way to the counter looking out over the busy sidewalk. He breaks the silence. "I feel like I owe you an apology, Steve. I should have told you about this a long time ago, but I was afraid you'd leave. I thought I could control it enough that you'd never have to deal with it. I didn't want it to touch you."

"I wish I would have known. I think it could have saved us a lot of trouble. And I wouldn't have left you."

"But you're thinking of leaving now."

"Not because of this. Because of the cheating. Because of the lying."

"I know it seems like cheating to you, but to me, it's not. I'm not your wife, Steve. I'm your roommate. And I have my own life. Besides, Liz and I aren't like that. It's complicated."

"I'm not sure I can get into this right after therapy. I'm just trying to get my feet under me. Let's table this for now."

"Agreed. This is pretty bizarre for me, too. I feel like you do know me. We've spent so much time together, but you didn't know I was a different person. Now it feels like everything is going to be weird. The main thing to remember is that I'm exactly the same person I was before you found out I have multiple personalities."

"I'm not sure that's true. I've experienced you as one person. Now there are seven."

"All that's changed is that you know now. That's a good thing, Steve."

We finish our coffee in silence, both lost in our own thoughts. Once home, the silence deepens and becomes uncomfortable, until I head to bed early.

I notice how everything suddenly feels unfamiliar. Our kitchen, which normally feels welcoming with it's deep blues, dark reds and sunflower yellows, now seems harsh. Our bedroom, which Sophie designed as a sanctuary with soothing gray walls and beautiful heavy drapes, suddenly feels like a cold, metal box. I can't sleep in here.

I grab my pajamas and as I reach into the medicine cabinet for my toothbrush, I see Sophie's Xanax and know I need one. I've been avoiding it for days, but I can't resist the feeling I know I'll get from it. I open the nearly full bottle, shake one out and feel relief the instant I swallow it. I head into the guest room, dumping my bag on the floor.

Dr. Newman's book falls out and I pick it up. I hadn't intended to do any reading tonight, but it was early and this looks like a quick read.

The book's simple to get through and puts my world into some sort of order. It explains the various stages of dissociation, how it works and why it happens. Apparently, we all dissociate from time to time—like when you're driving somewhere and all of a sudden you're there, but you zoned out on the way. Then there's the dissociation related to abuse—where you feel you're observing yourself from outside your body. It looks like torture is what it takes to create a large system like

Sophie's. I knew she wasn't close to her family and that there had been some mistreatment, but nothing like this.

I'm in way over my head. Even thinking that Sophie had been spanked as a child brought me to tears. But this? I'm not sure how to handle it. My life is beginning to take on a very "tip of the iceberg" feeling.

I never slept well after an intense day, but that night I sleep better and deeper than I had in weeks and it felt good. Sleep with Xanax feels like tasting my favorite food after giving it up years ago and I wonder why I ever let it go.

November 24, 2010

That week, I find myself trying to notice if different alter personalities are out. I'm especially tuned in and Sophie seems irritated with it. To be honest, I'm irritated with myself, too. The multiplicity seems so obvious to me now and I have no idea why I couldn't see it before.

I call home each day before I leave work so I know what to expect when I walk through the door. I notice when Sophie sounds like a child, she wants me to pick up fast food. When she cooks, she seems bossy. There are times when she's boisterous and other times when she's practically a ghost. I don't know if these are different people or if they're just Sophie in different moods, but I'm awake now and paying attention.

Friday arrives and we drive to Dr. Newman's together. Sophie seems more comfortable being her different selves now. She rests her boots on the dashboard, plugs her phone into the radio and sets the station to loud and obnoxious. She offers me a cigarette, which I refuse, and then cracks the window to smoke. While she feels more comfortable, I feel less and less at home. I don't know these people.

"Hey guys," Dr. Newman's greeting feels kind—like a doctor about to do painful surgery, but at least he's compassionate about it.

After a quick check in, Dr. Newman directs, "I think having a roadmap might help Steve understand The Timeshare. Does that sound do-able, Seb?" he asks, noticing that Seb is out now.

"Better than having him follow me around staring at me."

Dr. Newman purses his lips into a tight smile and shakes his head admonishingly at Seb.

I had learned some of the terminology around this thing by reading the book Dr. Newman had given me, but this wasn't one I was familiar with.

"The Timeshare? What's that?"

"That's what we call Sophie's community of alters. They share the body, so it's sort of like a timeshare."

"Huh. That makes sense." I respond.

"Steve, you've seen different moods as you call them. Let's put this into perspective. Can you describe some of the moods so The Timeshare can tell you more?

"Okay." I try to focus, suddenly grateful for my hypervigilance over the last week. I have to really think about it.

"There's one where she cooks French food and can get really bossy."

Both Dr. Newman and Seb smile as Seb answers, "That's Jamie. He's a best friend to the kids. He's sensitive but fearless—and he loves to cook. You can tell it's him because he's usually in a black tank top and wears a bandana. He also likes to wear an earring—just one—in his left ear.

"Well, Jamie's an incredible chef," I say. "Plus, he seems really friendly - easy to get along with."

"Who's the one that studied stage combat at college and goes to Krav Maga, and gets into bar fights?" I ask.

"That's Richard," Seb says without hesitation.

"I don't want to insult anyone, but I have to be honest. He's like a guard dog. I'm not crazy about that one. I do *not* want to get on his bad side."

"I hear ya, and it's okay that you don't like him." Seb laughs. "He's not concerned about that. He just wants to do his job. You can tell it's him because he has a New York accent and he smokes. He usually wears something New York related."

I'm surprised that it actually feels good to put a name to these moods, to have more information.

I continue, "I think there's an activist, maybe, but that might be Sophie? Sometimes she seems more intellectual and pensive—very academic. She likes to debate with me. She seems super brilliant."

Dr. Newman smiles knowingly. He's met this one, too. Seb looks proud of me for being able to differentiate—but now his eyes are different. They're a soft, light blue.

"That's me. No, I'm not Sophie. I'm Ellyn. And you're right, I'm an activist and I do a lot of volunteering. Primarily around women's rights."

I feel like I'm acing some weird sort of oral exam. "Then there's the one that's really quiet, that dresses in old clothes and hides. She seems like a housewife who's been beaten down. She's always cleaning something but I hardly ever see her. She eats under the table and sleeps sort of hunched over." During those times, I had just assumed Sophie was in a "mood."

"That's Elizabeth. She likes to keep everything cleaned up and organized, but she's 12 years old, so she's like an uber-responsible child. She feels like if she's good enough, her parents will take her back. I think she's stuck at 12 because her grandparents sent us away when we were 12. She generally wears her hair in braids, no makeup, very quiet. She holds the emotion around the abuse."

I wondered about the being sent away part, but it feels like we're supposed to move on, so I don't ask. They'll tell me if they want me to know.

"Makes sense that she looks and acts like she does, then. I'd like to learn how I can reach her. She seems so lost." I pause, hoping for some ideas. No one says anything. There are a lot of rabbit holes we can wander down and I get the sense they want to stay out of them.

I keep going, but feel a little stuck. Then I remember Saturday morning breakfasts...

"Oh, there's the cute one that wants to snuggle all the time. She walks around with a teddy bear or a doll. Hates waffles. Loves monkey bread."

Ellyn pipes up and says, smiling, "That's Rachel and she's a child— a little one—about five years old. She's aged a bit since we got together.

She feels safe with you and when alters feel safe, they feel comfortable enough to grow older. She likes to hug you and snuggle. She wasn't always like that. She used to hide all the time, but she really loves you."

"I like Rachel. She's sweet." She *is* sweet, but the deeper I go, the less capable I feel of handling this. Different moods were hard enough. But different people?

Dr. Newman interrupts my thoughts. "Anyone else?"

"How many is that?" I ask. You said there's seven main ones and a bunch of others, too. I mean, how many can there be?"

I sense a change in Sophie and wonder if Ellyn is still around. She looks a little on edge and says, "I think that's good for now. I don't think I can do much more today."

Dr. Newman steps in. "Okay, let's call that good in terms of introductions. Steve, what's important to understand is that dissociation is a coping skill. Let's say you smoke or drink a beer or pop a pill when you're stressed. How often do you use those crutches?"

"Any time I'm stressed out. So, a lot."

"Exactly. The way it works with multiples is that they get stressed and dissociate. It's how they cope. If there's an alter available who can handle that particular situation, he or she steps in. If not, a new one—or perhaps just a fragment that can help out for a short time, is created. The more an alter is needed, the more defined and developed their personality."

Ellyn nods and answers quietly, looking at the floor. "That's been my experience, but it might be different for others." Her voice has gone deeper and she sounds more forceful.

A sense of overwhelm creeps in and I think about that woman I saw in my bed with my wife. I was hurt by what had happened and wanted that acknowledged. "Then there's Sebi. The one that's screwing around on me," I add.

The Timeshare takes a deep breath and looks up at me. I couldn't read the emotion. "That's me."

"Well, I have a real love/hate thing going with you."

"Sorry to hear that, Steve," Sebi says, squinting at me. He sounds sorry that I'm hurt but not sorry about what he did.

"We'll get into that soon, but right now, Steve, I'm sure you have a ton of questions. What do you need to know?" Dr. Newman asks.

"I just feel like I'm lost. Like I'm stumbling around in a dark room trying to figure out where I am."

Dr. Newman is sympathetic. "I understand that. Deep end of the ocean. There's a support group for partners we can get you started with and I think that'll help. And I'm here to answer any questions you have. There are also a lot of books and resources. Just remember anything you see on TV or in the movies isn't the reality."

"I know you're not going to want to hear this, Seb," Dr. Newman continues, "but at some point soon we need to have a discussion with Sophie about what happened with Liz that weekend when Steve showed up early."

Seb lifts his gaze from the ground up to Dr. Newman. It's one of the looks that, when directed at me, drives me crazy. A smoldering, sexy look that's seductive and pouty. This doesn't look like Seb, but I have no idea who it is and he or she only flashes through quickly, moving back in when Dr. Newman shoots this alter a disapproving look.

All I know about it is that Sophie had mastered that look and pulls it out whenever she wants to persuade me to see things her way. Now I'm starting to see it for what it is—someone in her system being manipulative, not necessarily her. And it's pissing me off.

Dr. Newman is unaffected as Seb now steps back in and suggests, "That talk with Sophie about Liz? I'm not sure that's a discussion we need to have."

Dr. Newman is firm. "Seb, it is a vital discussion and until you guys are all completely co-conscious, this is how we have to do it—in therapy."

Seb shakes his head and crosses his arms. "It's like an emotional burn unit in here. Like getting little bits of my soul ripped off. I don't see why Sophie needs to know. There are compartments for a reason. Don't you get that?"

"I know this is hard, Seb, but she needs to know because you share a body. Everyone agreed to this a long time ago. You don't have to share things from the past that you don't want to—but if you want to get to co-consciousness, everyone needs to know what's going on now."

Sebi glares for a moment and then goes back to his staring match with the floor.

"Okay. Let's move on. Seb, I want you guys to write up some notes for Steve. Just let him know more about each alter—whoever wants to share. That way, he'll have something to refer to as he gets to know you. You might talk about your function or how you came to be, or how you feel about different things. Spread the word in The Timeshare, okay?"

"Got it," Seb says, still sullen.

Dr. Newman looks at his watch and asks, "Alright. What's the most pressing thing we need to resolve with the rest of our time?"

I speak up. "We need to talk about this thing with Liz. The cheating. The screwing around is a potential death blow to our marriage."

"Is that okay with you, Seb?"

He offers an unengaged, "Whatever. I don't think he gets it."

"Okay, then. How are you guys feeling about talking with me about sex?"

I'm taken aback by the abruptness and feel a flash of fear and shame around my own past issues. I defer to Sebi, who's leaning back on the couch, arms spread across the back, not wanting to speak first either. His jaw is set and he looks furious that we need to discuss this at all.

Dr. Newman assesses the situation, "We need to start finding a solution. I know you're dealing with a lot, but I think we need to take a step back and look at this. Steve, I know you've been thinking that if this is cheating, you're headed for divorce.

Dr. Newman looks to me expectantly. I respond, "I think our marriage is worth saving. I want to work this out but if we can't, then yes, I have to look at divorce."

"Seb, you're also here. I take it that means you want to work this out, too."

Sebi shifts in his seat. "I just want my best friend back."

"I'm right here, Soph," I say softly, moving from my chair to sit with her on the couch. I put my arm around her.

Sophie stiffens but doesn't shrug my arm away. She stares at the floor and shakes her head—"I'm Sebi."

"Sebi. Sorry," I say, feeling an aching sadness ripping me apart. I feel like I can't do anything right. "This is pretty weird to me because you look like Sophie. I don't see any difference."

Sebi can't contain himself and stands up to confront me. "I love Sophie, too, but I'm not her. She's falling apart. I'm not. Can't you see that? I am Sebi. It makes all the difference in the world that you see me. We're not two halves of the same person and I'm done being ashamed and hiding and hoping no one notices me."

Dr. Newman tries to smooth it over. "Steve, I'm sure you've noticed some differences and you'll get better at it over time. Seb is his own person and it goes beyond the clothes and cologne."

I open my mouth and Dr. Newman shakes his head slightly—warning me to stop before I put my other foot in my mouth.

"Steve, you understand the marriage to be monogamous. With Sophie, it is. But there are other people living in the body that feel her monogamy with you is pretty restrictive for them."

This sounds like double talk to me and I have to call bullshit. "If you're screwing around in *that* body, to me it means my wife is screwing around on me. I don't care what you call yourself."

I can feel Sebi go from seething to furious. Dr. Newman feels it, too.

"This is a complicated situation. There're a lot of moving parts we could focus on, but for now, let's just look at the fact that Sophie and Steve have made the agreement to be monogamous. Perhaps just for now, we need to see if monogamy with Steve is possible for everyone in The Timeshare. Consider it an experiment. If it doesn't work, we can find another solution. Is that something we can all agree on—just for now?"

Seb and I reach an unstable detante. He leans his head against the wall and looks at the ceiling. "I don't think it's going to work," he says, "but we can talk about it. If I'm putting things on the back burner, I have to call a couple people to let them know what's going on."

I'm blown away. "A *couple*? More than the girl I saw you with the oth...? Jesus, Sophie."

Dr. Newman tries to de-escalate things, "That's fine, Seb. And it makes sense. Steve, I know this is a ton of information hitting you at once, but the point is that Seb is agreeing to try monogamy. Let's call this a win."

But I'm seething underneath. I'm finding out that my wife leads a double life. Or seven other lives! I don't know if I'm staying with her at this point, or leaving. I'm on the verge of divorce, but another part of me feels that she needs me more than ever.

Dr. Newman reads me, "I can see that you're feeling really frustrated and you have plenty of reason to be. Can you trust me enough to give this a try for a few weeks? To stay with Sophie for now if Seb agrees to be monogamous until we can work this out?"

"I can agree not to file for divorce for a few weeks. I don't want to lose my marriage, but I'm not even sure what that means at this point."

"I know it feels like everything is up in the air, but there's a lot of good to work with. Not everything has changed, but some big things have. Let's see if we can put some sort of plan together, find some common ground."

"I'd like you both to close your eyes for a minute so we can set an emotional intention."

I'm willing to give it a try and Sophie seems to be willing as well. I close my eyes and lean back.

"Take a breath and let it go. Now take a deeper breath. And let that go. I'd like you to think about the first time you met."

A flood of memories hit me and carry me off. Sophie and I had met on Santa Monica beach as models for a fashion shoot. Neither of us did a lot of runway work, but we looked great in print. I never did any huge campaigns—just local stuff. But it was enough to help cover some expenses and it was a real ego-booster.

That day, I was in a tux and she wore a gorgeous wedding gown. She was stunning and the location was spectacular. Flowers, huge ferns, crystal orbs, flowing scarves and fans had been brought in. The photographer had chosen to shoot in the late afternoon, just before sunset. Sophie was fantastic to work with. She never complained, never needed a break and was willing to try any suggestion the director made without question.

In the last shot, she was lying on the beach with the cold waves inching up her body. I'm lying next to her with my arm encircling her waist and I can feel that she's there, but not there. Modeling can be like that at the end of a long day, but this was different.

"Sophie, give me some *life!*" the photographer shouts. She looked into my eyes and in a little voice said, "Don't let me drown, okay?" I held her tighter and told her, "I got ya." And I could feel a consciousness coming back into her. It felt like she was melting into my arms, now relaxed and happy. It drew me in. Even then, I could tell there was something different about her. At the time, it felt exciting to me.

After the shoot, it was late and we were tired. We'd both gotten up early to get to the location. Then there was hair, makeup, wardrobe, practice shots, prep and a lot of concentrating while being out in the hot sun all day trying to look cool and comfortable.

When we realized we were both students in the bay area, we decided to drive back together and spent the evening sharing details of our life and laughing over dinner. She had been charming and friendly but I wasn't confident enough to take it any further that night. Now, I wonder who that was. Was that Sophie? Or someone else? She had felt childlike at the beach, but at dinner came across as polished with something of an accent I couldn't quite place.

That memory filled me with love for her and sadness because everything was changing now.

Dr. Newman interrupts my thoughts. "Now, I want you to hold on to that memory. I want you to wrap yourself in that feeling. Can you do that?"

I nod yes and I can feel Sophie smiling.

"Lift your index finger when you've done that."

A few minutes pass and I lift my finger. Another beat and I hear Dr. Newman say, "Good. Let's start from this place. You can open your eyes now."

The room feels lighter, and both of us are less frustrated.

"Sebi, I trust that you're still here."

"Yeah," he says, a laugh in his voice.

"Okay," Dr. Newman begins, "From that place of remembering your first meeting and how that felt, tell me how you feel about Steve."

"How I feel about him...," he shoots a sly smile at me—like we had a secret.

Seb continues, "I care about him. I love him as a friend. He's been there for me like no one else and I trust him. We have a great time together." Everything Sebi says intones up at the end like it's a question. Then he looks at me and I think I catch him tearing up a bit. "I'm afraid of losing him," he says.

I want to answer, but I wait for some instruction.

"Steve, how do you feel when you remember that first meeting?"

"I feel happy. I remember how much fun we had. I wish we could still be that playful with each other. I wish we still had that level of trust. It's odd to me that we immediately had it, but that we seem to be losing it over the years. I'm surprised to hear that Seb trusts me."

"It can be different between different alters. I think we've got a good start." Dr. Newman shifts his gaze from me to Sophie and sympathetically says, "I know this is work, but we need to go deeper."

I wonder what he meant by work. I feel like this exercise was silly, but it's relaxing. Then I look at Sophie and she's rubbing her neck the way she does when a wicked migraine is coming, and I realize that *for me* to be here is an inconvenience at worst. *For her*, it's painful. She'll be down with a migraine tonight and the medicine will barely take the edge off.

"You okay?" I ask, thwarting my instinct to reach over and rub her back.

"Yeah, I'm okay. We need to do this."

Dr. Newman continues, "Okay. Let's keep going then. Seb, tell me about what you need in an intimate relationship."

"I enjoy flirting, the seduction. I like seeing the look in a woman's eyes when we go from being strangers to more than that. I like laughing together and connecting over something we have in common. And I like doing things for her like ordering her favorite meal when she doesn't even remember telling me about it, surprising her with stupid little things that make her smile, making her laugh. I like the physical stuff, too. But that's like playing to me. Sex is the icing on the cake."

I blink back the shock that keeps gripping at me. It comes in waves—like nausea. I'm shocked about the multiplicity, of course, but I never imagined other personalities could be male, or such different ages with very different ideas about sex. Sophie had described it to me as rare and sacred.

Beyond that, I'm just trying to keep my head above water—my wife thinks she's a straight, teenage boy, but from the outside, it looks like Sophie is a lesbian.

"Steve, what do you need?"

"I feel like I need to think about what Soph...Sebi just said before I answer."

"I have to challenge you a bit, Steve. If we want to resolve this, you need to speak up and tell Seb what you think. If you wait, your answer can be influenced by what he said. Please think about that first time you met and what you wanted in your intimate relationship."

"Okay. Umm. I wanted to be a part of Sophie's world, I think. I wanted to be close to her. I didn't want that night to end. It was fun, but there was also this connection and warmth."

Seb's rolling his eyes and Dr. Newman won't allow it. "Seb, I need you to just stay with that feeling—caring about Steve, okay?"

"Okay. Sorry. It just sounds so cliche."

"Go on, Steve."

"I wanted a physical relationship, but I enjoyed just being with her—talking, having dinner, working together. She was different than any other woman I'd ever met. I wanted to be as close as possible. I wanted to be whatever she needed."

I can feel a rise in tension and could literally feel Seb drifting away. I hear my wife take a sharp inhale as Dr. Newman looks to her. "Seb, you still with us?"

"Yeah, I'm still here. Can I take a Zomig?"

"Sure." Dr. Newman answers. Seb starts rummaging through his pack and pulls out a pill box.

"Ah, why don't you let me find it for you?" Dr. Newman says, holding out his hand.

Sebi gets a look like he resents being outsmarted, but hands the box to Dr. Newman, who opens it and gives him a pill to fight the migraine, but keeps the case until the end of our session.

"What's *that* about?" I ask.

"Sometimes, a trigger will bring a different alter to the surface. When that happens, it's unsettling and there may be a desire to take a tranquilizer and zone out. I'd like Seb to be present while we're talking today. Even if it's uncomfortable."

I feel unable to focus. "I gotta say I'm having a hard time knowing what to do here. I feel like I'm walking on eggshells, trying not to say the wrong thing."

"I get that. Don't worry about it. We can deal with the triggers."

"What are triggers exactly? I mean, I've heard of them, but what are they?"

"Triggers are words or phrases or experiences that are highly emotionally charged and bring someone back to another time, usually a trauma. Multiples get triggered a lot. The smell of toothpaste, a certain brand of soup, an old song, a specific word or phrase, even being touched. Anything can trigger them. So it's not about avoiding them. It's about learning to deal with them. Right, Seb?"

I can tell the migraine had settled into my wife's right eyebrow. She rubs it angrily as she nods and gives a sarcastic chuckle. "Working on it."

"Jesus. That must make the world impossible to navigate. She can just switch if she runs into the wrong thing?"

Seb looks up. "Yeah, and we never know when it will happen or what our reaction will be. It could be a switch and blackout and I might wake up at home, on a bus, in a stranger's bedroom or in a different city. And I don't have a lot of control over it. It's getting better, but it still happens sometimes."

"I know we're going down a lot of different avenues today, but let's get back to this discussion around your relationship. We can circle back to everything else later. I'll give you another book that'll give you some better insights about all of this, and the partners' group will help, too."

"So Steve, what else do you feel you need in an intimate relationship?"

"The bottom line for me is that I need to have affection in my life. There's always compromise. To be honest, I've always felt like there was something missing in my intimacy with Sophie, but I've never been able to get a handle on it."

"So, what I heard from both of you had very little to do with the physical act of sex. Intimacy has to do with connecting, having affection, feeling loved. Does that sound right?"

I hadn't considered it from this angle, but he was right.

"Do you notice how both of you mentioned sex in passing, but intimacy for you is much more than that? We're doing this exercise because I want you to see that there is some common ground. Seb is a straight male. I don't know how much wiggle room there is, but if you're going to be monogamous, I think we need to see what can be built. For sure, you can have a lot of intimacy without crossing lines you're uncomfortable with.

"So let's talk about where those lines are," Dr. Newman continues. He hands us both sheets describing everything from holding hands to things I'd never heard of. He asks us to circle everything that we're comfortable doing together.

Regardless of what name she went by, I saw *Sophie,* so for me this is a no brainer—though I keep that thought to myself to avoid offending Sebi again. I can only see differences in behavior—like my wife is acting like a boy or a 5 year old or whatever. I'm tempted to check off every box, so that we have options, but I know this is meant to be carefully considered.

After a few minutes, we hand him our sheets. Without looking at them, he hands Sebi's to me and mine to Seb. "This is your starting point. Go home, stay in the feeling of the first time you met and get rolling on common ground."

"And Steve…"

"Yeah?"

"You need to find a hobby. This is stressful stuff and we're building a lot of support for The Timeshare. You need to take care of yourself, too."

———

Driving home, I start getting irritated with Dr. Newman. I ask Seb, "What the hell was he talking about—a hobby? I don't have time for that!"

Seb looks at my white knuckles on the steering wheel and reads the tension in my jaw. He turns up the radio and starts scream singing along - loud and really, really bad. He's also dancing in his seat and he doesn't stop until we are both laughing so hard I can hardly keep driving.

I recognize him now—this is fun Sophie. This is how she was back in college. I didn't recognize that this was a separate person back then. I'd had a great connection with this part. He's magnetic.

The song fades out and he announces, "So, you know that I can't sing. Like, at all."

While Sebi sings like a cat in heat, Elizabeth, who I was just beginning to get to know, and Sophie both had amazing singing voices. I'd learned to never agree with a woman's self-criticism, even if a male alter is the one running the show at the time, so now I answer with a cautious, "Okay."

"Well, Sophie had this voice teacher who was the sweetest woman on the planet. Samantha something. She always gave Sophie these hilarious, upbeat songs at the start of her lessons. Technically difficult, but a lot of fun to sing. She wanted music to be a blast, so we'd only get into the serious work after we'd laughed a lot. Anyway, after her lesson was over, I'd come out and we'd cut loose and we'd just scream crazy songs at the top of our lungs. She was such a great lady. I loved going to see her. She made the work fun. Really helped with the stage fright."

I'm still mad at Dr. Newman, but Sebi's discussion about singing gets me thinking. The Timeshare has a ton of interests, lots of hobbies, so I say, "I'm glad you had such a great teacher. I have no idea where to start with this hobby thing. The only thing I can think of is handball. I enjoy it, but I don't have a gift for it. The last time I seriously played, I hurt my knee pretty bad. I'm a little gun shy. I'm good at running, though."

"Gifts are sort of a cool thing. It's like a reverse Catch 22, you know? I mean, you're sort of attracted to something so you try it out and you like it. You might totally suck at it, but you keep getting pulled back into it. Like me with drawing. And the more you get sucked into it, the more practice you get, and suddenly you realize you're not bad at it, you're just new at it. So if you feel drawn to handball, or running, do it! Your passion will mold your work into what looks a whole lot like talent. No one's born a prodigy."

"So you don't think we're born with innate talents?"

"I think we're born with tendencies. You see it in genealogy. There are tons of teachers in your family, artists in mine. My grandma taught piano. That goes back generations—her whole family is musical. But I don't think anyone ever sits down to a piano and plays a concerto the first time. You love to write, but was your first effort a masterpiece?"

"Hardly!" I laugh, thinking of the first book I wrote in elementary school. I still had it and it's cute, but it's not good. And I still have my first letter to the editor I wrote when I was 11 years old but it's not particularly powerful or persuasive. "I always knew I wanted to be a writer, but I didn't start getting good at writing until high school."

"How long until you wrote something you look at now and think of as strong writing?"

"Probably my senior thesis in high school."

"So you kept at writing for about eight years consistently before you produced anything good. How long have you been playing handball?"

"I played in high school and college—a few times a week. Since then, just a couple of times."

"And now you feel intimidated by it...like you have no talent for it. Imagine that."

We both laugh and I make Sebi a deal. "You need to take your own advice."

He eyes me with playful suspicion. "What do you mean?"

"You told me about drawing and how you want to get good at it, but it sounds like you have the same sort of relationship to it as I do with handball. I'll make you a deal. I'll give handball a decent shot if you'll do the same with drawing."

It sounds too fair to refuse entirely, but Sebi's reluctant. "That's not happening. But I will give pottery a go."

"Okay. And I'll get back into running to ease into the idea. That'll help me get into some sort of shape before facing an opponent."

"Deal."

As we pull into the driveway, I'm glad Seb's migraine has resolved. Blasting music and chatting up a storm didn't seem compatible with pain. But as soon as I open the front door, he bolts for the bathroom to throw up.

Apparently, Seb had gotten the effects of the medicine, but Sophie hadn't, and when she switched back, it hit her like a 2 x 4. I help her settle into bed and she stays there until morning.

I'm whipping up eggs, bacon, and waffles when Sophie comes down the steps. The morning after a migraine, she usually emerges from bed like someone with a bad hangover. She wouldn't speak until finishing at least two cups of coffee. Breakfast would consist of some fruit, if she thought she could keep it down.

But today, she bounds down the steps and comes up behind me asking, "Guess who?"

I love feeling her arms around me and I want to turn around and kiss her, but "guess who" takes on new meaning when you're married to a multiple.

"Hey there," I answer, leaving the door open for any possibility.

She leans around me to see what's on the stove and I can see her face in profile. Her hair is pulled back and a chain with a charm dangles from her neck—heart length. Sophie can't tolerate cologne because of her migraines, but this morning, she smells amazing—like leather and lavender, saffron and spices. She slides across the kitchen to peek into the waffle maker and asks, "Blueberry?"

"Yup" I answer.

"Sweet! My favorite!" she exclaims. *This* is not my Sophie. She can't stand waffles, and blueberries are a sort of trigger for her. She moves over to the bacon and takes in a deep nose-full. "*Extra* bacon, dude. Like a lot. I can down a pound of that by myself. Do you mind making me a couple eggs? Goopy ones with cheese and garlic that I can put on an avocado." Definitely not Sophie.

I realize now I often eat meals with this person. When I'd visited her at college, this was who I ate with. I thought this was just Sophie when she was feeling healthy and upbeat. While Sophie has a long list of food allergies, this alter can, and does, eat everything.

"Sure," I say, cracking more eggs absent-mindedly as I'm trying to sort things out.

Sophie, or whoever this is, answers, "Need help?" We'd recently purchased a pricey European stove and I had no idea how to work the damn thing. I was getting the hang of the stovetop, though. And I had to agree that it did look cool in our kitchen and Jamie's cooking had gone from delicious to spectacular.

"I'd appreciate it. Can you set the table and defrost more bacon? I mean, if you can really eat a pound of it, we'll need more." She tosses the bacon into the microwave and shuffles the plates, napkins and silverware onto the table. Then she pulls out an avocado and slices it up. She moves like this is a well-choreographed dance. This aspect of her always moves that way and I love the rhythm we fall into.

"Want some of this?" she asks, fanning the avocado out on a plate and sprinkling it with slow-roasted black garlic.

"Nah," I answer, "I think they're slimy." She laughs easily. Our conversation plays out like music and I feel like one of the popular kids.

She chops a tomato and tosses it on top of the avocados, then drizzles it with olive oil and a squeeze of lemon. She tears a few fresh basil leaves to sprinkle on top, then checks the waffles. "Dude, these look done."

"Pull 'em!" I say, gesturing like an ump indicating a player is out. She tosses them on a plate and pours two more.

We sit down to breakfast and Sophie is shoveling it in. She eats four or five buttered waffles with maple syrup, hopping up to get various things to add to our meal. She couples the avocado dish with the eggs I made her and thoroughly enjoys every bite. It's fun to watch her eat with so much passion.

As we finish up, I'm hoping she'll tell me who's out. She doesn't let me off the hook. I look at her and start, "I have to ask..." I look to her for some help but her mouth is full of waffles. She raises her eyebrows expectantly.

"Are you Sebi?"

She drops her fork on her plate with a loud clank and holds her arms out to the side like she's presenting herself. She gives me a smirk and says, "Live and in color. We have homework to do, remember?"

I smile, thinking about all the times I've interacted with him. He's a ton of fun, but he's also the one who broke my heart.

"I'm not sure where to start. I have your paper from Dr. Newman. Do you have mine?"

He pulls my folded sheet out of the pocket of his robe and smooths it. He shakes a cigarette out and lights it.

"I'd prefer you smoke outside."

"I know," he says with a laugh in his voice, "but truthfully, I smoke in the house when you're out of town and it just seems more honest to do it in front of you."

I both resent and admire the manipulation. He has a way of putting things so that you couldn't effectively argue the point.

"Okay. Well, for the record I'd like you to smoke outside."

"So noted," he says, taking a drag off the cigarette and exhaling smoke before asking, "Should we head out?" He gets up and pulls the robe tighter around his waist, indicating the back door with his cigarette.

I look out the window. It's snowy and cold. Now I feel like a jerk for suggesting that my wife stand outside in the freezing weather. I didn't want to be out there either. "No, it's cool. For future reference."

"Got it," Sebi says, like he's just won a hand of poker. Then he evaluates my homework from Dr. Newman again before offhandedly throwing out, "For future reference, does the smoke bother you?"

"Not really, no."

He looks to the side blankly—mocking me to an invisible audience —and I feel like an idiot. "Then why the *hell* am I smoking outside?"

"It gets in the walls."

"Who cares? We can repaint," he smirks, knowing he's got the upper hand.

"Okay. Well, let's table that discussion for now and get into this."

"This is pretty weird," he says, grinning.

I can feel the warmth in his voice and it makes me smile. I've never met anyone who could resist him. Oftentimes, I felt like Seb was a masterful manipulator. He'd make you feel stupid and then swoop in for the rescue and you'd feel grateful for it. It seems to come so naturally for him.

He continues, "Remember that we're supposed to go to our happy place. You know, when we first met."

"Oh, right, right, right. That was a great day."

"Yes, it was," Sebi agrees, smiling.

The memory washes over me and I remember lying in the waves. "Do you remember the water? It was freezing. Kind of felt good after being in the hot sun all day."

Seb leans in and looks confused, trying to remember but disagreeing. "The water? In the hot tub? Dude, the water was *boiling*. Remember, we both turned bright red? Toss in the tequila and I was trashed fast. I got so sick the next day. It's why I only drink beer now. Well, and vodka...and rum. Never mind. I guess I drink pretty much anything, but I stay away from tequila."

"What are you talking about? We met at the beach. It was that day we were modeling together, near LA. Remember?"

Sebi squints, considering what I've said. He's looking lost and I'm not sure he has any recollection of it.

"I don't know what you're talking about, dude. It was at that frat party. You rescued me from that incredibly boring discussion I got pulled into. We sat out in the hot tub with those girls and then jumped in the pool. I woke up in that damn pool! I was floating on one of those pink rafts and someone had put a bunch of empty tequila bottles around me. You jumped in and fished me out. You don't remember that?"

I suddenly feel sad. And very, very old.

Of course, Sebi wouldn't have been lying around on a beach in a gown, pretending to be deeply in love with a stranger. My voice cracks. "No, I remember that night but my *first* memory of meeting you is when we met at the photo shoot on the beach and drove back to school together. That was a couple weeks before the frat party."

He senses my sadness and says, "Sorry. Time's a little fuzzy for us. Plus, we all remember different things from different perspectives. If it helps, the first time I met you, it was awesome."

I trail off with "Yeah, it was. Well, let's close our eyes and I'll meet you at the frat party." I needed to touch my wife's hand and I reach across the table, but Sebi's eyes are already closed and he isn't reaching for me.

The extraordinary thing about being open to trying something new, to seeing a new perspective, is that wisdom sometimes finds you there. By shifting my understanding of our first meeting, I could suddenly see our relationship from Sebi's perspective. We were friends that night. There had been no vulnerability on his part, no flirting with me. Instead there was a "welcome to my team" sort of feeling. He was fun, but he tended to be reckless. He was the life of the party, but paid the price the next day. And, often, he took other people down with him.

I spend a few minutes there at the frat house and then open my eyes and I study Sophie's face. It's different. It looks more male, but I can't put my finger on *how* exactly. Something with her brow and jawline. She holds her mouth differently, too. Her lips are redder, but somehow that makes her look more masculine.

Her eyes flutter open and for the first time, I see it. The vulnerable green of Sophie's eyes has been replaced with Sebi's confident royal blue. If I'd ever wondered if this was real or not, now I'm convinced. And it throws me.

I think about Sophie and Sebi. In retrospect, I should have guessed something was up. I'd always been impressed with her wide range of interests and abilities. "Can I say something before we jump in?"

Seb is sipping his coffee, holding the rim of his cup with his left hand as he drinks. It's remarkable how even his gestures are different. I think he's ambidextrous.

"I always wondered how Sophie could have such diverse interests. She told me she had anxiety, and she was sick so much of the time, but she was the most fearless person I'd ever met—acting, singing, modeling all over the world. She was constantly thrown into new and nerve-wracking situations, but handled it all without missing a beat. And all while maintaining a 3.7 GPA. The confidence she brought to things was just unreal."

"I'm gonna say thanks, because some of that was me, but yeah. I mean, we get shit done. My first therapist, Dr. Ziegal, helped me see this as a superpower, so we never saw it as a disability. He expected that we could tap into it and do anything."

"I'm glad he did that," I say, feeling genuine gratitude for the man's ingenuity.

"When I was at Dr. Newman's office and was imagining myself with Sophie on the beach, there was a romantic feeling. Meeting you at the frat party, I got a completely different vibe. Like, more of a friendship thing. It was like I could stand where you are and see your perspective on us."

"Right? I don't mind a handshake or a hug, but after that it gets pretty uncomfortable for me. I just don't see you that way."

"I know. And I get that now. We just have to find a solution that's going to work. Sophie and I have agreed to be monogamous."

"About that: You know Sophie's asexual, right?"

"Asexual? You mean, someone who doesn't have any sexual attraction to anyone?"

"Yeah. Like, no hormones. Haven't you noticed that whenever she's out, she wears a silver band around her middle finger?"

"I know she always puts that ring on when she's out, but why is that important?"

"That's the symbol for being asexual. It's like an announcement."

I was taken aback. "I don't think that's what she means by it. It's not true that she's asexual, Seb. We've been together long enough that I think I'd know."

"Okay. Well, not to one up you, but I've known her slightly longer than you and that's a thing. She's never been sexually attracted to anyone—at least, not for a long time. She can fake it pretty well, but I think they sort of used up anything related to sex a long time ago and she's just happy not to have to do it anymore. I mean, she's always in pain, so sex is impossible for her anyway."

This is devastating news to me. And it's unsettling. I'm routinely having sex with someone in The Timeshare and I have no idea who it is. They're all in the same body and I wonder if it really matters. Then I'm sure it does—and that it's important. I feel myself going down a path that won't have any answers and we have more ground to cover this morning. Seb had told me that every alter personality has their own perceptions, so I need to take this with a very large grain of salt and not get upset. At least, not until I hear it from Sophie.

Seb doesn't seem to notice and keeps talking. "Something else has been on my mind. You expect me to be monogamous, but you aren't. You have sex with a bunch of different people in The Timeshare and you're asking me to settle for one person who's not even the right gender."

I raise my eyebrows at that one. I didn't know that I was having sex with different alters and now I'm not sure how I feel about it. "Who have I been sleeping with?"

"I'm honestly not sure. When you're in the mood, or they think you are, they come forward. But there are at least four or five that you've been with. Don't you notice any differences?"

I thought about it for a minute. "I do. But isn't that a normal thing? Sometimes you're in the mood for different things, different ways. Right?"

"Has that been true in your other relationships?"

"Seb, I haven't had many other relationships. But no, I guess you're right. We pretty much did the same things once the relationship was established."

"That's what usually happens. With multiples, any time you're with a different alter, it's going to be a different experience. It's not just that they'll have diverse preferences, but some are more submissive and others will be aggressive. They'll respond in dissimilar ways, too. But you'll know. They'll feel unlike one another to you. The point is that you have more than one partner."

I try to digest this news and also try to see Seb's perspective. To each one in The Timeshare, the alters felt like completely separate people sharing a body. To Seb, I was having relationships with a bunch of people.

"You're right. From your vantage point, I can see how it feels like I get a sexual buffet and you're just sitting there with your waffles. I never thought of it that way. It's not fair, and I don't have any answers. I wish I did. I'm just in a place right now where I feel like I'm absorbing—I'm learning everything I can and honestly, I feel like I'm cramming for finals."

"Sorry. I forget there's a learning curve to this stuff. This has got to be intensely bizarre for you. Plus, you're getting a lot of news you might not like. To me, you've got years of experience under your belt with it. But you're thinking of it in a whole different way."

"Yeah, I am. So, be patient, okay? For now, let's look at our lists."

"And I thought I was doing such a good job distracting you from it." Seb laughs. "Okay," he says, reviewing my list from Dr. Newman. "So I can do the hugs, a pat on the back, holding hands and the snuggling and spooning—as long as you're the spoonie. That's about as far as I can see taking it, but honestly, that's kinda pushing it."

Then Seb is quiet, considering something. "Look, I need to ask you something that's been on my mind since college."

"That long?" I tease.

"Well, yeah." Seb looks uncomfortable and serious. "Does it help or hurt when I hug you, grab your shoulder or whatever? I'm really tactile, but I don't know if that makes things better or worse for you."

"I don't know. This is just tough. I think sometimes it's nice, sometimes it's hard because I want more. Can I answer that as we go? Like tell you in the moment?"

"That probably makes the most sense."

"And can I make a suggestion?" I ask.

Sebi takes a deep breath. Considering the subject matter, there had to be cause for concern. Cautiously, he says, "Sssssssure?"

"I think we should try to do what we can and see if there's any sort of..."

"Spark?" Sebi offers, sounding unconvinced and looking a little squeamish.

"Well, maybe spark isn't the right word. But Sophie and I'd like to remain monogamous and you have certain..."

"Hormones?"

"Yes. That."

He nods. "I guess guys do it in prison, right?"

"Thanks for that. Yes. Super romantic way to springboard into this."

Sebi gives me a look that says he's willing to power through this, but it's not his first choice. "So, for me, this is a gay thing. Who's the Alpha dog? Don't they have some sort of pecking order—like a top and bottom sort of situation or something?"

We try to make sense of it, to understand how it all works and soon hilarity ensues. We're both tense at first and then can't stop laughing. This is such a ridiculous situation.

"This is just crazy! Who does this?" Sebi starts. "And why don't I have a gay alter who could work this all out? Or at least give us some tips?"

I get a strange feeling as we're talking. There's something he's not telling me. I know better than to ask. My inquiries sound accusatory to him.

Sebi pulls the vodka out—at 11 am on a Saturday—and we both take a few shots before heading to the bedroom. It feels like we have a mission to complete.

Sleeping with my wife, there's a connection, but there's always been a distance I've never been able to explain. It's good enough to sustain our marriage, but it's not totally fulfilling. With Sebi, even though he shares the same body, it really did feel like two straight guys trying to have gay sex.

We give it our best shot, but in the end there are just a lot of elbows, knees and awkwardness. Kissing feels uncomfortable. Embraces feel wrong. Even just touching one another in any way other than buddies feels foreign. It's obvious this is not going to be our solution and I know I have to crack my mind open in order to save my marriage.

For now, we chalk it up to getting a really good grade on our homework because, truly, we had gone above and beyond. Sebi heads to the bathroom for a shower as I grab my phone. It's my brother, David, and I immediately regret not checking caller ID before picking up.

"Hey, David. What's up?" I hope he can hear the impatience in my voice.

"Nothing, really. I'm going to be in Denver after the holidays. Thought we could have dinner."

I can not deal with any crap at this point in my life and it makes me more direct than I'd normally be. "No ulterior motives?"

David pauses and I know exactly what he's thinking—he has a very specific intention and doesn't want to tell me what it is. We're only two years apart in age and I can easily read every phrase, every intonation, every pause.

"David?"

"I don't want to get into it over the phone. And don't do your whole obsessing thing. I just want to catch up and make sure you're okay."

"Is Mom getting worse?"

"She's about the same. Try not to worry about it."

I hear another call coming through. Iowa area code. I have no idea who it is, but it's obviously someone from back home and I want to get off the phone with David.

"Fine. Dinner. Text me the details. I've got another call, so I gotta go." I click over before he can try to keep me on the line.

"Is this Steve?"

"Yeah. Who's this?"

"It's Kevin."

"Kevin?" I say out loud, trying to place the caller's voice.

"From high school."

Memories immediately flood me and I smile. "Kevin? Kevin Roberts? I haven't talked to you since the reunion. It's been years!"

"I hope you don't mind. I got your number from your sister."

He waits for an answer but I've got nothing. I'm shocked.

"From Rebecca. I got your number from Rebecca."

I snap back. "Right. Okay. What's up?"

"I know this is weird, but we could always talk. I'm hoping that our history outweighs the time and distance?"

He sounds defeated—beaten down by something he can't fight against. I'm immediately concerned.

"Are you okay? What's going on?"

"I've got a problem and I really need a friend."

I can hear the tears in his voice and I remember dozens of conversations starting this way with him when we were kids. He could talk, but I had to drag him to the starting line.

"Absolutely. You can always talk to me, no matter what."

"Okay. Well, this may be a touchy subject."

My concern shifts to worry. "Kevin, what the *hell* is going on?"

He doesn't answer but I can hear he's still there.

"Kev?"

"It's my wife, Shannon. Do you remember—Shannon Bruce? We were all in that advanced creative writing class senior year?"

"Vaguely. Sorry."

"No, it's okay. We were friends in high school and wound up going to Drake together. Anyway, we got married a few years ago."

Kevin pauses and I feel I'm supposed to say something but I'm at a loss. A long moment passes until I hear him clear his throat and continue.

"It's not going great and I don't know what to do."

Kevin's life always seemed to parallel mine. And here we are again. I wonder if Rebecca told him about my situation. She was the sort of person who wouldn't want to betray a confidence, but at the same time would want to fix everyone's problems. She often brought people together when they were struggling with the same issue.

"Did something happen?"

"She's just gone downhill lately. I know you got depressed in high school and Shannon is going through that, too. She's in the hospital now and she's coming home in a few days. I don't know if I can do this." His voice trails off, and I can hear him choking up.

All of my protective instincts come up. We'd been friends since elementary school and along the way, Kevin had skipped a couple grades. He's a little shorter than me with a thinner build. People joked around that I defended him like a little brother. With wavy, blonde shoulder-length hair and blue-gray eyes, we looked like kindred spirits, if not brothers.

A product of his parents, he was a hippie among farmers. Younger, smaller and wide open, he was a prime candidate for bullies.

I want to fix this for him, but know I can't. Depression is an enemy I'd barely survived. And having a chronically ill partner is like pouring your life force into someone only to have it consumed by a parasite that's draining them.

"I wish I knew what to say."

"What worked for you? What helped? I don't even know how to talk to her anymore."

I have no idea what to tell him, so I think about something I read. "Kev, if you care about her, she knows. I'm sure you just being yourself probably helps her a lot. Don't expect yourself to be all things to her. You can't be her husband and her doctor and her therapist. No one could handle all that."

I can feel relief on the other side of the line and as we continue, it feels like no time had passed. I'm glad he called, but I'm worried about him. Most of all, I feel grateful to have a friend who's sorta in the same boat.

With visits sometimes twice a week now, it's beginning to feel like I live at Dr. Newman's office. I don't know how Sophie maintains this level of intensity.

Dr. Newman smiles as he opens his office door and we file in. "So," he starts as soon as we're seated, "how did the assignment go? Did you have a chance to talk things over?"

"Yeah, we...talked," Seb says, his eyes laughing as he purses his lips to quiet a laugh.

"Find any common ground?"

Now I was trying not to laugh, "No, not really."

Dr. Newman offers a sympathetic smile. "In these situations, there's generally not a lot of agreement. The goal is to help you find that place of caring about each other and seeing one another's point of view."

"We don't think of each other the same way. In fact, Seb remembers meeting me at a frat party. I remember meeting Sophie at a photo shoot on the beach. So when we went to our happy place, I met him at the frat party and, yeah, completely different relationship."

"That's great that you were willing to meet him there. I think that probably gave you a lot of insight and took a ton of pressure off of Seb. So what did you come up with?"

I answer for both of us—a bad habit I picked up from my brother David. "We came up with the fact that while some parts of our relationship work great, life in the sex department isn't working for either of us."

Seb interrupts. "One big problem is that Sophie is asexual. Another issue is that I'm not. And I'm straight. We agreed that we can be partners in a lot of ways, but not in bed."

Dr. Newman nods his understanding, "I get that. So, what are you going to do about it?"

Sebi and I look at each other and I answer, "We have no clue."

"That's why we're here," Seb says. "You're the man with all the answers."

We look at one another, both wondering whether or not to share our best efforts that day after the vodka. It's too important and too funny to keep to ourselves.

Sebi starts and it feels like two kids admitting to an old crime. "After we did our happy place visualization—and a ton of vodka—we tried to see how far we could take things. Even pretty smashed, the answer is—not very far."

Dr. Newman surprises me by not being amused. Instead, it seems he's impressed with our commitment. "I'm really glad you tried. Sounds like you're starting to get the answers you need."

"Yes, we are," I tell him.

"Not necessarily helpful ones though," Seb adds.

"Well, I can give you some ideas, but it's up to you. Do you want me to tell you what other people have done?

"Please!" we both nod, feeling a cautious hope.

"Okay, I want you to really tune in and think about how you feel as I say them."

"Some people have alters who are dormant during the marriage. Others decide to be abstinent. Others will try to find enough satisfaction in what they *can* do within the relationship. I had one multiple who *created* intimacy between the alters. It was complicated, but really creative, and it worked for her. Other people will agree to some ground rules and allow some sort of relationship outside of the marriage. It can range from occasional dates, to kissing, to sex, or to full blown relationships." Dr. Newman pauses to take in our expressions and then asks, "Anything sounding like it would work for you guys?"

Sebi sighs and sits back, raising his eyebrow inquisitively. I know what he's thinking. And I know what will work for me—or more to the point, what won't work for me. I don't want to start the conversation, but find myself speaking up anyway.

"I'm still having a really hard time with the idea of anything extra-curricular. I have never in my life considered an open marriage. I think it's a recipe for disaster. Six months in and it looks like a zombie apocalypse. Everyone is hurt." Ironically enough, I'm beginning to grasp that it may be the only thing that will salvage my relationship.

Sebi finishes the thought with, "And an open marriage is about all that will work for me."

Dr. Newman asks, "Last time when we talked, it sounded like the chase is what you enjoy, Seb. You like flirting, finding out more about them and then making them happy, right?"

"Well, yeah. That and the sex. I mean, don't forget the sex," he's smirking now, both arms stretched out across the entire back of the couch, bouncing his foot on his knee.

"So Steve, I'm going to say something you might not enjoy hearing, but I want you to answer honestly because it's not a rhetorical question. How long would you be able to remain married if you had to be abstinent? Your wife could not have sex and you couldn't have sex outside of the marriage?"

He's right. I don't like the question because it won't prove my point. I don't want to answer. "I have no idea," I lie.

"Guess."

"Okay. I take your point. It'd be tough. I imagine even if I wanted to stay, we'd end up divorced if I needed sex and never got it."

"That's where Sebi is."

"Exactly." Seb says, slapping his hands on the back of the leather couch, looking vindicated.

"Seb, how long could you last in a relationship where your girl-friend was screwing around and cheating right in front of you and acting like it was no big deal? How would it feel if she was flaunting that in front of your face and telling you she didn't feel attracted to you?"

The arms come down and Sebi clears his throat as he adjusts his watch, "I see what you mean. That'd suck."

"That's where we are right now. We have to find a way to create some sort of a bridge. There has to be a compromise in here somewhere because without it, things are not likely to go in a good direction for your relationship. But you're better off than a lot of couples because you're willing to try—and you're having fun with this as well."

We're both quiet, wondering how we'll ever find a compromise in a situation like this.

Dr. Newman waits just in case some brilliant revelation is brewing in our minds. It isn't.

"Would you like me to suggest some more ideas?"

The room fills with our mutual discouragement. I don't think either of us feel much hope of resolving this, but we both nod for Dr. Newman to go on.

"Sebi, how often are you seeing these women?"

"I don't know—it's hard for them to get away. Liz gets out maybe four times each year. Laura and I talk more often but I see her less than Liz—maybe twice a year."

I wonder how long this has been going on but hold my tongue. Dr. Newman was getting information I'd been wondering about ever since this whole thing started.

"So you're involved with two women?"

Sebi shifts forward, looking at Dr. Newman but also being sure he can see me out of the corner of his eye for a reaction. "Mostly just one woman." If he's paying attention, he can see me bristle. I don't know if this is good news or bad news. My wife isn't out picking up strangers. That's the good news. But it sounds like she has an established relationship with someone else. The "mostly" concerns me, too.

Then he adds, "Steve knows them."

Shocked and confused, I immediately react with, "No I don't. What are you talking about?" It sounds like he was either trying to condone his behavior or make me an accomplice.

"Yes, you do. Liz and Laura. You remember? I dated them in college. We've been seeing each other ever since. I had some classes with Laura. And Liz worked at that bar," he snaps his fingers and points, trying to think of some cue that will help me out. "The one right off campus. By the pizza place? You've been there."

I must've gone completely ashen. I hadn't recognized Liz the other morning, but in retrospect, yes, I *had* seen her before. And I remembered seeing Laura leave Sophie's dorm room from time to time when I picked Sophie up for breakfast. These were very long-term relationships.

"I thought you liked reeling them in. This seems more serious."

"I do enjoy that part when I'm dating different people, but I also love my relationships with Liz and Laura. And they're free to leave at anytime, so I like winning them over whenever I see them. It's on-going. I don't think you can let that go in a relationship. You have to keep things fresh. Liz works hard, has a couple of amazing kids and she's an incredible woman. Her husband doesn't get that."

My blood is boiling now. He's romancing these women and I'm jealous. More than that, I feel that while he's working to win them over, Sophie wasn't putting much of an effort into our marriage. She couldn't put much in because her pain level has been so consistently bad, but I couldn't help feeling that a part of her cared more for these women than she did for me.

Dr. Newman interrupts my thoughts, "And that's a part of it. Am I right?" There's obviously something about Liz's husband that I need to hear.

I glance over and Sebi no longer looks playful. There's a different expression—like an assassin who's been caught but feels like he was in the right. "Yeah."

This look scares the hell out of me. I'd seen this before. He can go from lovable puppy to attack dog in less than three seconds. It generally means he's about to start breaking things. I hadn't seen it often and it was generally short-lived with a fairly low casualty rate, but it was intensely unpleasant.

I feel like I'm watching a horror movie unfold. Dr. Newman doesn't sound like Dr. Newman any more. He's still calm, but he's confronting—and he's offering Sebi an opening to share something I wasn't going to like. My body feels strange—like I'm no longer really here. I wonder if this is what my wife feels like all the time.

Sebi looks sly, devious. But there's something more there. He's pleased with himself. And he's not at all embarrassed that he'd been found out. Yes, he liked the women. He enjoyed the chase. But there was something about screwing over Liz's husband that pleased him as well. "Look, I love Liz. I mean, I care about her and what happens to her and her family."

I feel incapable of hearing any more. At home, I manage to stay out of the way when he's in this mood, but today, I'm angry and feel Dr. Newman can help me pick up the pieces if Sebi loses it.

"This is such crap," I explode, cutting Sebi off mid-sentence. "What the hell is wrong with you? Torpedoing our relationship isn't enough, you're going to take down theirs, too? Jesus, Sophie. This is wrong on so many levels."

While anything approaching anger in my voice usually makes Sophie crumble, Sebi is completely unaffected.

"First, I'm *Sebi*. Second, it's not *crap*. If Liz's husband found out, I'm sure it would just spice up their sex life." He laughs, but it sounds like a challenge. He's getting louder now, defiant. It's the sort of laugh you give when you've screwed someone over, but they don't know it yet. He stands up and begins shouting at me.

"Who doesn't fantasize about his wife being bi?" he aims toward me. "I mean, not you apparently, but pretty much every other guy. This is not a big deal."

He's pacing now. I join him on the floor, standing up to be face to face. I knew from experience that he hated this. He imagines himself to be taller and stronger than me. And it annoys him to see that I'm the dominant male—size-wise anyway.

"Wrong, Seb. WRONG. It's absolutely a HUGE deal. MASSIVE. The worst thing that could happen to Liz—who you say you love—is that she could lose her family. She could lose her kids. She could wind up completely screwed. There is no way to look at this and think it's okay. Did you think about any of this?"

"Alright." Dr. Newman is assertive but irritatingly calm in the face of all this. Did he know? Had they been talking about it and this was new information only to me?

"Let's take a step back for a minute. Have a seat and just reel in the feelings. Let's break this down a little bit. Sebi is responsible for his decisions and for how they impact your relationship. You've just learned that he's been involved with other people since before you were married and the entire length of your relationship. That's enough to keep us busy for awhile."

I feel Seb stand down as he tentatively takes back his spot on the couch. I return to my chair as Dr. Newman continues, "In terms of the women, they're making their own decisions and those decisions will impact their relationships. But that's up to them. We don't need to take responsibility for their decisions. We have plenty to deal with."

"I'd like to check in and see how you two are doing. This may be a good place to close today or we may need to tie up a couple loose ends before I send you out. Sebi?"

Sebi shakes his head no, but his face shows a mix of emotions I can't read. His eyes still have a coldness to them and I'm worried what he'd do once we get home. While I haven't experienced them often, I'm always worried they could boil over into something I can't handle. And I have no plan for dealing with something like that.

"Steve? You look a little pale. Do you need to say something?"

I have another hour's worth of things to say, but I start with this, "I'm seeing a different side of my wife and I'm not sure I like it. I have no idea how more time here today could fix anything, but I am not feeling okay."

"What do you feel like you need resolved before we close today?"

"No idea where to even start." I'm scared and I'm furious. "Is this a normal thing in these situations? The lying, cheating, betrayal?" Hearing the words come out of my mouth only fuels the anger I was feeling. I'm pissed about everything but also that this discussion hadn't brought any degree of resolution. I need this tied up and put away and it feels even messier than when we started. Now, I also have serious concerns about my wife's character.

"I guess I'm wondering if the sweet, caring person I fell in love with is even around anymore. She would never hurt anyone. I hope Seb isn't as cold and immoral as he seems right now. Seems like he has no problem hurting people and that freaks me out, to be honest. Those are some things I'd like resolved before I walk out of here."

Sebi is looking at the floor and I can tell he's crying now, but in this moment I don't care. I'm devastated. I want him to hurt as badly as he hurt me.

Seb shakes out a cigarette and waves it at Dr. Newman, who firmly tells him, "Outside if you want, but I don't want the second-hand smoke." Seb tucks the cigarette back in and replies, "I can wait."

Dr. Newman takes my questions one at a time. "Infidelity can be a major issue in any relationship, but it tends to be even more complicated with multiples. It doesn't happen all the time, but because they don't see it as cheating, it can be a real problem. There are a lot of different possible solutions. We're probably facing some trial and error to find one you can both live with. I don't believe Seb is cold or immoral. And I don't believe any of the alters are either. But I do believe that they were exposed to a way of thinking and doing things that's so far out of our comfort zone that we have no idea what influence that all had on her and we'll likely see more of that the deeper we dig. All of that can be reset."

He goes on to ask, "I know how unsettling this all is. What do you feel like you need?"

"I need some time to think," I tell them both. "I need a break...a few days away."

"That makes sense. Sebi, can you check in with everyone and make sure that will work out?"

Sebi nods and closes his eyes. His watch comes to his nose and he takes a breath. A minute later, he looks up. Tears are flowing from terrified green eyes and Sebi is gone.

Dr. Newman quickly assesses the situation, looks at the time and considers what can be done. I knew the first goal would be to stabilize everyone before we leave.

Then I wonder if this person sitting here is Sophie. Same eye color, but she feels different. This one feels more damaged and incapable of handling things. She's rocking back and forth now, chewing on her nails.

Dr. Newman kneels down next to the couch and tells her, "Elizabeth, it's going to be alright. We're going to work this out together, okay? Steve's here. Can I tell him a bit about you?"

She nods as she blows her nose, looking away from both of us.

"Steve, Elizabeth is agoraphobic. That means she's terrified about leaving the house to the point where she can't go anywhere. She's also not crazy about being there alone."

"I think I've seen her. A couple years into our marriage, Sophie told me she wanted to get a dog because of my traveling. One of her close friends from college gave her our Great Dane, Napoleon."

"Well, Napoleon has been great for her. He's been to my office before. Affectionate, balanced, friendly. He helps a lot when you're away. Right, Elizabeth?"

Dr. Newman motions for me to scoot in closer. I'm so furious and I don't know what to do. The *last* thing I want to do is sit next to her. There are doctors out there who feel multiple personality disorder (dissociative identity disorder) doesn't exist, but whatever *this* is, it sucks to be on the receiving end of it.

I bite the inside of my cheek and sit down next to her. Shaking and sweating now, she grabs on to me like she's drowning. I hate everything about this. I hate that she's multiple, that she's so terrified, that I'm angry about her fear. I hate that she's suffering and I hate that I can't deny that this is real.

Dr. Newman goes on..."Elizabeth holds all of the fear from the abuse, so she's very anxious. While some of the alters really appreciate being noticed, she doesn't. She prefers being anonymous. She'll talk, but she's very soft-spoken. Losing it like this is pretty much hell for her."

He quietly asks her, "Did you need to say something?"

Elizabeth looks strange and Dr. Newman gives her the trash can. She's so upset she vomits. Then she apologizes. Dr. Newman hands her a Kleenex and a bottle of water. "Take your time. We're not in a rush."

She rocks and sits with her nose on Sebi's watch. Then she reaches out for Dr. Newman's hand.

I sit and wait, but I'm growing impatient. It feels like whenever I had a need, it was always trumped by Sophie's problems and I was getting sick of it. Then I feel like a narcissistic jerk for feeling that way.

"Do you want some music?" he asks Elizabeth.

She nods and he puts on some classical piano music. I find this to be odd. Sophie abhors the piano and any time she hears it, she can't shut it down fast enough. We leave restaurants if someone is playing the piano.

Elizabeth's shoulders relax and she takes a deep breath into the watch before she finally finds her voice. She's so quiet, I have to strain to hear her. She says she's worried that I'm mad at her and that I'm going to leave her and not come back. Dr. Newman reminds her what they've been working on—less dependence on me and greater interdependence between the alters. "Steve isn't leaving forever and you guys can count on each other."

She's sniffling and gulping air. But she's calming. I never realized my being away was such a huge issue. I knew Sophie wasn't thrilled about it, but I didn't get that it was this bad for any of them.

"Steve has said he needs a few days to sort through things and I think it's a good idea. It feels like you came out because his going away is intolerable to you. Am I right?"

Elizabeth nods her head violently.

"Steve is going. That's non-negotiable. Let's brainstorm how we can make this easier for you. Did you want to ask a friend to come and stay with you? I think you've had your neighbor Carol over a couple times and Kathy, I think, stayed another time. Do you want to ask them?"

Elizabeth is still sniffling but nods in agreement.

"Yes?" Dr. Newman asks. "Okay, let's check in with them and if they can't stay, we'll find another plan."

"I don't have to go," I offer, feeling like I'll pop a blood vessel if I stay, but also feeling like I have no choice.

"No, Steve. This is one of those things where I want her to be able to deal with real-life situations. You're going to be traveling for work and sometimes you'll need a break. She needs to find solutions to this so she can be independent, so she's not crippled by triggers."

He turns to my wife. "Elizabeth, I heard what you had to say and we have a plan. If those friends can't stay, call me and we'll figure out something else, okay? And I want you to make a note in your book in case you're not out later and someone else needs to help make arrangements."

Elizabeth pulls out a small journal with a blue cover. On the front it says "READ ME." She opens the book and uncaps her pen, awaiting instruction.

"Make a note that someone needs to call Carol, and if she can't stay while Steve's away, to ask Kathy. See if they can stay with you two or three nights, okay? And make a note to call me if they can't. We'll put our heads together and figure it out. Everyone knows to check the book each morning, right?"

Elizabeth nods her head yes, as she jots down the note and slips the journal back into her bag.

"Do you feel better about this now? Did we handle it okay?"

Elizabeth is calm now, again nodding yes.

"Okay. Let's get someone out who can get you home."

She closes her eyes as Dr. Newman returns to his chair.

"Elizabeth, I want you to take a deep breath and let it go. And another—in and out. And just notice how your breath is like waves on the ocean and how very relaxing that feels. You can trust that the ocean will always be there. I'd like you to imagine yourself sitting in your living room and people of The Timeshare are there with you. Does someone want to come forward—someone who can get you home and then be there with you this weekend? Let's ask that person to take the wheel now."

The Timeshare knows I don't want to see Sebi right now, and the kids are too young to deal with this. The alters who hate conflict certainly aren't going to be coming forward.

My wife takes a sharp breath, shudders and sits up straight. Quickly assessing the situation, she grabs my hand to pull me in for a quick hug and several hard slaps on the back.

"Hey man, I missed you. Let's grab some burgers on the way home.

I'm starving!" Then she's digging in the bag and pulling out a bandana to tie around her head.

I look to Dr. Newman like, "*Help me!!!*"

"Hey, Jamie, good to see you," Dr. Newman says, "Take care of everyone this weekend, okay? And call if you need anything. I'll be around."

Jamie has a quiet, stable presence. He feels gentle, but he's also directive.

"I'll handle the kids, don't worry. I have a project in mind that'll keep 'em busy," he says with a wink and a reassuring smile.

On our way home, we stop for a burger. "Love these burgers, but I really miss In & Out sometimes, don't you?" Jamie says.

"So much!" I agree.

As we step inside the house, he asks, "Do you need help packing?" Not a lot of worry from this one about me leaving!

I throw a few things together and decide to go up to the mountains for a couple of nights. My parents had honeymooned up at a little one-bedroom condo on Red Feather Lakes and loved it so much, my dad bought it for my mom on their anniversary a few years later. We vacationed there all the time when I was a kid. They gave it to Sophie and me for a wedding gift. I haven't been up there in months, but I love it.

I always enjoy time away, but knowing now that Sophie was having a hard time with it made me feel guilty. On my way out, Jamie pats my back like a drum and says, "I got this. Have a good time."

———

As I'm heading out of town, Kevin calls to ask how things are going. With most people, the response is automatic. I don't think about it. I tell them everything is fine. If they press the issue, I tell them I'm just tired. With Kev, I can be honest. He knows my secrets. I don't give him the details, but I do tell him I'm having trouble in my marriage. Telling him Sophie was a multiple might blow his mind, so I tell him she has anxiety. It wasn't a lie. Anxiety attacks often precede a switch.

I can hear Kevin laugh sadly at my revelation before saying, "Why do we always seem to be going through the same thing at the same time?"

"I know, right? It's crazy, but I'm glad you called me. At least we can talk."

"Hey, I work for the airline and I'm in Denver a lot. I'm here for a few days right now. Do you want to grab a drink?"

"I have a better idea. I'm heading up to Red Feather Lakes for the weekend. Wanna join me for some fishing?"

"God, I haven't been fishing in years. Shannon hates that kind of thing. Sounds great."

I swing around and go back to pick him up from his hotel.

Sometimes you get together with an old friend and you realize why you don't see them anymore. Other times, it's obvious that the only thing you have in common is high school stuff. With Kevin, we fall right back into our old friendship. He knows me, my family, and he understands everything about me. He gets how I work through things and I don't have to explain anything or justify my perspective.

I see him now and, suddenly, I'm an 18-year-old kid again. It's familiar, but talking about my problems feels like a betrayal of Sophie. I push my guilt aside. I need some time to think, and Kevin and I have always helped each other work through things.

It's even cooler at the lake—a light snow drifts through the air, insisting that everything slow down and quiet itself. I close my eyes and take in the smell of the lake and pine, noticing that it immediately calms me. Kevin feels it too, and we spend the evening in a reflective, comfortable silence. I avoid trying to solve any problems and just stay in the moment. Everything here is different. No TV, no internet. We both fall asleep reading in the living room. I find I sleep more soundly here. For some reason, Kevin's steady breathing is comforting.

He's still asleep as I begin putting together the fishing stuff the next morning, but the condo is small and I'm loud enough that he wakes.

"What's up?" he asks, still groggy.

"Getting ready for fishing!" I respond brightly. A good night's sleep and a day of ice fishing to look forward to has put me in a good place.

Kevin looks at the sun streaming through the window and checks his watch as he yawns. "But it's like...? He stares at his watch harder, blinking and squinting. "Like 10. Isn't that too late?"

"Not really. In Iowa, yes. But, here you can kinda go whenever."

"Well, alright then. Let's do it," he says, sitting up and pulling his shoulder-length blonde hair into a ponytail.

We toss together a quick breakfast. I fry up some omelets while he makes pancakes. It becomes pure comedy when he burns the first few and the last one sticks to the pan and starts smoking. I assign him to toast and we laugh about how he never learned to cook.

We grab the poles and head out to the ice. It's a starkly clear, calm day. We usually have fog and gusts of wind that can carry off an ice tent this time of year, but we got lucky in our timing.

"Winter is so warm here," Kevin comments.

"You're just used to that brutal Iowa crap. No humidity here, so it's not nearly as bad. Summer is like that too, so a hundred degrees here feels like 80 in Iowa."

"No kidding. And you made me think you were such a bad ass at the reunion showing me pictures of you skiing in shorts."

"I am a bad ass but, yes, I do admit those pictures were a little misleading."

We only catch a couple of bass, but it's enough for dinner.

There's a fire pit out back, but I'm not in the mood, so I use the technique my mom taught me: cleaning the fish and wrapping them in foil with butter and lemon and dill. I toss them in the oven and tell Kevin, "I'm freezing. I'm going to take a shower."

"Okay. See ya in a few hours."

"Oh, shut up." I've always enjoyed notoriously long showers and everyone teases me about it. "But I *did* set the timer. Take the fish out when it goes off."

We enjoy fresh bass and a bag of chips for dinner before digging out a deck of cards to pass the time.

At one point, Kevin says, "Sorry. I'm not great company—sleeping all the time. I can't rest when Shannon's away and when she's home, I have to sleep with one eye open." He can read the concern on my face and continues...

"She did it in the middle of the night, you know? She took a bunch of pills and slept in the spare room. The only reason she's alive is because I couldn't sleep and went to check on her. It was totally random. When I couldn't wake her up, I called the ambulance. They're keeping her for 30 days."

"I'm so sorry. I didn't know."

"At least I know she's safe—for now."

"There's that."

That gets me thinking. I could be in the same boat with Sophie at any point. Beyond a suicide attempt, I didn't know what issues would call for a hospital stay. She told me she had tried to kill herself as a kid, but I hadn't even thought of it as a possibility until now. I imagine a lot of multiples end up in the hospital. It's sobering to consider.

As we're talking and catching up on one another's lives, it dawns on me how lucky I am. Apart from work friends or partners, no guy I knew really has any close friends. We compartmentalize—we have our high school and college buddies, people we've served with, acquaintances we know through our spouses, faith communities...but lifelong friends who have known us through everything? That's rare. And I have that.

After two days of fishing, poker, hiking and drinking too much, I feel like I have a firmer foundation. I drop Kevin back off at his hotel and head home.

As I approach the front door, I feel stronger and more capable, bolstered. I don't feel the need to brace myself, but still take a deep breath before going in. I find the house in perfect order. In fact, it's been completely decked out for the holidays. The tree's up and waiting to be decorated, which we always did on Christmas Eve. Stockings are hung, evergreen garlands have been wrapped around the banisters, the little ceramic Christmas village has been lined up on the mantle— the night lights inside glowing. Christmas lights twinkle against the brick wall of our living room, waiting to be decorated with cards from friends.

"Hello! I'm home," I proclaim, taking it all in. "Everything looks amazing!" The house is quiet and I wonder if Sophie is out. "Hello?"

I get to the dining room and see a plate waiting for me on the table. Warm homemade bread and steaming chicken pot pie with a glass of cold milk. She must've set this all out and rushed upstairs.

I quietly call out "Hello?" again.

There's a note next to my plate. It's a card made by Sophie's child alters—a drawing of me holding their hands and on the inside, scrawled in a child's writing, it says, "Welcome home! We missed you. Love, the kids."

"Do you like the card?" a gentle voice behind me says.

"I do. I really like it. It looks like it took a long time to make." I give her a hug, but immediately feel her pulling away. "Dinner looks amazing. Will you join me?"

Sophie is wearing her hair in two long braids. No makeup and she dons a long, shapeless, too-big brown dress, a darker brown sweater that's threadbare, and very worn, second hand shoes.

"Okay," she says, taking a plate of pot pie and going under the table to eat.

This is Elizabeth. I always thought this was my wife on a frumpy day, but there's more to it than that. This alter was the most fearful, the most beaten down, the most dysfunctional. Dr. Newman had said that she's the emotional container that carries all of the terrified feelings she couldn't express while being abused. I don't know how she can bear it.

She's startled as I lift up the tablecloth. "Sorry," I say, "can I eat under there with you?"

"Sure," she says quietly, but she seems surprised by my willingness. In the past, I'd rarely seen this alter eat anything. She'd usually switch out before it was time to share a meal.

I take my dinner and squeeze myself under the table. With my long legs, I'm not great at sitting on the floor.

"So, why are we eating *under* the table?"

Elizabeth shudders and someone else is there looking around, taking in what's happening.

"Oh, you're home!" she says in a tiny voice and gives me a big hug.

"I can tell you!" she says brightly in answer to my question.

"Papa took us out for fancy dinners with important people sometimes. When we were nine, we did something really, really bad. We forgot a lesson and took the butter from the plate with our own knife instead of the butter knife. So he made us eat under the table. He pushed my plate on the floor and said, 'Since you have the manners of a dog, you can eat off the floor like a dog.'

"Later on, I thought it would be okay to sit at the table, but when I tried that he said, 'I hate when you make me do this' and he ran a chair into my knees. But you know what? Elizabeth is smart and she pushed one leg forward so she could save her other knee. But that's why Sophie needs to use a cane sometimes. It's why she has bad arth…, arth… what's that word?"

I'm gritting my teeth hearing this. It makes me feel helpless and infuriated. "Arthritis?" I offer in a blast.

"Yeah, that—she has that in her knee." She notices my anger and starts whimpering. "I'm sorry. Are you mad at me?"

I'm frustrated with myself. I've been thrown into something I'm unprepared for and I don't remember all the names of different alters. I just want to be back at the condo where everything is simple and makes sense. At home, I need to be uber alert. I can never relax.

This young one can rattle things off like a nursery rhyme with no emotion, but I can't take it in without feeling practically panicked. It crashes over me like a tsunami and I feel like I'm drowning. I try to just listen and later deal with my own feelings—usually sobbing in the shower.

Now I say, "Oh God, no, honey. Of course I'm not mad at you. I'm mad at your grandfather for hurting you."

She smiles through her sniffles at that, glad to have an ally. I try to act like I don't know these things when I see Elizabeth again. I think she'd be embarrassed.

As Elizabeth settles back in, she starts eating dinner with perfect manners—polite, tiny bites but she's completely hunched over, her plate on the floor. I'm incredibly uncomfortable and my back is already starting to hurt. I'm beginning to understand at least part of the reason Sophie is always in pain.

I'm pulled from my thoughts as she asks, "How was your trip?"

"It was really fun, but I missed you guys." I don't mention Kevin because I want that part of my life to be separate. I love Sophie, but since learning of her diagnosis, it's multiplicity 24/7, and I just need a corner of my life that's untouched by it.

"How did it go here?"

"It went good. Jamie helped a lot and everyone was okay. He did a project with us. And Carol came over too and stayed. I think she had fun."

"I'm glad."

"We went to church yesterday," she offers.

"Which one?" I ask.

"It was Sebi's. St. Mary's."

"Who all went?"

"Just Sebi. Well, Sebi and Jamie went with him for support. The rest of us stayed home with Carol. We can do that, you know?"

"I didn't know. You can each go where you want to go?"

"Yup. So I don't have to go out."

I want to tell her that's good, but I'm not sure it is so I ask, "How's Sebi doing? Do you know?"

"He feels upset. He went to confession and everything." Elizabeth was not only the homemaker, she was the peacekeeper. I feel horrible. And I feel like a hypocrite. While I haven't actually cheated, I've thought about it. I think part of my outrage at Seb is to hide my fear of being called on my own mental infidelity.

"It does sound like he's feeling pretty awful about things. But I'm not mad anymore."

"That's good." Elizabeth knits her brow, looking like she's considering something. "Steve?"

"Hm?"

"Can I show you something?"

"Of course."

She takes my hand and pulls me up the stairs and into our storage room. Trepidation creeps in because I'm never sure what I'm walking into.

She sits down on the floor and pulls an old battered wood trunk out from under the wire shelves. It's stained dark with a faded pattern of wheat stalks around a pineapple that's barely visible.

"This is where I keep my things," she says softly, her words imbued with meaning. One leather strap on the trunk is broken so she gingerly lifts the lid to avoid damaging the other. I can smell its age as she opens it.

She carefully lifts out a stack of seven small books with green hardcovers, wrapped in a cloth ribbon. "These were my grandmother's," she says. "She was an English teacher."

"I didn't know that. I started off teaching English too," I tell her.

"She didn't teach for very long because then she had a baby and Papa wanted her at home. And then she had to take care of us." She gently brushes her hand across the books and seems sad for her grandmother. Then she brightens and with an air of pride tells me, "But she loved these books. They're Shakespeare's plays." She pauses to see my expression. "I can read to you sometime if you want."

"I'd like that," I tell her.

She pulls out an old stuffed rabbit made of black fabric. It's wearing a shabby brown gingham dress with a ragged, unfinished hem. She hugs it to her. "I saved up to buy this when we visited the Amana Colonies."

I remember going there as a kid myself. It's a chance to see the Amana culture. Big for tourists and kind of a cool place to swing by on vacation. She kisses the bunny and sets it aside.

Still in the trunk is another old baggy dress in dark brown, perfectly folded and wrapped in an oversized navy blue sweater. She pulls a case out from behind the trunk and opens it.

"This was my mother's. I probably should have returned it to her, but I love it so much."

She opens the old leather case slowly and the hinges creak. Inside is a violin and bow, which she handles with the utmost care. She tucks the violin under her chin and begins to play "Tis a Joy to be Simple" perfectly.

"That was beautiful! I didn't know you could play! I've never heard you practice."

I can see a flush rising from her neck to her face. "I don't like to bother anyone with it. I don't really play in front of people. I mostly only know hymns anyway," she says trying to discount her talent.

Then she switches gears. "Do you want me to read to you?"

"Sure."

Elizabeth quietly puts all of her things away and tucks them under the shelf. Then she goes to the books and pulls out an old copy of Aesop's Fables. "This was Grandma's, too."

We return to the living room and curl up on the couch. I try to put my arm around her and she tenses. Her shoulders feel like granite. I move my arm away and she pushes herself to the other end of the couch to read aloud.

Her selections are *The Oxen* and the *Axle-Trees* and *The Two Dogs*. When there's a picture, she turns the book around so I can see it. The stories reflect her own truth. The moral being, those who suffer the most, cry out the least. I find I'm fighting back my tears, but can't speak. Sometimes stories express our pain far better than we can.

"Thank you for letting me show you my things—and for letting me share my stories. I find washing dishes relaxing, so I'm going to do that and then I'm to bed," she tells me with a smile.

Elizabeth washes the dinner dishes by hand and refuses my offer to help. I feel like a 1950's husband reading my newspaper while she works alone.

After she goes up to bed, I feel lonelier than usual sitting in the living room. It's too quiet. I put on some music and crack open my most recent library find—a trauma book by psychologist Peter Levine. My attention wanders, so I head up early, checking on Elizabeth in the guest bedroom first.

I hesitate at the door, not wanting to invade her privacy or frighten her. Then I remember Kevin's wife and her suicide attempt. I knock gently and when I get no response, I open the door and I'm flabbergasted. The walls have been repainted light pink. There's glitter mixed in, so it sparkles in places. Netting has been hung from the center of the room so that the entire place is inside a sort of glimmering, beaded tent. Everything had been cleaned up and organized—puzzles on one shelf, dolls in a little wooden crib I'd never seen before, stuffed animals in a hammock, children's books on a small bookshelf. And the ceiling is decorated with glow in the dark stars.

Elizabeth is sleeping in her clothes, shoes neatly tucked under the bed. She sleeps bent over crossed legs with her head on her arms, which are also crossed. I wonder what happened to her that she slept all crunched up like this. It looks painful.

I turn in, but don't sleep well and, halfway through the night, I'm glad Napoleon has decided to crash with me. Normally, I'm not a fan of having a huge dog taking up half the bed, but this time, it's comforting.

When I wake in the morning, I feel like I haven't slept at all. I consider calling in sick, but know I have too much to get done at work. Sophie and I had an agreement that I'd tell her goodbye each day as I left. Those days when I didn't, she would feel upset—abandoned, she confessed. I knock on the guest room door and get a groggy "Mmm hmm."

My wife is lying on her side now, wearing her puppy pajamas. I walk slowly over to the bed, waiting for her to open her eyes.

She rolls away from the window, towards me and, rubbing her eyes, she yawns. Smiling, she says, "Oh, hi. Good morning."

"Good morning, sweetie. I'm heading in to work."

"Okay. Hug?" She puts her arms around my neck and snuggles in, whining a bit when I pull away to go. "I'll see you later, darling. Get some rest."

Napoleon pads in and takes up residence next to Sophie—she giggles as he pushes against her to get comfortable.

At work, though, I feel very distracted. With Sophie in my life, I always feel that I'm trying to put together an endless puzzle or untie an impossible knot. I don't know if I'll ever be able to get the answers I need in order to help her make sense of things, and it's been frustrating. It feels like we get one door open only to learn there's another, more impenetrable one behind it.

I shirk off the feelings and I get through the meetings I can't miss and do the work I must do...but I'm anxious to get home.

I dial Sophie around 4. "Hey, I'm heading home early today. What's going on?"

"Nothing much," she says, "Seb had a job earlier at the agency, but we're back now. It's pretty quiet around here. Just doing some research," she adds. "How are you doing? You sound tired."

"I am. All I want to do is eat dinner and get a good night's sleep."

"Sounds doable. Any special dinner requests?"

"Is Jamie willing to do that lemon chicken thing?"

A minute's pause, then I hear Jamie come forward. "I can do that."

I give myself a mental high five for catching that. "Thanks! Do you need me to get anything on the way home?"

"Nope. I think we're all good here. I'll text if I think of something."

"Alright, then. I'll see you soon."

When I get home, I hear Rascal Flatts playing. As I approach, I can smell the lemon chicken.

I swing through the living room to the kitchen. "It smells great in here!"

Sophie turns around. She's wearing a black tank top under an apron and has a red bandana tied around her head. An earring with a cross hangs from her left ear. Definitely Jamie.

Jamie takes a long drink of soda before saying, "Hey! We got salad on the table if you're hungry right now. Everything else will be ready in about an hour. Jesus, you look exhausted. Go take a shower and put on your sweats. It'll help you unwind."

Sophie is never this directive unless she's wicked pissed. And her chronic pain puts her in a place of being unintentionally more self-centered than she really is. But Jamie, I've learned, is the guardian of the kids and, as such, he's used to giving orders. Now that I've been brought into the club, it feels like he has taken me under his wing.

"A shower does sounds good. I'll be back."

He's right. The shower feels great and, as usual, I stay in too long. As I'm getting into my sweats, I hear dishes being put out. Dinner is ready. I head down the steps, letting the scent untwist my nerves.

The table is simple, but the food is plated elegantly. A perfectly prepared chicken breast with a thick ribbon of sauce, capers and slices of lemon sit next to asparagus with walnuts and cranberries. A perfectly dressed salad waits next to a loaf of still-hot challah bread wrapped in a towel. A bottle of beer has been opened for me.

I pull up my chair as Jamie takes off his apron and sits across from me, leaning back and drinking his soda before tearing the bread into pieces—steam still billowing out as he hands me a chunk.

I put my hand to my heart. "Thank you for this, Jamie. Really. Everything looks great."

"It's what I do." And I understand this is what he does. It's his role as the nurturer and guardian.

He takes huge bites through dinner and sops up the left-over sauce with the bread. After we finish eating, I feel full and content.

"Wanna tell me about the bedroom? It looks amazing in there," I start.

"You like that?" he asks. "Yeah, a little project with the kids. I hung the lights and the canopy, Richard put the shelves and crib together. Seb and Kalia painted the mural. Elizabeth made the canopy and curtains. Sort of a group effort. It helps when you have a team. But the kids like it and we wanted to do something to keep them entertained."

"Well, it blew me away. You guys are so talented!"

"Why, thank you," Jamie says proudly.

After dinner, we sit in the living room and I'm now aware of Elizabeth's quiet presence. We both pick up a book and read for a while and then she softly asks, "Do you want to hear about the mural at church?"

I put my book down and tune in. "I'd like that."

"Our minister was a really nice man and he always wanted the kids to help with fun projects. One Sunday he said that we'd be painting the church and he wanted us to come up with bible themes and paint the classrooms.

"My theme was chosen: Hagar and her son in the wilderness. Hagar was a slave who was forced to bear the children of Abraham and was then exiled by Abraham's wife into the desert with her son, but God provided for them. The theme was that God will always provide."

Her face begins to light up as she continues, "It was so cool! I got to the church and there were tarps all over the floor, buckets of paint and brushes everywhere. Our neighbor, Mrs. Moretti, who was a really good artist, was there to make everything look perfect. We were about eight years old and we got to paint the dots and spines on the cactus. It was such a great day!"

Sophie was in a safe place that she loved, with people she trusted and admired. I'm so grateful for these people, who probably did more to save Sophie than they'll ever know.

"It sounds like it was really amazing. That was such a good idea."

Elizabeth looks delighted as she goes back to her book.

I'm okay spending time with whoever, but after a while feel like I need to talk with Sebi. We still have some work to do, plus it surprised me but I found myself missing him. I didn't see him until our next session with Dr. Newman.

December 10, 2010

"Hey, come on in." Dr. Newman says, recognizing Sophie is Sebi, as he ushers us in. My goal is to be as perceptive at recognizing Sophie's different personalities as he is. I feel like I'm getting there.

"So, Steve, how was the time away?"

"It was good, Dr. Newman. I went up to Red Feather Lakes and did some ice fishing."

Today, Sebi is reserved and folded up—not himself at all. He mostly looks at the floor and when he does look up, I can see the pain in his face. This is such a different Sebi. I had really wounded him during our last session, I realize.

"Hey Seb, good to see you. How ya holding up?"

"I'm okay. Feeling like there's no easy answers. Feeling like I screwed up. I worked on changing, but maybe I was fooling myself. Maybe I'm still just a bad person that hurts people. Honestly, that's my greatest fear."

Dr. Newman's voice is gentle, "I promised I'd always be honest with you, remember that? So I'll be honest with you now, Sebi. There are no easy answers. But it doesn't mean that you did anything wrong. It doesn't mean you're a bad person.

"I'm sorry if what I said hurt you, Seb," I tell him. "I was angry, but I'm not mad anymore. We just need to figure out what we're going to do."

Seb looks like he's been crying for hours. It's killing me to see this. He looks resigned to whatever would happen to him—like a beaten dog. He nods his head yes, but looks pathetic.

I say out loud, "I'm worried about Seb. He's just not himself. He seems distracted and regretful."

"You know I can listen, but I can't give you any information without his permission."

I turn to Sebi then, hoping he'd nod an okay at Dr. Newman so he could talk, but it didn't come.

"I'm confused because my understanding of multiples from what I'm reading is that they're one dimensional, but Sebi seems to be an entirely different person," I say to Dr. Newman. "He's usually outgoing and happy, but lately he's been introspective. He has his own likes and dislikes, hobbies and talents, skills and abilities—a wide range of emotions and a long back-story. And he doesn't want the others to know what he's up to when he's out. Why is that?"

"Sebi, you wanna take this?" Dr. Newman asks.

"I've been with Sophie all along—her whole life."

"What happened that you came online?" I ask him.

"I'm not getting into that right now, Steve, but I can tell you that I'm different from Sophie. *She* tried to keep things as calm as possible. She thought the more compliant she was, the less Papa would hurt us. I'm the opposite. The one thing that infuriated my grandfather, Papa, was any damage to the body. He thought of it as his property and it drove him nuts when I hurt myself."

I'd seen the scars from the torture inflicted on Sophie's body by her grandfather—strategically placed burns and cuts so she could still work as a model and no one would know what was going on at home. I knew each scar had its own story. I was glad that Seb was opening up now.

"Papa was usually calculated about his punishments, but once when she was 12 she'd tried to run away from home. He caught her and whipped her. She lost a couple modeling jobs because of scars on her back...she still has them. Papa always blamed her—if she hadn't tried to run, he would not have had to whip her.

"Add to that self-harm," he continues, "which she generally did somewhere visible, and she had a lot of scars. She had said that she hoped someone would notice and help her. As an adult, she covered them with tattoos—her way of experiencing pain for something more positive, allowing her to see something beautiful when she looked at her body, rather than a diary of past hurts."

Seb continues, "When I was 12, I had a really rough winter. I was persecuting the hell out of the body. I'd been put into situations to endure pain and the only way through it was to learn to interpret it as pleasure. That meant that I was seriously injuring the body on top of what was being done to us. It was like I was addicted to it.

"And I didn't mind tormenting the other alters—physically and mentally. Papa had taught us to leverage pain—to augment it. He taught us how to make it worse. Anyway, when winter break started, Sophie was sent away—separated from us. It all culminated in a suicide attempt. That's how we wound up in therapy."

"I thought hurting the body might get us out of the work Papa wanted us to do, but it never helped. I even cut her labia in half with a pair of scissors. It didn't make any difference at all. So I stole things, broke stuff and got into trouble at school. I was on a first-name basis with the principal.

"We even made a really crazy video about what was happening at home. No one cared. I mean, beyond accusing me of being a bad kid from a perfect family. Sort of fit in with their little narrative."

I could feel myself grimacing more and more as he spoke. I wanted to close my ears. Why did I ever ask questions about Sophie's past? Jesus! I tried to pull myself together and think. I'd just read *Trauma & Recovery*, and things were starting to come into horrible focus.

Sebi had aligned himself with the abuser, believing if he hurt himself enough, his grandfather would leave them alone. He had started out differently. He'd started as a persecutor alter but he was really trying to protect everyone in his own way.

At this point, Dr. Newman steps in, "Early on, therapists used to believe integration was best. Some of them tried to weed out the more destructive alters. Their therapist, Dr. Ziegal was bleeding-edge progressive with his philosophy that each alter serves a specific role and should be retained. I've heard him lecture. He's brilliant."

Seb continues, "I was the first alter—in a way—and, yeah, I was pretty intense—and not in a good way. But instead of getting rid of me, Dr. Ziegal helped me. He asked me to find some role models, to look for hobbies that seemed fun, to look through books and talk with friends so that I could enjoy life more than just surviving. As a result, I'm pretty complex."

Dr. Newman turned to me and said in explanation, "Multiples are chameleons. They're able to take on the qualities they observe in others really easily. One of their super-powers."

Seb smiles, but is quiet. I want to know more about where he came from but I know I need to wait until he's ready to share.

"Dr. Ziegal could only help so much. My grandparents were powerful in the community, so the abuse didn't stop. My gym teacher tried to help me by reporting the abuse and he wound up getting fired."

"I didn't think that was possible. I mean, I thought there were mandated reporters who *had* to call the police. I thought they were protected."

Sebi looked upset at the memory. "That's how it's supposed to work, but they came up with some other excuse to fire him."

Dr. Newman filled in, "The situation that most often creates multiplicity not only involves horrendous abuse, it's also inescapable. Fortunately, Seb had some good stuff in life, some good people, and that helped an enormous amount. So The Timeshare is pretty high functioning. She's able to hold down a job, take care of the household obligations, maintain relationships. And, for the most part, she's co-conscious. The alters are aware of each other and what's going on. Seb has a number of different roles and..."

Dr. Newman looks at Seb who shakes his head no. Our therapist nods and stops.

"Why is this making me feel so edgy? I mean, seriously, the hair on my arms is standing straight up," I say now.

"I can't answer that, Steve," Dr. Newman says. "That's something you'll need to explore. I can tell you that I get why all of this is unsettling."

Seb pulls a piece of paper out and looks at Dr. Newman, who gives him a reassuring nod.

"Steve," Seb begins, "we made something for you. A list of some of us and what we do. No one really wanted to talk about how they were created, but I think it will help, maybe. I hope it does."

Recognizing what a huge leap of faith this is, I take the paper he's offering and thank him. Opening it, I see, in several different handwritings, information about Ellyn, Elizabeth, Jamie, Richard, and Kalia. Rachel had drawn a picture.

"Thank you so much, guys," I say, looking over what had been written. "Can I ask a question?"

"Sure."

"I'm not sure I know Kalia. Did we talk about her before? The name sounds familiar but I know nothing about her."

"She helped paint the mural in the kids' room. She's a fragment that helps with the art stuff. You won't see her that much, but she wanted you to know she's vegan in case she's out at meals."

"Good to know. Another question. You said there were seven main alters—and Kalia is a fragment. Is someone missing?" I ask, looking over the list.

"Yeah, well, Anna didn't really have anything to say and you're already getting to know me, so I didn't write anything either."

Dr. Newman fills the pause, "I feel like it's important to do some more work around the intimacy issues. Okay if we switch gears?"

Sebi's smile fades in favor of a furrowed brow. "I'm okay switching gears, but I'm not sure we'll find any answers."

Dr. Newman responds, "I'm not sure either. I told you all the options I could think of. This is up to you two. I'm just here to help you brainstorm."

I had done nothing but obsess about this. I couldn't get it out of my mind. "Sebi," I start, "I've been thinking about this a lot. I've come up with three choices. You could be celibate, which would make you miserable. You could cheat, which would make me miserable. Or we can have some sort of an open marriage. I think we need some ground rules, but we can talk. I kept thinking about what you said—about how I get a sexual buffet while you're starving. That's not fair. What do you think a compromise would look like?"

Sebi eyes me suspiciously, but when he realizes I'm serious, I can see gratitude in his gaze.

"I think ground rules are fine, but can we call them *agreements*? Agreements feel like it takes everyone into consideration and that they can be adjusted as needed. Rules make it sound so black and white— like it's set in stone and some sort of polyamory SWAT team will break down the door if we screw up. What are you thinking?"

"Can you limit it to Liz and Laura?"

"For now I can, but if I'm out more, I'm not sure that'll work. I only see them a few times each year. And I'm not sure you understand my relationship with Liz. It's not what you think."

"But you were in bed together."

"We're close, but she's straight and she's not really my type. So, we're more friends. I mean, we kiss sometimes but..."

I can feel my heart in my ears. "First agreement," I interrupt, "...I can agree with the relationships, but I'm having a really hard time hearing the details."

Dr. Newman sees the tension rising in me and interrupts. "So, we've got a strong start. Keep in mind that open marriage can mean a lot of different things. Then there's polyamory, which is a whole different option. There's probably more to research. Let's launch the discussion here and then you can finish this up at home. Steve, what sort of agreements do you want to set up around these relationships?"

"I don't want to know about them. And, will it work for them to be at the house only while I'm away?"

"We can do that. We might need to coordinate," Seb says.

"That works for me," I agree, but I feel like I need to ask for what my heart really wants. "Is there any chance you and I can have something together—something beyond a friendship?"

"I think we explored that already. Didn't seem to work out too well. I think we're good where we are."

"Can we leave that door open?" I ask.

"I'm straight, Steve, and I don't see that changing. I'm naturally pretty touchy with people, so there's that. And the hugs, spooning... but I don't know if it can ever go beyond that. I'm sorry, I'll try to think of something."

Dr. Newman offers, "What if we say that any sort of intimacy beyond what's happening now will be initiated by Seb?"

"That works," Seb and I agree.

Then Dr. Newman brings up something I'd never considered. "Keep in mind that intimacy isn't just sex. There's a whole continuum and we get it from a lot of different people. Hugs, compliments, handshakes. There are a lot of ways to fill that bucket.

"We have a little more time but you two look lost in thought. Is there anything else we need to discuss?"

"I think we're at a stopping place. We have a lot to think about," I say, looking at a very distracted Seb.

———

As we start driving home, it feels like a dark cloud has been lifted just in time to make way for the grand opening of Pandora's box.

"Coffee?" I ask Sebi before looking at him in the passenger seat. Sophie looks like a young man with a baseball cap and sunglasses on, earbuds in with music seeping out.

He removes one earbud and waits for me to ask again.

"Coffee?"

He looks up and squints. "Actually, I'm starving. Grill?"

"How's the budget looking for that?" I ask. I hate doing math and Sophie's a whiz with it, so she (or someone in The Timeshare) has taken care of the books. They've done a great job managing money and budgeting. We have no credit card debt and both the truck and car are paid off.

"No worries," he says, "but you're right. We should skip it for tonight. So, burgers?"

"Sounds good, buddy."

Seb snorts out a laugh, "Did you just call me buddy?"

"I think I did. Is that okay?"

"It's fine," he smiles. "Just reminds me of something funny," he says, putting his earbuds back in and giving me no more of an explanation.

We hit the drive-through and eat at home.

———

A few minutes later, Sebi is stuffing bunches of fries into his mouth, but pauses as he says, "You know how Dr. Newman told you there were some great people around me as a kid? Can I tell you about one of them?"

I'd learned Seb liked to reset to pleasant memories after discussing anything dark. "Absolutely."

"I was just starting high school," he begins, "when we visited this gallery of local artists. I could not stop looking at this one painting by an artist named Constance. There was real depth to it and the brightness of this old red truck leapt off the canvas. The rust on the truck was perfect—the shape, color, placement. A white fence ran along the edges but the perspective blew me away. I could tell that she used different brush strokes on each item and the shading was so accurate. It just drew me in.

"A few days later, I got a call from the artist. She was offering a class to students and had seen me staring at her painting. She asked if I wanted to join. It was an amazing opportunity. I learned so much from her, and it was like being around your favorite rock star for a few hours every Wednesday night. I was in heaven.

"There was a lot of bad stuff that happened to me growing up and I'm not denying that. But there were also some awesome people who changed my life for the better. I was really lucky in a lot of ways."
It always shocked me when any of the alters described themselves as lucky. I just couldn't see the silver lining.

"In one of our classes," he continues, "as we were working on our paintings of fruit, Constance asked if we'd ever heard the story of the orange. She was working on showing us how to shade and texture as she talked.

"Constance sounded absent-minded as she asked, 'Two kids are fighting over the last orange. How should their mother handle the situation fairly?'"

We all offered our ideas—cut the orange in half, take it away from them, go get more oranges..." Seb shudders and blinks. "Where was I?" he asks, forgetting what he'd been telling me.

I look up and notice his eyes are a lighter blue. He's pulling his hair tie out and running his fingers through his hair.

"Umm...the orange? You were telling Constance about how to divide the orange."

"Oh. Right. Sorry. Well, Constance was focused on her work, holding her paintbrush lengthwise against the subject and then her painting to get the angle right. It was as if she forgot she asked us a question. We quieted down and asked her if any of us had gotten it right.

"'No, you didn't,' she smiles. 'Apparently, none of you squirrels understand integrative negotiation. It's all about understanding the interests and priorities of each party. The first step to resolving any conflict is to listen to the other person—to understand what everyone needs. If the mother had done that, the kids would have given her the solution. One child needed the zest of the orange for a cake she was baking. So she just needed the peel. The other child felt like he was getting a sore throat and wanted the juice. Divided correctly, one orange was all they needed.'"

Whoever this was smiles at me—watching it sink in.

I have to smile at the brilliance. What a gift to hear this lesson at such a young age—and to take it to heart.

"Smart lady."

"I imagine Constance never knew this, but that was the best part of class for me," whoever this is continues. "It saved me from so many internal conflicts between alters. And I think it helped me in all my relationships, too. So often there's no need for the conflict in the first place."

We both sit with that for awhile. It was a good lesson and it stuck with me, too. Sophie did have some extraordinary people in her life. Thank God.

The posture changes again and Seb pulls his hair back into a knot. I catch a passing wink, too. I want to ask what had just happened, but feel like that might be an invasion. I can tell Sebi has come back to himself and I'm relieved he has come back to me, too.

December 17, 2010

I've been doing a lot of reading on the subject. Finishing up the latest book I'd borrowed, I order a bunch more on Amazon. The more I learn, the more complex this all seems. I'm looking for answers, but all I find are deeper holes. It's not just the multiplicity, it's the post traumatic stress, the anxiety, the depression, night terrors, and all of the physical issues. Sophie has (among other issues) arthritis, bursitis, IBS, bone spurs, back and neck pain, chronic migraines, glaucoma and fibromyalgia—all connected to the abuse when she was young. Some alters are crippled by the pain, like Sophie. Others manage it better, like Sebi.

I hope that the more I learn, the more it will make sense—and the more answers I'll find. I'm doing a ton of research, but every multiple is different, so I ask Seb to tell me more.

He holds me in his gaze for a long moment. He knows I've been learning all I can. I get a sense he feels I've earned this and that I can be trusted.

"Okay, Steve. I'll start at the beginning. I was diagnosed at 13. That's really unusual. Most people don't know until their 40's. After the suicide attempt, my grandparents had no choice—they had to send me to therapy, but I knew I couldn't say too much. They told me no one would ever believe me—or if they did, they'd commit me. That's when I started seeing Dr. Ziegal."

"The cool thing about Dr. Ziegal is that he let me set the pace and he never pushed me. In addition to trying to off myself, I had really bad migraines and blackouts. They checked me for epilepsy—which I don't have. Then they did this super long personality test. I didn't want to take it, so Elizabeth did and came out as reserved, quiet, somewhat paranoid, and nervous. They said they suspected schizophrenia. Elizabeth is great, but she's too honest. She told them she heard voices—the voices were us. They re-tested to confirm a diagnosis. The second one, taken by yours truly, showed we were outgoing and gregarious, an impulsive risk taker, trusting and positive.

"Thank God Dr. Ziegal asked a critical question: *'Do the voices come from inside or outside your head?'* I told him they came from inside. With that information, the personality test showing at least two distinct personalities, and after a few more talks, the Dissociative Identity Disorder (DID) diagnosis was confirmed.

"But he still didn't push it, you know? The alters are my family. Hearing they're just delusions would have been cruel, but that's how some doctors approach it. The way I think of it is that we're housing different souls."

As we spoke, I saw Sebi's demeanor change. His pitch rose, his voice quieted and his pace slowed. A sort of southern accent slipped in—but it was subtle, gracious..."I didn't believe the story about the alters and didn't follow up. To me, this was normal. I'd lived with all these other people inside me my whole life. We're convinced our experience of the world is normal or right and we typically don't like our reality challenged. When the other doctors wanted to integrate everyone, we refused. I think we felt that if we didn't get help, we had plausible deniability.

"Then in high school," he continues, "at an eye exam, my vision was way off. The follow-up eye exam showed completely different results. The doctor wanted further testing, but I said my eyes were just tired that day. I never went back to her, but I did eventually find someone I could trust enough to tell. That's why I have four different sets of glasses. It's not a fashion thing. They're different prescriptions."

"I got in the habit of making excuses, creating stories to explain things away, faking memories when people would tell me things we'd done together. I preferred to live that way, fearing that seeking treatment meant we were crazy—or that it could make things worse. The Timeshare is a delicate balance. I could at least marginally hold things together—treatment meant falling apart and also giving someone else control. Falling apart is terrifying and handing over the wheel was unbearable. But once I did that, things got better.

"But, yeah, getting started was rough. We didn't want to admit it for a long time," Seb adds.

"I finally told Dr. Ziegal that a guy named Sebi was sharing my body and sometimes I had conversations with him and sometimes he was cutting me, burning me. I think admitting this was the bravest thing I've ever done. But the doctor was great. He didn't freak out. He told me that it all made sense and that it was okay—that we'd work on it together. Still, we didn't want to talk about the alters and we didn't want to talk about what had happened. We talked more about how to handle the anxiety, depression and OCD. I mean, it all helped but it didn't resolve anything.

"Then at college, I had to go to the campus doctor. I thought Sophie might be pregnant. I had some bad bruises and it was pretty obvious we'd been raped, but Sophie didn't remember anything. The doctor suspected DID and asked how many alters we had.

"Listening to that campus doctor, I felt seen for the first time, and I appreciated that. But it scared Sophie. She felt like if this doctor could see our truth, the veneer was cracking and other people would soon discover our secret. She wanted to get help so that no one would find out about us. She got into an incest survivors group, but we didn't really address the multiplicity head-on until a couple years ago."

I was quiet, caught up in Seb's story. But I was also aware of a shift. "I was speaking with Sebi, but you seem different," I say.

"I'm sorry. I'm new to this—having to tell you I'm here. I'm Ellyn."

"Ellyn. You wrote me a note on the paper that Seb gave me. You're 21, right? An activist? And you're the one who spoke with me about the art class—you told me about Constance's oranges, right?"

"Yes, that's me. I step in to help if someone can't remember certain details. I hold a lot of the memories—both good and bad. I thought it critical to hold on to the good stuff—to provide a different perspective—to remind people in The Timeshare who we are—and that we're good."

"That makes a lot of sense. It's pretty brilliant, actually. Can you tell me more about yourself" I ask, "...how and when you came online?"

"If you don't mind, I'd prefer not to," Ellyn says. "We can talk later, but I'm a private person. I just know about this area, so I wanted to talk with you. I know you've had questions."

"I get that. Thank you for telling me. It helps me make sense of things and I appreciate it. You hungry?" I ask, turning to the kitchen and rummaging through the fridge.

A long pause is followed by, "I am!" I hear another alter. Rachel, I think. I feel like now that I know about them, the different personalities seem to be okay popping out all over the place. But I still don't feel quite ready for them.

I have no idea what to say, so I do what I've always done. I just keep going. "What would you like to eat?"

"Mac and Cheese! I like the box kind and not the restaurant kind," she scrunches up her nose in little kid disgust.

Frowning, I pull out a box of mac and cheese and start boiling water. I'm feeling yanked around. I just get used to one alter, relax into the conversation, set my expectations, and then she switches. I can't keep up and I'm feeling pissed about how much my life is changing.

"I'm sorry that you're sad," she says, noticing my expression. The floodgate breaks and I fall apart...

Since I have no idea how to speak with a child alter about what I'm feeling, I try to hide it, telling her it's okay, that it's not her fault, that I'm just sad because of what she went through.

"That is sad. But now I get to be here with you," she says in a tiny voice.

She takes about three bites of her mac n cheese before bolting from the table to watch cartoons and play. I have no appetite, so I skip dinner entirely and opt for a mineral water.

"You know how to play Chutes and Ladders?" she says hopefully as I plunk down on the couch.

"I don't," I say, thinking about how I interact with my nephews and niece. "Can you teach me?"

Rachel jumps up and down and smiles bigger than I've ever seen Sophie smile. "YES!" she shouts and pulls me over to the coffee table where she clumsily sets up the game and tells me everything she can about it, giggling as she's teaching me. I find myself fascinated seeing her like this. She's entirely charming. Going with the flow makes things easier—at least for tonight.

December 23, 2010

I'd been avoiding the partner's group. I felt that by going, I was admitting that my situation wouldn't improve as quickly as I'd hoped it would. I was admitting I was one of those husbands who needed support. I'd been in a couple other types of groups and I never liked them. I'm all for whining, but group whine is just too much.

But I know I need help. I could talk with Dr. Newman about Sophie, but would feel weird discussing my own struggles with him. And getting my own therapist seemed over the top. So, partner's group was the best fit.

That first day there, I'd felt intensely uncomfortable walking in. Six guys and two women sitting on hard plastic chairs in a circle in the middle of a too-small, too-warm room at the psychiatric branch hospital just a few miles south of Denver. All eyes turn to me as I enter, and it stops me in my tracks.

I look at their faces, trying to assess if I'm one of them. Somehow, I feel that I'm not. *My* life hasn't completely fallen apart. We were working things out. I'm not as *exhausted* as these people appear. They look completely drained and it scares me. I don't fit in. And I don't want to head in this direction.

I scan the circle for Dr. Newman, but he's not here yet and I wonder if I can turn around and leave. I decide that I can't, and take one of the last two chairs as I announce, "Hi, I'm Steve."

"Welcome, Steve. Dr. Newman said you might be joining us tonight. I'm glad you could make it," one of the guys says.

"Is he running late?"

"Oh, I'm sorry, Steve. This is more of a peer support group. My name is Brad and I've been here the longest—6 years—so I'm the default leader. We take turns." Brad looks to be in his mid-50's, graying hair, and portly with a voice that sounds kind. "My partner of 30 years was diagnosed about 8 years ago. He's got two alters—one male child, one female adult."

The others introduce themselves—just their first name—and then everything else is about their partners. The entire focus for the next two hours is on our spouses and sharing survival strategies. Which insurance is best, how to submit claims so they're more likely to be paid, which free resources are best. We discuss medications, home health care, talking with family. How do you handle night terrors? How do you navigate food allergies from one alter to another?

One gentleman talks about how the chronic pain and constant migraines had reduced his wife from a competitive athlete to a couch potato. One of the women has a husband addicted to pain killers. The other had divorced her husband after he had an affair, but his child alters kept calling her—not understanding why she didn't want to see them. They have kids together and she's still trying to co-parent with him. Another just found out his wife was working as a prostitute.

A guy named Brent, who looks to be around my age, tells us, "Karen was diagnosed three years ago. Everything changed. She had been working less and less and finally had to quit. I had to take a lower paying job so I could be home more. The yard and garden went to hell, friends dropped away and we were at the doctor all the time. She has the mental stuff, but also tons of physical issues."

Brent tells us about a book he's reading that suggests we embrace the new normal rather than trying to get back to an old one. "That helped a lot. There's good and bad in everything. And if you're grieving your old normal forever, you can never see the positive in what you have now," he comments.

I knew I had to do the same. T*his* is my new normal and maybe it's time to accept that, but somehow it feels like that resignation might swallow me up.

"Tell us about you, Steve," Brad asks a little too brightly.

"Well, I'm Steve and my wife is Sophie. Umm...I just found out about this thing a few months ago and our life is kinda upside down. Not that it wasn't before, but I didn't really have a handle on it. I thought having a label would help, but it's just freaking me out."

Brent nods. "It's like your whole life revolves around it, right? While other people are spending money on vacations, you're investing in treatments that insurance won't cover. While other people are researching which car to buy, you're researching different treatment methods. Someone else may lose their house because they chose to do something stupid. You lose it because your health care costs are three times your mortgage."

Everyone in the group nods in agreement and this feels like a foreshadowing of awful things to come. I came tonight hoping to find inspiration here, encouragement. Instead, it feels like more of the same. I can see why so many people just give up and walk away. Overwhelm seems to be my new default setting.

At that point, Brent must have felt the crash of group morale because he tries to turn it around. "I do have to say that, for me, there's a richness in all of it—in knowing all of Karen's facets, in having relationships with them, in helping them achieve little victories, in seeing her progress and heal. Being with her while she has this condition is both achingly devastating *and* remarkably rewarding."

We're all lost in our own thoughts. Brad breaks the silence with a check-out statement and asks each of us to do the same.

We'd meet once a month to help each other through this. We'd share what we were learning in therapy, suggest books, brainstorm solutions. And when we didn't have any answers, we'd just listen.

I leave that first group feeling overwhelmed but understood. Brad hands me a sheet with everyone's names and contact information. "Call any of us day or night. We probably won't be sleeping, so don't worry about bothering us."

———

After group, I do my Christmas shopping. I always waited until the last minute because I wasn't sure who would be out or what they'd want. I load up on candy and little bags of different coffees and cocoas and teas. Then I stop at toy store and spend entirely too much. When I get home, I stay up wrapping everything.

I discovered that some environmentally friendly alter from The Timeshare had made several dozen fabric bags in different sizes. All I had to do was slide stuff in and tie a ribbon on it with a gift tag. Made life a lot easier. I sign "Santa" on the gifts for the kids.

On Christmas eve, Jamie prepares a feast of Romanian holiday foods along with some of my Scandinavian favorites. Saying he was Sophie, he'd called my mom for her recipes and made them as part of his gift to me. We pop on Christmas music and decorate the tree.

The kids are always out more this time of year, so we leave a note and cookies with cocoa for Santa, carrots for the reindeer and bird seed for good luck. I read Rachel, "The Night Before Christmas" and she's in bed early.

Then I put all the gifts under the tree and fill a stocking for the kids. Candy and nail polish, crayons and pens. I break off the carrots, eat most of the cookies and drink the cocoa before leaving a note from Santa.

Sophie and I never made it back home for any of the holidays. My family would never understand the multiplicity. Even more challenging was trying to navigate visits from family here. They wanted to come to the house and hang out, explore Denver and Colorado Springs, take us out to nice restaurants. In the past, Sophie was on edge the entire time they were here and begged out of a lot of plans, claiming to have a migraine. Anxiety is not something my family understands. Depression is just an excuse for laziness. Multiplicity would be complete fiction to them.

Christmas morning arrives and Rachel is up with the sun. She races out to see that the "reindeer" have eaten the carrots she left for them. Then to the note from Santa. She squeals in excitement that he's eaten the cookies.

Then she sees all the gifts and jumps up and down. I pop in Christmas music and hang with her as she opens all her gifts, switching throughout the day depending on the gift tag.

My family calls and we catch up. Jamie cooks more food—surf and turf, beautifully done. Friends are in and out all day and Jamie sends them home with containers of left-overs. Most of the visitors don't know about the alters, and assume Sophie is just in a really social, really productive mood.

In the evening, we watch Christmas movies and then a parade of alters present me with their gifts—everything from drawings, to movies I've mentioned I want to see, a gift card for new running shoes, a nice pen and a plaque that says "Life is better at the lake" to hang up at the condo the next time I'm there.

My life is so full. Dozens of cards from people we love fill up the display on our wall. They overflow into a large basket. We've spoken with family, hugged neighbors who dropped by to trade treats—knowing that "Sophie" is a talented baker. We've shared meals with friends, had an amazing day full of blessings and smiles.

So why does it feel to me that something is missing? Why do I feel so lonely?

January 7, 2011

We're due to see Dr. Newman on Friday. On Wednesday, my morning meeting wraps up early and my first afternoon meeting wouldn't start until two. I call home, but get no answer, so I decide to drop by the house to make sure everything is okay.

Generally, if Sophie's not at a modeling job during the day, I'll find Ellyn working on her volunteer job at the dining room table. The car is still here, but no one is in the living room. I head upstairs to find Sophie napping. Seeing her sleeping there makes me fall in love with her all over again. Her hair is spilling out over the pillow and a teddy bear is tucked in with her.

Napoleon is curled up behind her and shifts when he sees me, waking her. She opens her eyes and stares blankly at me. Then confusion flashes across her face, followed by terror. She leaps from the bed and races into our walk-in closet to hide as I'm yelling at her to calm down, telling her it's just me.

I suddenly become aware that my freaking out is not helping. I can hear her crying but have no idea what to do.

I've frightened a child alter—probably Rachel. I text Dr. Newman— "911, Rachel."

Within 5 minutes he calls me, "What's going on, Steve?" His calm voice sounds reassuring, but I'm in a panic.

"I came home for lunch and Soph—I mean, Rachel...I think, Rachel was napping and I scared her. She's in the closet crying. I don't know what to do."

"First, take a breath. She's safe. She's upset, but she's okay. We have time."

I recognize that I'm actually not breathing.

"Seriously, take a breath."

I take an audible breath in and out.

"Okay. So you came home for lunch, she was napping and you surprised her. You didn't do anything wrong. Let's talk about what to do to deal with this today and later we'll talk about what we can do to prevent it in the future. Are you still feeling freaked out or are you able to tune in?"

"I'm still rattled, but I can tune in."

"We're going to figure this out together and it's going to be okay. You're still upset, so grab a piece of paper and a pen. That way, you'll have the information if you forget or if this happens again. I'll wait."

I'm shaking. I can still hear Rachel crying and I feel horrible. I get a pen and paper. "Shoot."

"I'm going to talk with Rachel, but I want you to take some notes first. Let her stay in the closet as long as she wants. When she comes out, just make sure she has water and food. Let her watch what she wants on TV. There's an old Cat Stevens song that will help Rachel hear that you care about her. It's called *Sad Lisa* and you can pull it up online. That'll help her feel safe.

"Some things not to do: Don't tell her she's safe. Abusers say this to get kids to put their guard down. You'll want to hold her. Don't. It will make her really uncomfortable, but she won't be able to tell you that. Don't sit next to her unless she asks you to. She'll probably be back to Sophie in a couple hours. You okay?"

"I think so. Thanks," I tell him, still shaking, but grateful that I have someone who knows how to handle these situations.

"Okay. We'll talk about preventative stuff when I see you next time. And call me later to tell me how things are going. For now, can you put your phone outside of the closet and let Rachel know I'd like to talk with her?"

I take the phone upstairs and knock on the closet. "Rachel, Dr. Newman wants to talk with you if you're up for it. I'll leave the phone here and go downstairs."

As I walk out, I hear the closet door creak open and the crying slows as she talks to him quietly. I set a glass of water and a box of cereal on the coffee table by the couch along with the iPad so she can watch her movies when she comes down. I pick up a book to read as I wait. I'm concerned about my afternoon meeting, so I text my boss to let him know I may need to call in for it. I was getting why some people in my shoes wound up needing a different job. Fortunately, I had some flexibility. But I still needed to be reliable at work and somehow always available for Sophie.

Twenty minutes later, she's out of the closet but embarrassed. She slowly navigates the steps to the living room, looking like she'd prefer to be invisible. Still in her pj's, bear in hand, she gives me my phone and then sneaks onto the couch and pulls the throw over her entire body, hiding beneath it.

I ask if she wants to hear a song. She pulls the blanket down momentarily and I can see the caution in her eyes, but she agrees. I find the song Dr. Newman suggested and let it play. It was obvious why it spoke to her—and why it was important that I offer it to her. It's about a man trying to reach out and help a traumatized little girl who doesn't want to be seen. At least that's how I heard it.

She needs me to be there so she feels safe, but having me there is a leap of faith. I need to be nearby but not too nearby. And though I'd felt perfectly at ease with my wife playing cute before, now that I understand the darkness that creates alter personalities, I feel sad and uncertain. I worry about saying the wrong thing.

——

As the people of The Timeshare and I have grown more comfortable with each other, I have learned from them that this child alter, Rachel, would answer every question completely, honestly and unemotionally.

She would rattle off the most grizzly, appalling, horrible, torturous details with no feeling whatsoever. It was the creepiest thing I'd ever seen. I learned that she held the memories, but in order to survive, she had none of the emotions attached to those memories. Elizabeth, on the other hand, held the feelings, but few memories, and she was a wreck.

"Rachel, there's water and cereal on the table for you. And the iPad is there if you want to watch a movie."

A tiny "Okay" drifts out from under the throw. I feel like I'm dealing with a wounded animal.

Another half hour and Rachel has longingly looked at the cereal box but hasn't eaten any. She's taken the iPad with her under the blanket and I could hear "Peg + Cat" playing. The show helps little kids problem solve.

She starts moving a bit more and the blanket comes down as the end credits to her show begin to play. She looks around as if she'd just woken up, sees me, looks deathly embarrassed, tucks the teddy bear into a blanket and slinks upstairs.

I hear the shower running and a little while later, she comes downstairs wearing jeans and my Stanford sweatshirt. In it, she still looks like a child and I'm not sure who's here. She curls up on the couch and clicks the iPad back to life, selecting HGTV. I smile at her and keep reading. She glances at me and then looks away. "Sorry. I'm okay if you need to get back."

"I have time. Want some lunch?"

"That would be great. Thank you."

"I think we have turkey, tomatoes and cucumbers."

"Yum. Yes, that. No turkey though."

"Is Kalia out?"

"No—but you're doing good remembering she's vegan. I just can't handle meat today."

"I get that." I go to the kitchen to start lunch and Sophie offers to help. I imagine she's tired, so I tell her, "I'll get it. Just chill."

When we sit down to eat, she picks her sandwich apart and pushes it around, only occasionally taking tiny bites.

"You okay?" I ask.

"Lump in the throat," she whispers. "Steve, I'm so sorry for hurting you. I handled everything badly. I'm sorry for freaking out today, for not telling about all of us a long time ago, for...just for everything." Tears were falling onto her plate and she couldn't look at me. "I'm not sure how long I'll be here today. I'm having a really bad pain day."

"I suspected. I'm sorry you're in pain. Sophie, I told you that we're in this together. I appreciate your apology, but I know you weren't trying to hurt me. You were trying to protect yourself."

I worried about how Sophie would take the news about Seb having an affair. She was feeling the crush of guilt just for not telling me about her diagnosis and, as far as I was concerned, that wasn't anything to feel bad about. I'd struggled with my own demons and didn't want to share them with anyone.

She was sobbing now. And I knew that after she cried, the pain would be even worse—headaches and agonizing joint pain. I walked upstairs, got the heating pad and Advil and brought them down to her. Then I sat down and put my arm around her.

"If it makes you feel better to apologize, you can, but you don't owe me anything."

She gasped and pulled away, searching my eyes for a lie.

Confused, I shook my head and asked, "What?"

"How can I not owe you anything? I owe you *everything*, Steve. I do."

"I don't see our relationship as a quid pro quo. You're working on getting well and while you're doing that, you're still holding down a job, helping out with everything around here, and investing time in our relationship. Believe me, I have heard some things in the partners' group I go to that I'm so glad I'll never have to worry about with you. Why does it surprise you that I'm happy to help?"

"I think I just feel like a bad person."

Sophie's posture changes and she clicks off the iPad.

"I knew the principal by his first name," she begins. "I was always in there for beating up the boys or for flirting with the girls or for breaking rules I thought were stupid. That guy was so cool. He knew something was off at home. We'd have lunch together and he became a friend."

"I'm glad you had him in your life. I'm sorry, but your grandparents were just assholes."

The Timeshare laughs and as I glance over, I see that her eyes are Sebi's now—clear, deep pools of blue.

He looks around, assesses the sandwich and goes into the kitchen. "Do we have any left-over bacon? Never mind—found it." He returns with a reconstructed sandwich. This time with a mountain of chips, plenty of bacon, an avocado, and a soda.

"About that—the asshole part. I have got to tell you a story. Kinda long, couple of rabbit holes, starts out sad, but stick with me because it's hilarious. You know this picture?" he says indicating the huge black and white print of dandelion seeds blowing across the sky on the wall behind him.

"Sure. Rachel loves it. She told me it reminds her to make wishes."

"Okay. Well, I have a different story. Do you have time?"

I check my watch and I do. I find it fascinating that each alter personality has their own story about special items in our house.

"Papa used to pay a buck a bucket for dandelions we dug up. He hated those things. So, when we were little, we'd fill up a bucket and go show him, but he'd tell us he was busy and would look in the morning. By then, of course, they'd be wilted, so the deal was off and we had to start all over again. We always had something we were saving up for, so we'd get practically despondent.

"But remember that gym teacher I told you about? The one that got fired? He was smart and he knew something was up. He thought if he could build Sophie's strength and confidence, it might help. So he started training her in gymnastics.

"For me, it firmed up my work ethic. He taught me that it's always worth trying because, no matter what happens, you wind up stronger. Every effort pays off in some way. He taught us how to be innovative instead of giving up.

"So, one fall, Papa caught us outside blowing dandelion seeds all over the lawn. When he asked "What the *hell* do you think you're doing?' we told him that we were planting more dandelions so we could fill more buckets."

Seb was laughing so hard at this that tears were pouring down his face.

"Grandma just about died laughing hearing that. She admired our spunk and how we infuriated him with our logic and innovation. Papa was less amused."

"That is brilliant," I say, laughing with Seb while admiring the bravery.

"Those dandelions behind me aren't about wishes. They're about rebellion—to me anyway. Hey, thanks for lunch—and for..." he points upstairs "helping us with that. I know you need to get back to work, so I'll see you tonight."

⸻

Friday arrives and Sophie is impatient in the waiting room, pacing. Dr. Newman opens the office door and ushers us in.

"Hi, Sophie. It's been awhile. How are you?"

"Not good. I can't wait any longer. I need to know what happened."

"Tell me what you know," Dr. Newman asks as he shuts the door and we all sit down. "You've worked hard to be co-conscious so let's start there."

"I know the others are out a lot more. They're being more obvious. Is that why everything is such a mess?"

I reassure her, "No, that's not a problem."

Dr. Newman steps in, "Sophie, I need you to bring Sebi into awareness. I know it's hard to maintain, but I need you to try."

We wait silently for a few minutes as Sophie sits with her eyes shut.

As she opens them, Dr. Newman squints to check her eye color. Still green but now lighter with a ring of sky blue. Again, I'm blown away.

"Is Ellyn here, too?" he asks, still squinting.

"Voice of reason," Sophie admits and I can hear Ellyn in her voice.

"Okay. Are we ready?" Dr. Newman asks Sophie. She gives a quick nod and although her eyes remain green, I can sense a subtle shift in her posture as she adjusts the watch.

"Steve, did you want to start?"

I want to launch in, but try to be measured. "Sophie, I know the last few weeks have been really hard for both of us. Do you remember someone named Liz being at the house?"

"Liz? No."

"Well, there was a Liz here a few weeks ago. She was visiting Sebi. What do you know about Seb?"

"I know of him, but I don't know what he does. He likes to stay hidden from me. I know he's a guy, he's about 20, I think. He can't sing, but he's very creative. Fun to be around. He's also impulsive and can do crazy things. I'm rarely co-conscious with him or with Anna."

"We're having an issue with Sebi and we need to tell you about it and then ask for your help. You might have some ideas."

Sophie was one to take the blame for everything. She had grown up the scapegoat and it had become habit—not only within her family but within The Timeshare as well. "What did I do?"

"That's a loaded question, Sophie, and we're going to get to that, but first, I want you to take a breath. We're walking that fine line between your responsibility as a system and Seb taking responsibility for his behavior."

Dr. Newman looks at me to go on.

"Sebi is a 19 year old who sees me as a roommate. He and Liz have a relationship."

"Okay...," Sophie says, not taking in what I mean at first and then wilting as it dawns on her.

"A relationship. Wait. Like...do you mean that I've been cheating on Steve? With a woman?"

Dr. Newman steps in with some direction. "No. Sophie, we've talked about how this works. Together, you need to consider each other—the commitments you have, the agreements you've made and the things you need to honor. This was one of those things that slipped through the cracks. You didn't know this was going on and Sebi sees Steve as a roommate."

"Oh my God. I've always been terrified that something like this would happen," she says, collapsing. "Steve, I am so sorry. You must be feeling incredibly hurt." She was sobbing now, worried that our relationship was over, that this was the last straw and I'd be leaving her.

"Dr. Newman, we need to make this stop."

I reach for her hand and tell her, "Well, we're not sure that that's the solution. But we're working on it."

"What do you mean it's not the solution? We're married and I don't want to lose that. This is cheating and I'm sure it really hurts you. I don't think the solution is to bring other people into our marriage. The solution is to figure out how I can make it stop."

I went from being furious about the affair to stepping into Sophie's world for just a moment. I was beginning to realize what this must be like for her.

"Sophie, look at me." She shakes her head no and continues to stare at the ground. I put my hand on her back and tell her, "I'm not leaving you. I know you're working on it. And I know it's complicated. This was not you."

Sophie takes a deep breath, sits up, and softly pounds the back of her head on the wall several times. Her jawline becomes more defined and as I look over I see the ring around her iris becoming deep blue. It was like touching a paintbrush to wet paper and watching the color spread out. Mesmerizing. Dr. Newman catches it, too.

"Seb," he says, "you're here as an observer. You need to step back and let Sophie handle this."

Sebi pops up and takes a defiant stand. "This is not her problem. It's mine. I should be the one to work this out. It's my job to protect her and you're trying to make her pay for something I did and making me watch. You're breaking your own rules and, if you keep going, I'm not going to trust you anymore."

Sitting there watching, I take a deep breath. I'd never been more grateful for Dr. Newman. This was not something I wanted to handle on my own. Sebi was growing louder and there was a palpable feeling of rage behind his shouting. Dr. Newman quietly tells him, "First, I need you to sit *down*." Seb stops but holds his ground. He looks like he's feeling suspicious of both of us. "You know you can trust me on this. Sit down." Sebi sits on the edge of the couch and Dr. Newman tells him to close his eyes and take a deep breath.

For a beat, Seb looks like he might run, but Dr. Newman keeps him locked in eye contact until Seb closes his eyes. Then he helps him to step back into The Timeshare and Sophie comes forward again.

Sobs shake her body. "Why do you stay with me, Steve? I need you, but I can't stand hurting you. Maybe it's time to talk about some other solutions. Maybe your brother is right and we should just divorce. It doesn't matter who cheated or that I didn't know about it. The bottom line is that this has got to be intolerable for you. Now I know why things have felt so tense between us."

No longer angry at her, I respond, "Sophie, I love you. I want us to work. I don't know if we'll be able to find a perfect solution, but I know without any doubt or reservation that we have to try."

Her sobbing slows to tears of relief. "This is on me. I have to take responsibility for it."

Dr. Newman answers, "You *are*. By being here. But there's a balance. You need to be gentle with yourself—realizing the problem is the memory loss and the other side effects of the multiplicity. But we're working on it. If you have to be angry, be angry at the side effects—not each other. That means that you're not mad at Steve *or* Sebi. We need to hold alters responsible for their behavior, but also recognize where it comes from. If we start judging and blaming, this all goes to hell."

"Sophie, I don't want a divorce," I say. "I don't want to leave you. I love you and our relationship means the world to me. I *need* you, too. And we *will* get through this. We'll find a way to make it work. But we have got to be honest with each other."

"I just feel like we work so hard to get things organized and in order and then a hurricane comes through and destroys everything in its path. And I'm the hurricane. I don't want to hurt you. I don't want to hurt anyone."

"Sophie, I have not had one relationship with anyone where I didn't get hurt. And I've never had a relationship where I didn't hurt the other person. That's just life."

"But," I continue, knowing this is the time to bring it up, "I need to ask you something and I want you to be totally honest with me."

"Of course."

"Seb told me that you're asexual—that you have no attraction to other people."

"I don't want to talk about that," she says, spinning the silver ring on her middle finger. She looks to Dr. Newman for some help.

"Sophie, if you want to resolve this, we need to talk about everything, he says. "There's no need to feel embarrassed."

"I'm not embarrassed. I'm mad. That was not Seb's to tell. He keeps his life hidden from me, but knows all about mine and then spills my secrets. Plus, it's more complicated than what Seb said."

"Can you tell me, please, Sophie? I just need to know so that we can find the best solution," I say.

"I love you and I feel attraction to you. I like to be close to you. I like to kiss you and curl up on the couch with you. I love being in bed with you—being held. I love talking with you and feeling safe. Sex is not a safe area to me. It never has been. Plus, I'm in pain so much that it's not something I enjoy."

I clear my throat before responding. "That's actually a lot better than the road I wandered down when Seb said 'asexual.' I feel a little thrown though because I've been having sex with someone in The Timeshare pretty regularly since before we were married. And there's been a huge shift since I found out about the multiplicity. Feels like a different person. Who are they?"

Sophie looks hurt but unsurprised. "I wish I could tell you that, Steve, but I honestly don't know." And then she starts crying.

"God, everything is such a nightmare. I know it's absolutely insane, but I haven't been having sex with you and I don't know who has. I remember being close to you, kissing you and then fading out. It's totally my fault, but it feels like you're having sex with someone else and it's just killing me."

I take a deep breath and put my arm around her. "Sophie, we're going to figure this out."

Dr. Newman smiles. "Well said, Steve."

I feel guilty that Dr. Newman seemed to be looking at me like I'm some sort of saint for sticking with Sophie. I'm no saint. Sophie was sticking with me, too, and I had my own faults and flaws. But unlike my brave wife, I was keeping mine hidden. It's easy to lie to yourself when you're just thinking about doing the wrong thing.

January 11, 2011

All too soon, the date arrives for the dinner with my brother David and nothing in my life seems good enough. I change clothes three times, but I don't own a $3,000 suit. It doesn't really matter anyway. He'll find *something* to criticize.

I go through my closet, trying things on like it's a first date. Nothing looks right. "Screw it. He'll hate anything I wear. I'm going to be comfortable!" I defiantly throw on my generic jeans with a blue button-down and gray sweater, but concede to vanity with a spritz of Seb's cologne. My logic is simple: when I try and David is critical, it hurts more than when I don't try at all.

My whole life, I always found myself just on the other side of "good enough" with my family. The black sheep with my career in education. Yes, I like nice things but I see so many kids who'd starve if not for free lunches at school. Spending $1,200 on a pair of shoes? I'd feel like a hypocrite. Now, as I drive through heavy rush-hour traffic, I find I'm gripping the steering wheel hard and yelling at the other drivers, regretting my decision to meet David at a steak house. Why hadn't I suggested he uber to my neighborhood for a Starbuck's? That would have been quicker...and easier to escape. But instead, I'd committed myself to a three-course meal and hours of the verbal onslaught that is my brother.

I spot him immediately. Slicked-back dirty blonde hair, icy blue eyes, cleanly shaven...a tailored, charcoal gray suit and matching shoes. His entire look screams *divorce attorney*. I'd hate to face him in a deposition.

"Hey, Steve!" he says as I come into view. He grabs me by the shoulders and looks straight into my face.

"Jesus, you look like *crap*! Who dressed you today?" He laughs out loud. I move in for a hug and he whacks me on the back. "Nice cologne though."

He's setting the tone for our evening. I was excellent with words, but not conflict. "Thanks. You too" is all I can force. My reply is weak and he laughs at me like I'd just struck out. I always felt like the pathetic little brother trailing after a successful sibling. I'd never catch up.

The pervasive scent of grilled beef, low lighting, leather booths with grommets and pretty waitresses in sexy uniforms firmly establish this place as a man's domain, fueled by testosterone. David's right at home. My family admires his ambition and my sister Rebecca's commitment to her family. Their lukewarm approval of my integrity and their total rejection of my liberal mindset continues to make me feel like the misunderstood misfit.

I come from a conservative, traditional family where the men are men and women are women. In their world, no one is poor unless they chose to be, mental illness is a weakness and homosexuality a character flaw. The only hint of liberalism comes from my mother's commitment to feminism but, even then, it's more of a libertarian bent on the subject—women need to muscle their way through any oppression and are absolutely capable of doing so. Perfectly valid reasons for failure were seen as excuses.

We slide into the booth and begin looking over our menus. This is not my sort of food.

"Rocky Mountain Oysters?" I ask, remembering a similar evening years ago when I convinced him to try our local delicacy before telling him he'd just finished a plate of cattle testicles.

"Hilarious, Steve. No. Fool me once."

The waiter smiles. "Can I get you started with some drinks?"

David grabs my menu and hands it to the waiter, "Actually, we're ready to order. I'll take bourbon neat and a local craft beer for Steve here. We'll both have the porterhouse—I take mine rare, Steve's—medium well. And the cheddar potatoes. Lava cake for dessert."

The waiter finishes writing down our order as David asks about his favorite brand of pretentious scotch. They don't have it so the waiter offers something else. David shoots him an unpleasant glare as he disapprovingly resigns, "That'll be fine."

The waiter smiles at me like he knows what I'm in for—or maybe to see if I have anything to add or change. My brother just ordered for me like I was his date. It's degrading. I just smile back and take a deep breath. And as soon as the waiter leaves, David starts a ten-minute dissertation on bourbon.

I'm grateful for any discussion apart from the topic I know he's itching to bring up. As he finishes, the drinks arrive and he shifts gears.

"You know Mom's not getting any better. She had that surgery and has gone downhill ever since. Did you know that medical mistakes are the third leading cause of death? I tell ya, I picked the wrong specialty. I always make fun of the personal injury guys, but they are *raking* it in."

Dinner arrives, interrupting David's stream of consciousness. Huge steaks swimming in butter and potatoes smothered in cheese. The waiter can see my discomfort and tries to lighten the mood. "Nice sweater," he says to me with kindness in his face. Out of the corner of my eye, I can see David is pissed that the waiter didn't notice his expensive suit. He was always in competition mode, even if no one else was playing.

The waiter then sets down a big pepper mill and, as he walks away, I say, "He seems nice."

David mocks me, "He's a fag, Steve. He's flirting with you. Plus, I'm pretty sure he was being sarcastic."

David was brilliant at taking out multiple targets with his insults simultaneously.

Throughout the meal, I learn that most of the medical errors that lead to death involve surgery. Too much anesthesia, cutting the wrong thing or nicking some other thing. Second most deadly, prescribing the wrong pills—or the wrong combination or misdiagnosis. I smile and nod, finishing ahead of David, partly because I can't eat this kind of food and partly because he's doing all the talking.

I feel like I'm waiting to be scolded by the principal—dreading it, but wanting to get it over with.

Dessert arrives and I desperately need a glass of milk or at least water, but David would see that as a sign of weakness. I wouldn't hear the end of it. Four beers and I was feeling buzzed. I subtly signal the waiter, who says, "Oh my gosh, I'm so sorry. I never brought your water. Let me get that for you."

We've arrived at the main event.

"Steve, I know you love Sophie and she is beautiful, but honestly, how are things going?" He doesn't wait for an answer. I had opened my mouth to say something and he ran right over me.

"I ask because I'm worried. I know she's dealing with some stuff, but I'm worried she's taking advantage of you. You really do look like crap."

"Sophie has some things she's healing from. You know, she has some health problems that have come up."

"Uh-huh. Like terminal laziness? I've always thought she was sort of neurotic. Is this a mental thing?"

I feel pinned down by his question and stuff my mouth with the sickly sweet lava cake to give myself a second to think.

"Because if that's what it is, you might as well get out now. These things *always* go downhill," he continues. And from his perspective, he was right. Divorce lawyers don't see the other side. They don't see the people who heal, only the ones who have gotten progressively worse and more difficult to live with, more hostile.

"She's getting better. Look, Dave, I really just want to enjoy a nice meal with you. Do we have to have this conversation again?"

"I'm just looking out for you, Steve. Rebecca's worried too, but she can never get away to come out here, she's so busy with Mom and her own family." This was code for the fact that he'd spoken with Rebecca and brow beaten her until she reluctantly and half-heartedly gave in just to make him stop.

"Sophie didn't grow up like we did. She has a lot of crap to deal with because of the abuse she went through."

"Oh, please! Is that what she's telling you? She was abused? Last Christmas when we called, she told us about that teacher at school that taught the kids to speak Dutch and gave them all wooden shoes filled with candy during the holidays. She's told us about how her grandparents arranged for her to take classes with famous painters when she expressed the tiniest interest in art. World travels, an arts high school? Sounds like a living hell. Steve, she is playing you. It sounds to me like she's just an immature, spoiled brat. Did she not get the right color of car when she turned 16? Is that what traumatized her?"

At that, I want to punch him in the face, but in the past I'd always just walked away. This time I try a different tact. I push my plate away and get out my own soap box.

"David, you hear divorce stories from guys who hate their wives. That's not me. Believe me, she went through some horrible things growing up."

"I don't buy it."

"I really don't care if you buy it or not, David. She's been through hell and she still came out extraordinary."

David swallows hard, knowing there was more. Now he looks like the one that was pinned down and wanting to escape. But his standard operating procedure has never been to flee. His default setting is to fight.

"If it was that bad, her grandmother would have left," he says.

"Really, David? Because you work with some of these guys. Do their wives file the first time he hits them? Or do they make an excuse—he was drunk or he had a hard day? What if he makes a good living and you're home with little kids? What if you want to keep your family together? What if there's *good stuff* too? Do you leave if he cheats? Hurts one of the kids? In our minds, this is so easy. It's black and white and we think we're so clear on it. But get into the reality and it's pretty damn murky."

The waiter brings our bill and can feel the tension. David picks it up and tells me, "It's getting pretty late. Maybe we should finish this later," like he's patronizing a crazy person.

He notices I've hardly touched my steak and smirks at me as he mocks me, "Did you want a doggy bag for that? Or are you 'off red meat' again?"

He wants to win this fight, even if he had to play dirty. But I've moved past that part of my life and his comment misses, instead nailing down for me how much he'll never change.

"I'm fine, David. Thanks."

"Alright," he says in his best patronizing, big brother voice, "it was good to see you, Steve. Let me know if you need anything."

David is a terrible tipper, so while he's distracted with the bill, I slip some money under my plate. Our waiter had gone out of his way to make tonight tolerable.

We get up and give one another perfunctory hugs. As we leave the restaurant, I tell him my car is parked in the opposite direction and, as he fades from sight, I call an uber. I'd never live it down if he knew I was too buzzed to drive home.

The driver tries to engage me in conversation, but I'm quiet and feeling like a total loser. I work through this and recognize its just a David thing. I refused to compete with him, but I had done better in school, I had more friends, and I had Sophie. He's not concerned, he's jealous, I conclude.

———

I throw off my coat and slip out of my shoes in the living room and then head to bed. I'd learned not to stand in the doorway staring. Instead, as usual, I'm loud enough that Napoleon stirs and wakes Sophie before she sees me.

I go up to the bedroom, and Napoleon casually looks over at me but Sophie's not in bed. Momentary panic strikes me, but then I feel cool hands on my shoulders from behind. I'm enveloped in an embrace and the scent of lavender with leather seems to intensify the effect of the alcohol. I feel soft kisses on my neck and hear sighs.

"I've been waiting for you."

I melt into her, soaking in the experience, but at the same time am trying to figure out who this is. It *sounds* and feels like Sophie. But I need to be alert enough to catch any inconsistencies telling me to stop. That's a tough balance when you're buzzed, but since learning about the multiplicity, I've learned to be more aware.

Moreover, now that we'd been having conversations with Dr. Newman, I wanted to learn who it is that I've been making love with for years. Now, I try to keep her engaged in conversation, but she's less and less talkative. I give her a few compliments hoping she'll respond. She only nods or makes sounds letting me know that she likes what I'm doing. I ask questions, but she only answers with an "uh huh" or "no."

The person in my arms is very clearly an adult, which is a huge relief. The more I read about multiplicity, the more I fear that child alters were triggered into thinking they had to be with me sexually and that thought horrifies me. I'd feel like a pedophile.

I softly run through the names I know, but I get no response. I ask in my most approving and nonjudgmental voice, "I want to say your name. Tell me."

Sophie suddenly stops, holds my face and looks into my eyes.

"Please," I ask.

My request is met with more kissing and I don't want to stop. We've been having sex only a couple times a month and it's not enough. She's become more submissive and proper than when we were first together and I miss our old sex life.

It's not until she's lying in my arms afterwards that she tells me in a slight, polished English accent, "I'm Anna."

I close my eyes and let the tears silently flow as I wonder if I've ever made love to the woman I married.

———

The next day, Ellyn drives me down to the restaurant to pick up my car. Sophie isn't crazy about Denver traffic, but it's nothing to Ellyn.

On the way, we talk and I'm hoping to get some answers. "I need to ask—who's Anna?"

Ellyn sounds playfully defensive. "Why are you asking?"

"I ran into her last night, but I know nothing about her."

Ellyn is amused, apparently guessing how I ran into Anna. "What do you need to know?"

"Anything you can tell me. I'm in the dark."

"I'm not sure how much I *can* tell you. She's 28 and she works at the modeling agency. She stays hidden from the rest of us for the most part."

"What does that mean? Why would she do that?"

"There could be a lot of reasons. She might just be a private person or maybe she wants to have her own relationship with you."

"Are there other reasons?"

"I'm sure there are more reasons than I can think of right now. We can't guess at the motivation of others. It's generally a recipe for misunderstanding and disaster."

"I appreciate your insights," I tell her, wondering if I should dig deeper. I decide to go a different direction.

"Speaking of disasters, dinner with David was a mess." She listens patiently as I rant.

"Why do I even try with him? God, he makes me crazy! He refuses to even listen to anyone who disagrees with him. He is such a jerk. He thinks Sophie is making this whole thing up."

She just smiles and tells me, "Don't take it personally. He comes from his own pain. It has nothing to do with us."

"How can you be so calm about this? He's saying that you're manipulating me— 'playing me' were the words he used."

Ellyn shrugs her shoulders and nods. "His pain. Not mine. If you felt that way, I'd be concerned, but I don't live with David and while I hope that he can heal whatever this thing is that makes him so hateful, it's not my responsibility to fix it."

I appreciate her perspective but am not ready to let it go yet. While Sophie had alters to offset *her* emotions, I couldn't turn off my feelings. Her alters who didn't feel the emotions could easily sit in the observer position and talk to me as Ellyn just had. They seemed wise and egoless. Me? I have to rant and drink, swear and vent.

When Sophie is upset, she just switches. And if she can't do that, she'll go on autopilot. That means no one is home. I had no idea how to handle it the first time it happened, but these days, we have a workable plan.

April 19, 2016

Friday morning, a little after 10, Sophie calls me at work. I see that it's her, but I'm in a meeting and it's a crazy day, so I don't pick up. A minute later, a text from Sophie. "911." The last time I got this message was years ago. It was reserved for the most dire of circumstances.

I call home and Sophie picks up right away but doesn't say anything. "Sophie? Sophie? It's Steve. I got your 911. What's up?" She doesn't answer. In fact, there is no sound at all. "Sophie? You there?" No answer.

That twenty-minute drive home never seemed longer.

Napoleon greets me at the door, but I push him to the side and bolt up the stairs. Sophie, but not Sophie, is sitting on the couch staring at her computer. I approach to see the screen has gone dead. I call all the names I know to see if she'll respond to any. "Seb, Sophie, Richard, Ellyn, Rachel, Anna, Jamie, Elizabeth, Kalia?" She doesn't even look at me. I put my hands on her shoulders and look right in her eyes. If anyone is there, they'll either hug me or pull away. She neither tenses nor melts. Her eyes are dead. No one is there.

I push power on her computer to bring it to life. An email from her old art teacher comes up. "Honey, I heard about Becky's passing from breast cancer. I know you two weren't close, but I also know you admired her so much. Hope you're doing okay. Please call if you need anything. xoxo, Constance."

Constance's words were kind, but the message was too much.

This is autopilot. She'd been doing so well, which meant she was taking on more responsibilities. The Timeshare was busy with a full schedule. It could be managed, but they couldn't handle one more thing. This news brought everything to a crashing halt.

We've been through this before and it had been the equivalent of a three-alarm fire. Not the end of the world, but I'd need help. My sister, Rebecca, is too busy with her own family. Seb's girlfriend, Laura, is not my biggest fan and Seb hated for her to see him on autopilot. Liz made the most sense.

Sophie is scary calm. No expression. Everything is in perfect order. Her calendar is out with her daily and weekly checklist. Sebi's pottery sale, Richard's Krav Maga test and Ellyn's presentation to the governor to raise awareness of human trafficking...all were on the agenda.

Autopilot means that she has no ability to make decisions. The only thing she could do was follow simple instructions. And if she hurt herself—burned herself making toast, cut herself shaving, sprained an ankle working out—she wouldn't stop. Pain didn't register when she was on autopilot. And that made it dangerous.

I call Dr. Newman and leave a message. Next, I call Liz. "I'll be right there," she promises.

Most people have an evacuation plan in case of a fire or earthquake, emergency contacts in case of illness. We have a disaster plan for autopilot.

I ask Sophie, "You okay? Thirsty?" She doesn't answer, but I make her a tepid cup of tea and set it on the coffee table next to her.

I check the notes that she wrote before fading into autopilot. She didn't choose this, but she could tell it was coming. Like being able to pull over when you get an aura before a migraine or making a pot of soup as you feel a terrible cold around the corner—Sophie could let us know what she needed before she went away.

Richard's Krav Maga test was coming up tomorrow. That would definitely have to be canceled. There's no way she'd be back in time for it. Ellyn's talk with the governor was coming up in four days so that was a toss-up. I'd call her friend Anne at the center that morning if she wasn't back. Sebi's art show, the most critical thing on the list because of how disappointed he'd be to miss it, is thankfully, still a week off.

I call the gym. "Hey, I just need to let you know that Sophie Benjamin will miss testing tomorrow. She's not feeling well."

The woman on the phone sounds confused and I hear the clicking of a keyboard. She sounds distracted as she tells me, "We don't have anyone by that name testing tomorrow. Could it be under another name?"

"Sorry. Yeah, Richard. Richard Benjamin. He's testing for his green belt."

"Oh, yeah. Here he is. Okay. The next test isn't happening until November. You sure he can't make it?"

I look at Sophie, who's still staring at a blank computer screen.

"I'm pretty sure."

"Okay, well, we can transfer the fees and application for him. Tell him to get better soon."

I look back to the notes. In Sebi's handwriting, a sticky note tells me, "Please price everything on rack 3—prices on clipboard. DON'T CANCEL SHOW."

That was the thing about Sebi. Even though this happened rarely, he was always prepared. He had everything ready just in case. And he'd fight his way back to do the show.

I'm aware Sophie hasn't touched her tea, so I hand it to her and tell her "Drink this now—slowly." She does as I ask and then waits for me to get the cup from her. I put it in the kitchen and tell her to go to the bathroom.

My phone buzzes and I pick up. It's Dr. Newman. I tell him Liz is on her way. "I just want you to be aware in case things go sideways, but I think we've got it covered," I say.

"Sounds like it. I'm glad Liz can come out. Wish I could tell you something to fix it fast, but you just need to wait it out until it passes. You know the drill. What triggered it?"

"Sophie's mom died. Breast cancer."

"I'm sorry to hear that. It's interesting, though."

"What is?"

"Breast cancer. If I were a metaphysician, I'd tell you that breast cancer is a manifestation of something unexpressed—a betrayal or something that happened close to the person's heart that was never resolved. If I were into metaphysics."

"Okay," I say with more sarcasm than I wanted to express. "I just hope we can resolve things for Sophie."

"We will certainly try. You're not alone in this. Remember that I'm here and you can always call people in the partner's group. They've been through this autopilot thing, too."

I order pizza and wings for dinner. I make up a plate for Sophie and set out a can of soda, hoping that might bring Jamie forward. He had been the first one out after autopilot last time. Sophie doesn't respond, so I tell her, "You need to eat that." She doesn't move. "Soph. Eat that now." She eats what's in front of her but leaves the soda. I trade it out for water and tell her to take sips as we wait for Liz.

By 9:30, Sophie has fallen asleep on the couch. She sleeps sitting up, the empty dinner plate on her lap. I take the plate to the kitchen, refill her water and cover her shoulders with a blanket. I know not to move her because waking up in a different place will add to the disorientation she's already drowning in.

Liz arrives just after 11, taking an uber from the airport, so I don't need to leave Sophie alone or take her out of the house. I welcome her in the entry with a hug and point to Sophie on the couch. She nods as I pick up her suitcase and we head down to the basement to talk.

Our basement is rarely used, so it looks brand new. Gray carpet and walls give it the feel of a hotel. The bed is made up with a crisp blue and white quilt. The bedside table has a small alarm clock on it next to a glass and small pitcher. Books, a deck of cards and some movies sit on a shelf in case a guest is bored.

A jetted tub, fresh towels, a robe and a small basket with soap and shampoo make the bathroom look like a spa. A mini kitchen is all set up with a coffee maker, small fridge, microwave and a little basket of snacks.

"What happened?" Liz asks me quietly, as I put her suitcase in the closet.

"She just found out that her mom died of breast cancer."

"Oh, my God."

"Yeah. It's not good."

As Liz thinks about it, she calculates the impact. "She and her mom never resolved things...and if she goes to the funeral, it'll be a disaster. If she doesn't, she'll feel like she didn't get a chance to say goodbye. And breast cancer. Does that run in families? Sorry. This is just...no wonder she went on autopilot."

"Yeah. Autopilot is always bad. Did you know that when she was in college and on autopilot, she went in for a chiropractic appointment and wound up in Atlantic City with the doctor for three days? He recognized something was off and when he realized she was confused and being ultra compliant, he told her they were dating and they had this trip all planned out. She came out of it on Sunday night, punched the guy in the face and came home. Still no idea what went on that weekend but we can guess."

"That's terrifying. She is so vulnerable."

"I know, right? So, I canceled some of Sophie's obligations, but I'm waiting on Seb's art show. Sounds like he wants to do it if he can."

We formulate a game plan for the next few days. Liz would take the day shift so I could go to work. I'd take the night shift, so she could sleep. I wouldn't sleep soundly, but I could get some rest sleeping next to The Timeshare.

Neither of us cook that much or that well, but Jamie had thought of that, too. In the past few months, he'd frozen several dinners, so we'd use those up and then resort to take-out.

Liz and I stay up half the night. I try not to violate Sophie's confidence, but I need to tell Liz about some things, so she knows what's going on.

I wanted to understand how Liz perceived the multiplicity, too. It was obvious she knew something about it, but I wasn't sure how much.

"So, can I ask you a question?"

"Sure."

"How much do you know about Sophie?"

"Do I know he's transgender? Of course. That's why I accept him as male. I call him him."

I nodded. That's how Sebi had spun it. That he was transgender.

"Or about the alters? Of course. Sebi prefers we pretend the others don't exist, and I play along," Liz continues. "But I went home with Seb a few times in college and met his family. It was obvious something was seriously wrong. His grandfather took me down to the basement and made a pass at me. But the feeling I got from him was malevolent. It went beyond the dirty old man thing, you know?"

"Sounds scary. I only met them briefly, but I got the same feeling."

"Yes, it's easy to see how Seb's multiple. I've seen autopilot before—just didn't have a name for it."

"But Sebi's story with you is that he's trans, right?"

"Yeah. It's fine. I mean, it sort of works. A man in a woman's body and all that. But I've seen other alters—the kids call me sometimes just to talk. I saw someone different once when we were out and a guy wouldn't stop hitting on us and Seb punched the guy in the face. Not really Sebi-like. And whenever we're in bed, I swear his eyes get lighter.

"I don't know how many there are," she continues. "I don't know their names for the most part. I know Rachel because she's introduced herself. I've always sort of thought of it as Seb and Sophie. And Rachel is just Sophie acting little. I don't know. I have no idea how to make sense of it, to be honest.

"When I've asked Sebi about his family, he's only shared the basics. But from what I've read, things have to be pretty bad to develop multiplicity, right?"

"That's my understanding, too." I left it there.

"I asked Seb point-blank once and he denied it. I honestly believe he doesn't think there actually *are* others. I get the feeling he's playing along when people have told him he's multiple. But once I knew that's what was going on, I read a bunch so I could understand it better."

"I'm in a little bit of a weird area here," I say. "I don't want to violate Sophie's trust, but at the same time, you need to know who's around in case she comes out of autopilot when I'm not here. I think they'd be okay with me giving you an overview and then they can fill in the rest later.

"You said that you'd spoken with a child alter, right?"

"I think so. Really little voice, giggles a lot?"

"You're right, that's Rachel. She's about 5 or 6 and she's pretty happy, but she can get frustrated. You have to watch her like you would any little kid. She loves junk food and cartoons, but she needs some help washing her hands and pouring milk and all of that. Make sure she doesn't eat too much crap or you'll hear from Seb. She has a lot of memories from the abuse, but none of the feelings, so brace yourself if you ask her anything.

"Oh, you mentioned the bar fight. That's Richard. I doubt he'll be the one to come out first. It sounds like he knows you, so worst case scenario, he'll try to protect you.

"There are fragments—pieces without a full identity. With those, you just have to go with the flow. They seem to have just one purpose —they may have no name, no history. They can surface sometimes during autopilot if something is intolerable.

"Then there's Elizabeth and she may cry if she's the first out. She's 12, dresses really frumpy and doesn't like to be seen. She holds the emotions around the abuse. She's very sweet, but very timid.

"Jamie is the most likely to be the first one out," I add. "He sees himself as a best friend of the kids. Very sweet guy. No worries there. You obviously know Seb and Ellyn, of course. I think that's it in terms of who you may run into."

"Wow. That's a lot. I guess I thought it was just shades of Sophie and shades of Seb. I didn't realize..."

"Yeah. It's a lot to keep track of, so don't feel like you need to know it all. It's mostly trusting your instincts. If you run into any issues, you can call me and we'll figure it out together."

The next night, I come home from work and Liz runs to the grocery for recovery food. If the kids came out first, we'd need to have junk food on hand.

We try to get Sophie in for a bath. Sometimes this can help her come back. But this time, it just results in a primitive fragment coming out grunting and fighting until both of us give up. This was actually a good sign. Normally she just dead weights us.

Night three and Liz and I have just defrosted and finished eating an amazing Lamb Navarin and French brioche by Jamie. Sophie is sitting in the recliner with a bowl of mac and cheese that has grown cold, the movie Elf playing in the background.

I look over and see the recliner is moving—it's almost imperceptible, but Sophie has started rocking and her eyes are shut. If she were on autopilot, she'd be staring at nothing, motionless.

I have to just allow this, rather than rushing over to her with a million questions. It's a little like letting ice melt away.

I shoot a look at Liz and she looks over to see The Timeshare re-acclimating and smiles. Then she nods at me, relief in her face.

Sophie looks around, shifts to get more comfortable, tunes into the movie, notices the macaroni and cheese in her lap, and starts eating it with awareness. She sets it aside, gets up, wanders into the kitchen and comes out with the family-size bag of chips, grinning at me and Liz with what feels like gratitude. This is Rachel. We're here for her and she knows it.

She sees the movie has ended and starts to cry. She points at the TV. "I missed it," she says, her voice dripping in sadness.

"It's okay, honey," I tell her as I hit play again. Now she's upset because she didn't get to see the puffin at the start. I restart the movie so she can watch the puffin.

After autopilot, it was like this. She would feel overwhelmed and intensely uncomfortable with the depersonalization and it would manifest in general dissatisfaction with everything. I had learned that she also needed to reassert the control she'd relinquished.

Once I had a handle on the "why" of things, it made it easier to be patient. I just tried to remember how miserable she was and how terrifying it must be. Depersonalization is not really an "out of body" thing. It's more the experience of wanting to be in your body but not being able to get there and you can't coordinate your movements with your brain. Like a bad acid trip, your body doesn't look like your own, nor does it respond to commands the brain gives it. Lots of short circuits.

After crunching down a fair amount of chips, Sophie goes for the cookies. And then she starts to cry from feeling so weird. She had dropped chips as she ate them and had resorted to eating her macaroni and cheese with her fingers because she couldn't work the fork. Then she was biting her fingers, which hurt. She was phasing in and out and missing her favorite parts of the movie. She'd cry in frustration and tell me, "I missed the narwhal!" "Did I miss the spaghetti and pop tarts?" We replay some parts and fast-forward to others.

She begins rocking harder. I'd learned that she did this to help her come back into her body.

The next few days are spent recovering. It feels like Liz and I were Sophie's parents—being sure she ate, drank water, took a bath, used the bathroom.

Seb hates it. He considers himself to be strong and capable. He wants to be dependable and hates looking flakey. Dr. Newman had done some work with him on this. "Life happens," he explained, "to everyone." But the perfectionistic part of Seb had a hard time acknowledging that.

It is true, though. Everyone has family emergencies, illnesses, and other problems. Autopilot is ours.

Sophie is still having trouble coordinating and dealing with double vision as she tries to put together everything that happened while she was away. Liz and I try to fill in as much as we can, but we don't know what's going on inside—or why.

Sebi wants to do the art show and it would be happening at a safe place among friends. He seems a bit like someone coming out of the flu, but the charisma is coming back. He's embarrassed that he'd gone on autopilot—feeling like he wasn't strong enough to fight it off. This would be hardest on Richard. To be Seb's bodyguard and to be psychically bound and gagged and thrown in the corner had to be humiliating.

We get all of Sebi's pieces priced and packed up and remind him about the schedule for drop-off, when he's to be there, and other details. Because this is so close to an episode, Liz and I will go with him and be available to help.

On Saturday we're at the art center early. I know that Seb does better when things are calm and he has time. Rows of tables are neatly set up. He has a double table on a corner. It's labeled "SEBI G DESIGNS" and he smiles when he sees it. The 6-foot tables are covered with a stretchy black cloth. Seb throws a muted green beaded linen square over each table and then sets up collapsible black risers.

We're getting into a routine with these shows. I push three boxes off the dolly and run out to the car for the rest. Seb unwraps each piece carefully and positions it perfectly to highlight each one.

We all stand back to look at the display. It's perfect. We have nearly an hour before the show opens.

"Sushi?" I ask.

"That'd be great," Seb says. "I'm starving."

We hit a fusion spot we've been meaning to try and it's amazing. Seb gets sushi but also fried wontons, sweet and sour pork, and ginger ice cream. He forgoes the alcohol because he's already on Xanax to help even out the anxiety around being out of body for so long.

Back at the sale, we arrive as other people are finishing up their displays...watercolors, drawings, stained glass, metal work, jewelry. Seb's sculptures are unique. We notice the older woman in the booth next to him has some wild-looking animals with porcelain bodies and very long wooden legs painted in crazy patterns.

"Hey, Dot, how's it going?" Seb is outgoing and friendly as he gives her a hug. She seems sweet.

"Hey," she answers, "didn't know you were doing this one. Did you want to give me a couple sculptures and I'll trade you some beasts?"

"That'd be great," Seb says, but looks confused and responds flatly, and I can see concern starting to settle in Dot's face.

Normally, Seb would introduce me and Liz, but he's not on his game, so I step over to her and say, "Hey, I'm Steve. Seb's hus... room-mate. And this is our friend Liz."

"Well, it's nice to finally meet you. I was beginning to think he was making you up!" She smiles warmly at me.

Seb and Dot look over each other's creations. Seb looks slightly lost and Dot takes over in a motherly way. She mixes and matches their pieces on Seb's table and then hers, asking if he's okay with what she's doing. By combining pieces, they effectively double their space while helping each other out. It's a good strategy.

The first art lovers begin to filter in. They look at all the offerings and chat, taking pictures and asking questions. Seb is in his element, excited to be talking art with people. He refers to his notebook when people ask questions, but gets stumped from time to time, so I step in and hand them his business card.

"I'm so sorry," I say, "Seb is just recovering from a virus, so he's a little out of it. Give him a call next week and he can answer all your questions."

People who've been around know Sophie goes by "Seb." They assume he's transgender. New people are confused, but courteous. Artists tend to be pretty open. Besides, dressed this way, Sophie looks like a diminutive man.

Seb is fine when things are quiet, when he could handle one thing at a time. But as things heat up and get busier, he begins to get flustered. He's trying to answer one person's questions while another lady waits. Becoming overwhelmed, he begins to get abrupt in his answers, the charm falling away in favor of short, factual statements. I knew what would come next—he was edging back towards autopilot—just when it was so important for him to stay on keel.

Then Seb looks over to me and motions for me to come closer. It's not his usual funny frat boy "come check this out" beckoning. This is a panicked "throw me a life preserver" situation.

At one point he stumbles while answering a woman who had bought a number of pieces before and wants to hear about a sculpture she's interested in now. The woman asks if he's okay and he hugs her and says, "Yeah, of course, sweetie. I'm just having a panic attack right now." She puts her hand on his back, apologizes and asks what he needs. He just shakes his head and looks at the ground.

"Okay if I call you next week?" he finally says.

She gives him an adoring look full of sympathy and says, "Of course. Take care of yourself. Are you okay if I buy this now and call you next week for coffee? Can I bribe you with chocolate?" Seb smiles and takes both her hands in his. "I would love that. Thank you."

I ring up her purchase and turn my attention to Seb, who has gone ashen.

Dot is guessing at what's wrong. She puts her arm around my waist and directs me, "Darling, I've seen this happen to him before. He's going to be fine. He just needs a cigarette to calm down. Go on. I'll watch his booth."

I love everything about this woman.

"Seb, cigarette?" I ask. Seb looks dazed as I wrap my arm around his shoulders and lead him out. Liz stays behind with Dot and is already chatting with people at Seb's booth.

We make it to a bench near a small pond just outside the side entrance.

Seb looks at me. "I'm okay. I just need a second. And a cigarette. I just...can't...get my body...to coordinate with me." He pats his jacket, but can't find his cigarettes. His hands are shaking so hard, I don't know if he'll be able to hold one anyway.

"It's okay, Seb. Hang on. I reach into his jacket and pull out the Marlboros. I hand one to him, then reach into his side pocket for the lighter.

"Thanks," he says gratefully as I light his cigarette, but I can hear frustration in his voice. He draws the nicotine deeply into his lungs and closes his eyes. But a little while later, he's still out of it. He tries to downplay what's happening—the panic, the shaking, the inability to think straight, and his body's unwillingness to obey the brain's orders—by confessing, "I'm just wiped out."

I kick myself, thinking we probably should have canceled the show, but I hate to override The Timeshare's instincts about what they need.

"I'm sure," I say. "This show came pretty quick on the heels of an episode. You can use some rest. Should we let Liz handle things? Head home?"

"I'll get some rest after the show, Steve. I owe that to everyone who came out and the people who set stuff up. They put in a lot of work and it'd be disrespectful to leave now. I can wrap it up. It's only a few more hours."

We re-enter the sales floor and find Liz speaking with a group of men who had gathered. She's describing Seb's technique, why his pieces are so valuable, and how they can be displayed.

She spots Seb and grabs his hand. "Hey baby, I missed you," she says, giving him a long kiss—more for appearances than anything else. Dottie and I exchange an eye roll and knowing look. After the guys leave with their statues, Seb smiles at me and raises his eyebrow. "Damn! I should bring her to all of these things!"

But Seb is slightly dazed the rest of the day, able only to engage with Liz when she prompts him. By the end of the show, he's mentally exhausted, but they've nearly sold out. Even had a couple of friendly bidding wars.

I was jealous of the connection Liz and Seb shared, but I admire this about Sebi. When he commits to something, he does his level best to follow through.

It takes us less than half an hour to pack up and I go check on Seb. He's not sitting on the bench or hanging out by the pond. I find him around the corner, leaning against the building, making out with the woman who won the bidding war. She looks to be in her mid 20's.

"Seb," I say as I near. He doesn't hear me.

"SEB!" I say loudly. Now I'm pretty sure he hears me, but is ignoring me.

The woman he's kissing puts something on her tongue, and Sebi smiles as he opens his mouth to take it from her.

I stop where I am, shake my head and yell, "*Seriously*?"

He pulls himself away from her, but it's obvious he's going to be completely out of it soon.

"Art student. Big admirer," he says as he stumbles past me and ruffles my hair. At the car, he falls into the back seat face down and passes out.

Liz looks at me. I no longer get angry about this sort of thing, but instead have fallen into a giggle fit.

"You okay?" she asks, starting to laugh herself.

"Yeah, I'll tell ya later. Is there more in there or is this everything?"

"One more load, I think."

"Can you stay with him and I'll go get the rest?"

"Is he okay?"

"He took some sort of pill."

"Super," she frowns. "What was it?"

"No idea, but it looks like he's going to be sleeping it off."

She reminds me to take the dolly and I load up the rest.

Later at home I carry Sebi to the couch, pull off his boots and let Liz tuck him in. Then Liz and I sit down at the dining room table for a debriefing of the last few days.

"So, when I went to get him after the show, he was making out with some woman..."

"Yeah, well, that sounds about right," Liz says. She isn't upset, merely amused.

"I thought you might be pissed."

"Are you?

"Well, no, not really. We have an agreement. I was a little jealous of you guys at the show. You two just click in a way I don't with him. These random hook-ups scare me, but they don't upset me, if that makes any sort of sense at all."

"Yeah, totally," Liz offers. "They never go that far anyway. He's just flirting. It makes him feel more normal after autopilot."

"I was a little worried about the pill that woman gave him."

Liz shrugs. "Unfortunately, certain drugs bring him back into his body. And sometimes it's not about getting back in—sometimes it's about getting a break from it—just knocking himself out so he doesn't wind up on autopilot again."

I'm glad not to be alone in this situation and as I glance at Liz, something moves through me. I'm starting to understand the appeal of an open marriage. At this moment, monogamy no longer feels realistic to me—or even desirable. I have to be honest with myself and, if I am, I have to admit that I feel an attraction to other people. I still feel an open marriage is playing with fire, but I can also see some of the benefits. And even though it's acutely uncomfortable and I feel a surge of shame, I'm coming to grips with my own truth.

I pull some pie out of the freezer and sit down with Liz to discuss the past week. I can't help but laugh as Liz teases me. I'm putting whipped cream from a spray can on my slice until you can no longer see any trace of the pie. I try to do the same to hers and she pulls her plate away so whipped cream goes all over the table.

We laugh together and I find myself staring at her.

"What?" she says, smiling at me.

"Just thinking how far we've come. I didn't really even meet you during college. Then I pretty much hated you after finding out about you and Seb. Finally, I'm getting to know you and now I'm calling you for help and you're always there. I feel like we're very nearly friends."

"Yeah, I think if we weren't there before, this trip definitely sealed that up."

"I'm curious about something else," she continues, "...so, can I ask you a question?"

"Absolutely," I say, taking another sip of my drink.

"Sophie is female. Sebi is male. So, are you gay? Or straight? Bi?"

"I'm not sure how to answer that because I'm still trying to sort it out myself. I can honestly say I have no idea."

She nods as I ask her the same question.

She laughs uncomfortably and moves her glass in a circle on the table before responding. "I don't know either. I drove myself into an existential crisis over it for a while and then I just let it go. I'm straight, but I'm in love with Sebi's personality—not the body. When I talk about it, I just feel like it sounds crazy."

"I hear you." Then I take a chance and ask, "Does your husband know?"

Liz looks a little wounded. I can tell there's more to this story than I'd considered. It's painful for her to talk about.

"I'm sorry. You know, that's none of my business. This is a very complex situation. I'm sure you're doing what's best."

"It is complex. But yes, he knows. You've trusted me. Now I'll trust you. Charlie and I are married in name only at this point. He put in overtime trying to prove he's not gay. I know he screwed around with high school girls. I know he was seen as a letch. But he is totally gay. I think it was just hard for him to admit. When he finally did? Well, he has his life and I have mine. And the kids have both of us. Seb doesn't know. He just knows I'm not happy."

"Oh God, I'm so sorry. Sounds rough."

"Yeah, we've had some rocky spots. Lots of fighting. Coming out here, just being held by Seb—it's a life-saver. I don't know. Is it me or is there something remarkably healing about him? Or am I just drunk?"

"No, you're right. I've felt it, too. Like a charisma, but warmer than that. Like being accepted by the most popular kid in school, right?"

"That's it exactly!" she says, taking another drink as she nods her head. "Anyway. Chuck. I just feel like a moron. I should have known. All the time at the gym, the plastic surgery, the apple-tinis. Like he didn't drop enough clues!" she says.

"I don't think that's how it works, Liz. We see what we want to see. And when you're married, the only choice is trust. If you don't have that, the whole thing falls apart. The cheating? That's on him. Not you." And suddenly I'm able to hear myself and something lets go. I feel lighter. It dawns on me that I can help The Timeshare, but I can't be responsible for their choices. That's huge.

I snap back in as Liz tells me, "Do you know how many times we've had sex in the last 10 years?"

I raise my eyebrows in question and Liz answers.

"Keep in mind we have four kids. We've had sex less than a dozen times. He told me he was very conservative. He said he'd sown his wild oats, but in marriage, sex was only about producing children. I found all of this out after our first baby was born. I was sure it was just because my body had changed. Now I know it had nothing to do with me."

She takes another bite of Jamie's blueberry pie. "At this point," she continues, "I've gotten used to it. It works—in a way. He has his boyfriends on the side. I have Seb. And as long as it works, Chuck and I will try to stay together—at least until the kids are out of the house."

"Sounds like a lonely way to live." Then something else occurs to me and a fear runs through me like cold electricity. Chuck is sleeping around. Liz is sleeping with Chuck—and Seb. And I'm sleeping with someone Seb shares the body with. I have to ask. "Liz, have you been tested?"

"Tested? Oh, for STI's? I haven't. I know it's really stupid, but I'm sort of worried about what I might find. I should do it, but it's humiliating."

"Would it help if I did it too?"

"You would do that?"

"I probably should. It seems like a smart idea, but just thinking about it makes me nervous."

"I know. Me, too. But it makes sense to keep an eye on it. We should have Seb go in, too."

"I'll talk with him," I tell her. "Staying with Chuck sounds so painful. How do you tolerate it?"

"The kids need a dad. Besides, Sebi makes it better. Knowing that I can come out here a few times a year has been a lifeline. I love him more than I can express. More than friends, but not really a romance. Nothing really happens when I'm here. There's a closeness. I mean, I know he loves me and we have something special, but he's in love with someone else."

I knew that someone else was not me. And I could tell that not being with Sebi full time was breaking her heart. But no one got "full time" with a multiple. I didn't get Sophie full time and Liz didn't get Sebi full time either.

"I found his Facebook page years ago," I say, "and there's a picture of the three of you at The Grill. I always wondered—is that how you guys always are or was that sort of a staged picture?"

"No," she laughed. "That's just us whenever we're together." My heart sinks with her words. "You saw him with that girl today," she continues. "That's him. He makes everyone around him feel great—like they're the only person in the world that matters. I can't believe how someone that tortured could come out of it with such a sweet spirit. But he did. He really deserves all the love he can get."

"About the picture? We were just out having fun and we were a little drunk. There were these guys there that kept staring at us. I'm sure they had all sorts of ideas. So they were happy to take pictures of us when we asked. Some of them were racier. I mean, not super racy. We were in public. But, you know. Sorry if that's not what you want to hear but when the three of us are together, it's sort of a big party. I consider myself straight, but there's something really hot about watching Sebi and Laura. He's just so into her."

She's lost in her own thoughts, not considering the weight of her words. "Sorry. TMI probably," she finally says.

Then she asks, "Can I show you something?" hesitating as she speaks—as if she were regretting asking as soon as the words came out of her mouth.

"Anything to shed light on this."

She pulls out her phone and flips through pictures and videos. "This was last summer..." she trails off, inviting me to change my mind if I wanted to.

"Was Laura here?"

"Yeah, she was," she answers distractedly as she scrolls. "Okay, here it is."

She finds the video. Liz is doing a half selfie, trying to catch Sebi and Laura in the frame, too. She's explaining that they just woke up. Their hair is a mess and they're still in their pajamas and robes. They're laughing their asses off as they get breakfast ready. Upbeat music is playing and every now and then, they break into dance.

Sebi is laughing harder than I've ever heard. He can barely stand up.

"No, you guys, we *have* to decide what we're doing for breakfast! I'm *starving*! Do any of you bitches cook? I mean, seriously!?" he was saying.

More laughter. "No one in this house knows how to fry a damn egg? What. the. Hell?" He's laughing because he can't cook either.

Laura has been digging in the pantry and pulls out peanut butter and honey. She shows it to the camera. Sebi laughs, "Oh, yes, that's brilliant, Sunshine! Yes! Awesome." The camera pans to a jumble as Liz roots around and finds something to put the peanut butter on. She pulls out some crackers and hands them to Laura.

"Open face, ladies, *open* face! The honey squishes out otherwise! Oh my *God*, Laura, you are doing that so wrong! And where's the cinnamon? The cinnamon *makes* the whole thing work. Jesus, you guys!"

They look as if this is the most fun they've ever had.

Laura holds up a sandwiched example and says, "No, it doesn't. Look! Sebi, see? It's fine!" And as she hands it to him, it starts dripping honey. Liz moves from a blurry close-up of the cracker sandwich to her face and she opens her mouth in a mock scream. Back to Sebi saying, "This is what I'm saying. No one listens to me. Seriously! Look at this—honey everywhere!" And he's kissing honey off of Laura's hand and down her arm as they all laugh until tears are rolling down their cheeks.

The camera swings back to Liz, who's saying, "So, I think we've got breakfast figured out. See you for lunch!" And as the video closes, you can hear the conversation trailing off with Laura asking Liz for the milk so she can make Sebi's coffee. Sebi's laughing, saying, "She sucks at the sandwich thing, but she does make an amazing cup of coffee."

No wonder Sebi was in such a good mood after the girls visited. Who wouldn't be happy? He's completely at home with them.

I'm now feeling left out, like I could never provide this for The Timeshare. I wonder why they were even with me when they had this option. I have to get ahold of myself. I know I may never have another chance to ask the questions I've had for years. So, feeling now was my chance, I ask, "Tell me about Laura."

"Laura. Well, Laura is his great love, isn't she? I know it sounds corny but the best way I can put it when I see them together it's like she feeds his soul. Laura has been with Carla since college —you know why they're not married yet? Because Laura won't marry Carla unless Carla agrees to accept her relationship with Sebi unconditionally. I don't know if you've heard Sebi talk about her, but I'm Sweetie and she's Sunshine. There's a reason for that. Laura lights up his whole life. He's told me I make his life sweeter, which is nice, but I don't think he could live without her."

I hadn't recognized the depth of these relationships. Seeing the pictures, it was easy to think this was just a fling. Now I had to admit to myself the importance of these women in Seb's life. I sat with that a minute and felt a spark of jealousy tempered by gratitude for the role Liz and Laura played in his life. I wondered if Liz was jealous, too.

"But you know about each other—that you both have a relationship with him. That always struck me as strange and difficult."

"All relationships are strange and difficult," Liz says reflectively. "Look at us. Here we are, friends because of Seb. You and I would never have talked if not for him. Your relationship with Sophie? I imagine it's an uphill battle every day. Maybe that's not how all relationships are. Maybe you and I are a couple of drama queens. If I'm going to be honest, I could never really be happy with Sebi. The whole second-choice thing. In high school, and even through most of college, I was always the first choice. Did you know I was homecoming queen?"

I could feel the scotch making me more honest than I would have been sober. "I can see that. That was actually my first thought when I saw you. You're beautiful," I offer. "I was never the typical popular kid, but I knew I had looks going for me. In high school, I had the same thing. Homecoming court, anyway. I feel like I'm third choice now—after you and Laura."

"I don't think so, Steve. I think, for Sophie, you're it. For her, you're the great love of her life. *I really believe that.* You should hear how she talks about you. She feels like you're her hero. She feels like she doesn't deserve you and she's more grateful than you'll ever know. But I know Sebi struggles with your relationship with him. When he talks about you, he's passionate about your friendship. He doesn't talk that way unless he really cares for someone."

I nod and then think about how strange it is to be talking about my wife's affairs in this way—detached and yet caring. I feel sad but the jealousy has melted away for the most part and find that to be really odd. "How do you deal with it?" I ask. "How do you deal with knowing that she has me and Sebi has you and Laura? I always had a traditional idea of marriage. I can't get my head around it."

"I had that traditional view growing up, too. I never saw anything different. It was one man, one woman. I never thought of myself as bi. I always thought of myself as completely straight. And I think of Sebi as a man, but obviously, the body is female. So what does that make me? And I'm married to Charlie, but it's certainly not traditional."

After a moment, she goes on, "If I take it down the rabbit hole even farther, I'm straight, married to a gay man who doesn't want me, committed to another man who's married to you and lives in a woman's body who is in love with a lesbian who is, for all intents and purposes, married to another woman. If that doesn't mess with your head, I don't know what will!"

Both of us had, like most married people, wandered inch by inch, sometimes leap by leap, farther and farther away from what we signed up for.

I drop Liz at the airport and we share a hug. We'd been through so much together, neither of us wants to let go. We've reached a new point in our relationship and, like two soldiers who've been through a battle together, we know in this moment we will always remain close.

Kevin calls as I'm driving home from the airport and a wave of relief washes over me. Over the years, I'd found myself relying on him more and more. I loved my partner's group, but Kevin and I had a history. He'd known me almost my whole life. We met in elementary school and he was one of a handful of lifelong friends.

I tell him about autopilot, as well as my latest conversation with Liz and everything that's going on with Sophie. The problems with his wife are intensifying. She was back in the hospital and they were talking about trying to find a permanent solution—like some sort of long-term residential treatment center.

Kevin gets to Denver fairly regularly, but I still wish we lived closer. Sometimes I feel I really need to grab a beer with him in person. That day, he tells me he really needs to get away too, so we set up another time to get together.

Sophie sleeps pretty much solid for the next week. Compared to the previous week, for me, this is a breeze. I go to work and Sophie rests. In the evenings, Rachel and I eat the left-over junk food and watch children's movies. Things needed to be fun and light as Sophie did the hard work of returning to her body.

Liz and Laura check in daily. Laura would have been there, but with her teaching schedule, it just didn't work. Her visits were longer but less frequent. For Liz, things are falling apart with Charlie and she can't take more time away from work. She had wanted to try and stick things out until the kids were done with high school, but it had just been too painful—and probably not that great for the kids anyway. Charlie had never been very attentive as a husband but, until recently, he'd been a great dad. However, over the past few months, he had fallen in love with someone at work and they were spending all their time together.

I'm happy to be there for Liz. It feels good to be able to actually help. I hate to admit it, but with Sophie it sometimes feels like a losing battle.

Sophie got in to see Dr. Newman a couple of times. I drove her, but she wanted to speak with him alone to sort out what had gone on internally during autopilot. I was okay with that. I didn't know what I'd say anyway. I did tell her I was going to go to the mountains soon and she understood. Things had been so intense.

I help Sophie reschedule things. Seb had another art show coming up so he needed to get to work. Pulling more creativity from his mind is actually a healthy exercise that helps him sink into the body more. Dr. Newman says it's a way to get the brain back on track—like art therapy."

When Seb's feeling better, I sit down with him and tell him Liz and I had spoken. I tell him that we both respect his privacy, but I had needed to give her an overview of the alters.

"How did she take it?" he asks.

"I think she was surprised, but not shocked. She thinks of the system as just you and Sophie with the other alters being parts of you, but not completely different people."

Seb nods his head but looks somber.

"You okay?"

"Yeah, I'm okay. It's just...." Seb sighs. "I don't want her to see me as a condition, you know?"

"I don't know that anyone could ever see you that way, Seb. It was so strange to be talking with Liz like this, but we talked about how healing it is to be around you—how charismatic you are."

Seb is suddenly very uncomfortable. He looks suspicious and a little hurt, which really confuses me. Hadn't I just given him a compliment? I can see him choosing his words carefully now and settling on "Thanks. I'm glad you guys are becoming friends."

"Seb. What's going on?"

"It's just...look, I know that I have some sort of quality that draws people in and I'm grateful for it, but sometimes I wonder where it comes from. In high school, I was one of the most popular kids but I had no idea I was until someone told me. People roll out the red carpet for me and I appreciate the hell out of it, but I don't know why they do that. And people get attached to me in really weird ways. I've actually had stalkers. One guy had a whole wall of pictures of me in his bedroom. I feel sort of like an addiction and it's unsettling. I have to wonder if this is me or if this is something that was trained into me—to draw people in.

"Papa was charismatic too and he used it to hurt people and get away with it. My biggest fear is that I'll become my grandfather. I don't want to hurt people. I'm worried this charisma is like a poison."

"I don't know, Seb. I think there are so many threads we could start pulling on and maybe it's better to deal with what's in front of us and not worry about anything else. I can't imagine you being anything like him. You have a kind soul."

He puts his hand over his heart and nods as the tears steal his voice.

"Sebi, can I ask you a difficult question?"

"You mean this is going to get more intense?" he laughs, wiping his eyes. "Jesus, let me get a drink first." He gets up and grabs two beers, opens them and hands one to me.

I take the beer, but don't drink. I don't want the distraction. I need the truth.

"This may be crossing a line, but what exactly is your relationship with Liz and Laura? I've wondered for years."

He squints his eyes and puts on a crooked smile as he reaches across the table. He slides my beer away from me and teasingly scolds me, "You just lost your beer."

"Seb. Come on, I'm serious."

"I know you are."

Seb's phone begins vibrating on the table and the sound is jarring. I try to never check my phone when we talk and it irritates me that he's so afraid of missing something that he's always checking his. He looks at the number.

"Sorry. It's someone from back home."

He picks up his phone and stands up.

"Hello? Oh, my God," a beat later and his eyes are filling with tears.

"Yes, of course... Yes, I did. Thank you... No, I won't be there... I know, but..." Seb is crying now. "That would be incredible. Thank you. Thank you so much."

He turns the phone off and puts it back on the table as he wipes the tears from his cheek.

"Sorry."

"What was that about? Are you okay?" I ask.

He smiles and shakes his head. "It was incredible. That was Constance. She wanted to know if I was okay because I never answered her email. She asked if I'd be at the memorial for Becky and when I told her no, she offered to bring a rose from us. Isn't that beautiful?"

"It really is, Seb. You know some amazing people."

"I do. Sorry about the interruption. I know that bugs you. I turned off my phone. Where were we?"

"Liz and Laura. Your relationship with them."

Seb sits down and takes a sip of beer. "Steve, I'm not sure this is a conversation you're entitled to. You told me a long time ago you didn't want to know anything about it."

"Liz and I have talked. I think I'm past the jealousy part. I feel sad sometimes—wishing I had with you what you have with Laura, but it's not jealousy."

Sebi winces as he shifts in his seat. "I'm still not sure how much you want to hear. I get that this is a sensitive area and I'm walking the line between not wanting to lie to you and not wanting to hurt you."

There's something noble about that. Someone who's been through so much abuse wanting to protect others from pain. It's a trait I admire.

Seb pulls me back, "Do you really want to hear about this?"

"Huh?"

"Do you really want to hear about this?"

"Yes, I do want to know."

"I think the best way to describe what I have with Liz is to say that we're friends with sort of kind of benefits, I guess."

"Well *that* clears things up," I say, shaking my head.

Seb ignores me. He's doing his best.

"I know she wants more," he says. "How do you handle that, you know? If I back away, I'm a jerk. If I keep seeing her, I'm accusing myself of leading her on. But, I do love her and I care about her as a friend. Ellyn is in love with her but I don't think Liz could ever really be happy with us. We sleep in the same bed, we make out a little and I hold her. That's it. I think mostly she just wants to feel loved. That closeness. But I've never been attracted enough to her to go much beyond making out and she's too straight to do much of anything while I'm in this body."

"What about Laura?"

And there it was. He looked down, his hair hiding the blush that's moving across his cheeks. He pauses for a moment and when he speaks I can hear the affection in his voice.

"Laura is my sunshine."

To hear those words from my wife's lips, regardless of who's speaking them, rips my heart into shreds.

"You love her."

"I do."

"I'm assuming when she's here it goes further."

"It does."

"I have to ask you a question that I'm really uncomfortable asking."

"We're already in a pretty uncomfortable area. Shoot."

"Liz and I were talking about getting tested for STI's. It seems like a smart thing to do. Will you go with me?"

Sebi answered quickly. "It's not a big deal, Steve. Sure, I'll go with you."

I'm surprised by his instant willingness and the lack of concern.

"Why do you seem so okay with this?"

Seb's eyes widen a bit as he shrugs his shoulders. "It's just a blood test, Steve."

"But this feels monumental to me and Liz. What's going on that this seems like it's a non-issue for you?"

"I...I mean, I grew up with those tests, Steve. Every six weeks. I still go in for a test every few months. Don't worry about it. So far, so good. Plus, I'm careful. I wouldn't want to put you at risk of anything."

The grip around my throat loosens a bit but it's replaced with a sinking feeling in my heart that there's more to this story. I sense both fear and guilt from Seb. Still, if Seb's okay, I assume I'm okay. But I still resolved to go in for a test.

My next question is one that had been on my mind. One that I was afraid to ask, but I had to know the answer. "Are you going to leave me for Laura?"

"Sophie would never leave you and, while it kills me to not be with Laura, she's with Carla and I only get to see her a few times a year."

"Did you know that you're part of the deal?" I ask. Sebi's eyes narrow. He doesn't know what I'm talking about.

I continue, "...that Laura said she won't marry Carla unless she can keep seeing you?"

"I didn't know that." He smiles. "Makes me love her even more."

"Liz showed me the breakfast video. You guys have so much fun together."

Seb reads the sadness in my voice, but says nothing about it.

A competitive wave runs through me and I need a win: "When they come to visit, do you play the piano for them?"

Seb looks offended and it surprises me. I feel the question is so generic.

"No, I don't. That's a you-thing. I don't think you get the significance, but now's not the time to get into that," Seb says.

"Can I ask you something about Sophie? I know it's hers to tell, but I so rarely see her anymore. Maybe you can ask her for me?"

"Okay."

"I'm seeing less and less of her these days. What's up? Has she been integrated or something?"

"No, it's not like that. She's resting."

"Any chance she'll take the wheel again anytime soon? I miss her."

Sebi's quiet. Maybe going inside, maybe evaluating if he should share this with me. He takes a deep breath, bites his bottom lip and almost imperceptibly shakes his head no.

I had already felt Sophie slipping away, but now I have confirmation. All I can think about is how desperately I want to escape to the mountains.

———

As I drive up to the condo, I can feel the stress peeling away from me. The early May sun barely manages to steal the April chill from the air and it's refreshing. The closer I get, the more the traffic thins and eventually, the road opens up and a sense of freedom allows me to take the first deep breath I've had in weeks.

I turn off the main road and click off the music in my truck. I like the sound of gravel crunching under my tires. There's something satisfying about it that invites a feeling of contentment. I used to feel that way about coming home to Sophie. There were harbingers along the way that I looked forward to seeing—the feeling of happiness growing as I got closer to her. But the condo is beginning to feel more like home than my house in Denver, and I'm not sure how I feel about that.

Rolling down the windows, I take in the sounds and smells around me as I drive. Fragrant pine trees line the road, and now seem to provide a feeling of shelter. It's so peaceful. An occasional deer wanders along the road picking at a bush. Prairie dogs sit atop rock outcroppings, keeping watch. I wonder if they feel fierce and protective. To me they look like cute little stuffed toys.

At the condo, I pull into my spot and see Kevin's rental car. I step out onto the gravel, take in the fresh air and stretch. These first moments of arrival are always my favorites and I savor them. I do a 180 to see everything, to acclimate, to be present. Then I close my eyes and breathe, soaking everything in and allowing the feeling of peace to envelop me.

I climb the steps and push the door open. Kevin looks up from his book. "Oh, you're here. Hey. Gorgeous drive today, huh?"

"Yeah, it was," I say, tossing down my bag and sinking into a chair. "What are you reading?"

"I don't know. I just found it here and it looks nap-inducing."

Kevin never could read very long without falling asleep.

While we'd talk on the phone about our marriage problems, at the lake, we just wanted to escape from them. We'd made an agreement not to talk about our problems here. It needed to be a place where we could recharge. Kevin adored Shannon but, like Sophie, she was no longer really there. She'd be going to long-term care soon and would remain there. Kevin is a mess, but he has no choice.

For the next couple of days here, we get to be in charge of our own lives, our own schedules. Life is calm and predictable. It feels simple to sleep when we're tired, eat when we're hungry, and just be able to catch our breath.

Mornings, we'd wake with the sun and then quietly sit at the lake with a thermos of coffee, fishing. When it got warmer, we'd explore a new area, hike and take pictures. Evenings, we'd build a fire and make dinner. When we talked, we mostly joked around about high school, fishing, our bucket lists. Nothing heavy. It was a relief punctuated by the fresh coolness of the mountains.

I was still feeling really discouraged after this last autopilot episode and the talk with Liz hadn't helped. Revelations by Sebi about Laura had made the wound sting even more. Then hearing that Sophie wasn't coming back anytime soon? I felt pretty despondent about my marriage. I didn't know if we'd make it past this. I wanted The Timeshare in my life, but wasn't sure I could be their sole support anymore.

Sitting around the fire that evening, I break down. I'd had no intention of spending this tiny slice of normal being upset, but I can't shake it...I feel so hopeless. I'm grateful that the moonless night hides my tears.

Kevin pretends he doesn't know I am crying. Instead, he haltingly says to me, "I think if we're lucky, we feel this perfect love as children and then we spend our whole lives chasing after it. Some idiot said it's better to have loved and lost than to never have loved at all, but he was a God-damned liar. I wish I'd never met Shannon. Watching her being eaten up by depression is worse than any pain I've ever known. She's given up and won't even try any new treatments. I know I'm going to lose her completely very soon and there's nothing I can do about it."

I can't hide my tears any longer. Kevin knew exactly how I felt and he was going through it, too. I'd never felt a closer bond with him and that feeling of betrayal of my relationship with Sophie was growing deeper. This bond we have makes me feel understood and also lonelier than I'd ever felt. I don't understand it and can't make sense of it. The loneliness, anger, frustration and sadness overtake me and I completely lose it, and as the refreshing chill of evening gives way to the pitch black, dark and cold of night, I let all of it go. I cry and yell, kick a few rocks and wring out every feeling I'd been holding in for years. Then the rage burns out of me and I'm suddenly aware that I'm freezing.

———

We meet the warmth of the condo with a shiver and both grab sweatshirts before looking for something to do. We play a few hands of cards, but get bored quickly.

"You don't realize how addicted you are to the internet 'til it's gone," I quip. "I feel like a spoiled kid without it!"

Kevin laughs at me and says, "I thought this might come up. I brought something." He goes to his pack and pulls out an old yearbook.

"Remember that time we all went to the mall in our PJ's and crashed the Santa line?" he asks, opening the book to a photo of all of us—me, him and six of our best friends with the mall Santa.

"God, that was such a great night! He was a pretty good sport about it. I wish we could get everyone together again."

"When was the last time you talked to anyone else?"

I reflect a moment. "The reunion, I think. You and I kinda picked up where we left off, but with the rest of the group, it wasn't like that. Even with Kimmie and how close we were. Our families had camped together since we were in elementary school. But that night at the reunion, we just stuck to small talk."

"Yeah, I felt the weirdness too. Maybe it was because of all the time that had passed." Kevin looks at me and reads the sadness. He adds, "I don't know. Maybe it wasn't the time. Maybe it was just the venue. Or do you think they found out about that camping trip at the end of senior year? Kimmie was acting pretty distant and embarrassed. Maybe she told everyone? I mean, that could make things a little weird, too."

I have huge, mixed emotions about that camping trip. I still feel fiercely protective of the memory, both because of the intensity I'd experienced and the shame around never quite getting over it. I wouldn't change anything about that weekend but I felt terrible about the people I hurt. I'd cheated on my girlfriend and it was a whole thing. And now, I feel accused of breaking up our group, though I know Kevin didn't mean it that way.

I try to laugh it off, "You sound like a self-help book."

"I read a lot. But it's true. You see it at companies all the time. It's why they don't allow fraternization. When it happens, it screws everything up."

I hadn't considered that it could be my fault our little group had fallen apart. I had consciously put that night out of my mind and tried to avoid wandering back to it. But now, sitting out here with no distractions, I can't stop thinking about it, and the memory is dragging me back in, bringing up old feelings that are better left undisturbed.

Five years earlier, February 18, 2011

I had put off my promise of getting back into running for too long and stop by the local rec center to see what they have available. Usually I like running outside, but this time of year is unpredictable— snowy and cold on too many days for me to develop the habit. The rec center has an impressive number of treadmills and an indoor track. I also notice they have handball courts. I grab a flyer that lists the hours and then see something about pottery classes, so I grab that flyer for Seb.

Immediately I sign up for a membership and vow to get started this week. The "how" comes back easily, the execution will be a bit tougher. My body remembers what to do but feels a little less capable of it than in my high school days. But over the course of weeks, my body would get more used to the workouts.

Seb gets back into pottery right away. But since he's frustrated with the wheel at first, his teacher suggests hand-building. He starts making masks and tiles, and enjoys talking art with the other students. He enjoys working with the clay, but the studio is crowded on Saturdays and the commotion is distracting. Once the session ends, he switches over to a weekday class and his love for pottery is rekindled.

This new teacher, Pete, is patient, consistent, and encouraging. He tries to understand how each student learns, so he can teach directly to their strengths. He lets Seb work independently without disturbing him, but he's there to answer questions. Through him, Sebi learns a lot of special techniques and when he brings in pictures of projects he'd like to start, Pete helps him figure out how to accomplish them. There's a nurturing component to what he offers. All in all, class is very therapeutic for Sebi as well as giving him a real sense of purpose.

The rec center has a pottery sale and one day Seb ends up submitting everything he's made. At the end of that day, he packs up what's left and isn't sure anything had sold. He's discouraged, but a few weeks later, Pete asks him if he'd picked up his check from the show. Seb is shocked as Pete smiles and hands him the check. "You're a professional artist now."

Hearing Pete call him a professional changes everything for Seb and he starts taking himself seriously as an artist. He's worked hard and now sees this as his craft. He treats it like a job and I often find him looking through library books about clay and glazes, learning how to achieve certain effects, studying hand building, immersed in his passion. His real goal, I know, is to build sculptures. Dr. Newman remarks that this is a huge step in the right direction. I have to agree.

Seb had grown to trust Pete, who handed him a flyer one night after class. "I'm teaching a drawing class starting next week if you'd like to join us. I'd love to see you there. I think you'd really enjoy it."

Sebi puts the flyer on our bulletin board. He wasn't ready to commit yet, but he was willing to think about it. There's healing to do here as well and I see him staring at the flyer all evening. I encourage him to sign up, but notice the mix of pain and embarrassment in his face.

"I'm scared to try. I really can't draw," he quietly reflects one evening.

"And I really can't play handball," I say.

I'd heard him rave about his teacher, so I tell him, "Talk to Pete. If you do the drawing class, I'll sign up for the handball league. Deal?"

The next evening, I get home from work and ask, "So, how did it go? Did you get a chance to talk to Pete today?"

"I did. I talked with him about sculpting and clay bodies and glazes."

I laugh. "Oh thank God! I'm not ready to jump into handball yet! But I do have an idea. How would you feel about turning the storage shed into an art studio? I mean, right now it's just full of lawn care stuff we don't need, a couple broken bikes we're never going to fix and a potting table we can put outside."

There is so much joy shining back at me. By suggesting this, I was telling him how seriously I take him as an artist, how I understand his commitment and want to support him.

He jumps up from his chair, leaps over to me, grabs my face and kisses me on the lips. I'm not sure what to make of it. It wasn't a romantic thing. It was a gratitude thing.

We started working on the shed the next Saturday. Sebi is full of ideas—where we could put different tables and shelves, where he would glaze things. He was passionate about his work and wanted to get it right.

While Sophie often started one thing, got bored, and went on to another—which had both its own drawbacks and benefits—Sebi went deep. He was single-minded and devoted to one thing at a time. He had always been an artist. He just needed a platform and a little support.

"You know, we don't need a lot of this stuff—the mower, the edger, the lawn stuff, the wheelbarrow. If you want to list them online, you can use the money to buy shelves and tables and stuff," I say.

Seb runs with it. He sells everything from the shed and buys used equipment and, as more of his art sells, he invests in a used pottery wheel.

He then spends nearly all his free time in the shed, honing his skills. He learns to throw on the wheel by watching videos online and then working with Pete. He makes tons of cups and bowls, but is beginning to play around with sculpting too—simple pieces to start. He's driven about it. At times, I wouldn't hear him come in until after 2am. Beyond the art, I didn't know much about Sebi or his life. I didn't know what he was doing, but he was gone a lot—telling me he was at work or an art class, or that Ellyn was volunteering or some other excuse that sounded like a lie.

I had to know more.

At that point, I do something I'd never considered before. I go on Facebook and look up Sebi Benjamin. He doesn't come up. I'm not sure what last name he used. I try just his first name—Sebi—and I find a long list but nothing matches. Maybe Sebby? Sebastian? There are too many to check out.

I type in the last name of his grandparents...and every ex he had that I could remember. I try everything with no luck.

After a couple dozen tries, I remember how into ancestry stuff Seb is, so I go to our online genealogy account and begin typing in old family names.

Finally, I find him. Sebi Godwulf. Godwulf was an ancestor on his bio dad's side of the family—the grandmother's line. I wonder why he chose that name so I read more about the family. Apparently, they came over from Germany late in the 1700's. They were Catholic. I follow a few more clues and learn his family had been sent here. It doesn't sound like it was a choice. That's all I could find.

The profile picture was the one used for a theater production Sophie acted in a few years ago. She played a woman trying to pass herself off as a man. In retrospect, it was a perfect role for her.

Sophie has said she loves the feeling of family she finds in the theater. She started acting and singing in local productions at just 5 years old. At her high school, the arts were valued as much as academics were. She loved every teacher there—except the French teacher. Not a mean woman, just outrageously pretentious. From time to time, she'd imitate her when the situation called for a good dressing down.

As I continue surfing, the larger picture across the top of Seb's Facebook page ignites a flash of jealousy. There he is—wearing his signature black skinny jeans, freshly pressed white button-down shirt, black tie under a gray vest. His head tilts back in laughter, one hand holds a cigarette, while the other, a short glass filled with ice and booze.

One arm is around Liz—she's taller than Sebi with long blonde hair and brown eyes. She's bent over laughing. I remember her clearly now. She had worked at a bar. I think she's a couple years older than Sophie and a couple years younger than me. The other girl is shorter than Seb, heavier. This is Laura. She has pixie-cut black hair and big blue eyes with full lips. I think she was an education major at school —same age as Sophie. In the picture, she's kissing Sebi's cheek and laughing. Liz and Laura's hands meet on Seb's stomach.

When *was* this? And *where*? Why did it matter? I guess I just needed to get my bearings. It had to be in the last couple of years, I think. I look at the background. This is The Grill. That hurts. This is the place I take Sophie for special occasions. I had always thought of it as our place exclusively.

Did they all know each other? Was it okay with them that Sophie was having a relationship with three different people?

"Oh my God!" My hand flies to my mouth. I'd once seen them leaving her dorm room at college when I came by to get her for breakfast. They *did* know each other. And they must know that Sophie goes by Sebi because here they are on his page. Did they also know this was an alter—an aspect of Sophie and not actually Sophie? Or did they think she was transgender or something?

I feel so disrespected, but there's something more, too. It creeps into my stomach and takes up residence there—a sadness, a loneliness, and a gnawing longing for something I feel I could never have in my life.

I glance over at Sebi's friends' list. Over 1,000 people. The number is completely out of character because Sophie is so selective with friendships—or *any* relationships. Seb, apparently, wasn't.

Sophie often told me that she felt she was consumed by people. She would start a relationship with a friend, as a volunteer, at a job— whatever—and people would just ask her for more and more and more. It was different from the day-to-day thing we all experience.

This was predatory. I remember that she had a couple of guys in college that were obsessed with her and followed her around. She felt she brought it out in people.

I type "Liz" into Sebi's friend list. I scroll down the list and find her. She's a pharmaceutical rep in California. It would have been easy for her to slip away to Colorado. Her banner is a photo of her family. Her husband is a doctor named Charlie and they have a couple perfect children. Gorgeous family, of course. They look like a cologne ad, all curled up together on a beach in blue jeans and white sweaters, with their golden retriever.

Then I type in Laura. Laura Edmonson. Same name as in college. Her girlfriend, Carla, is a professor. Laura teaches high school. They're still in Berkeley. They also have a Great Dane.

I go back to Sebi's page and look through posts and comments. Lots of pottery demos, lots of modeling photos where she looks like a tomboy. Art, theater references, some selfies with various people, lots of men's fashion articles. And lots of comments from lots of people. Men and women saying, "Love it!" "Love you!" "Can't wait to see you again!" And from Liz and Laura: "I love you more than life," "Just want to kiss that face!" "You're so talented!" And after each comment from Liz or Laura, Sebi has responded with "xoxo, Sunshine" or "Love you more, Sweetheart" or something equally heartbreaking.

Why didn't I know about this? Why didn't I see any of it before? And who were all these strangers commenting from such a place of familiarity? Someone named Robert is on there a lot. I look him up. He's older, maybe in his mid-50's. With dark hair, green eyes and a slight cleft in his chin, he's wearing an oatmeal-colored turtleneck sweater. He's beautiful. His comments are all in German and as I run them through Google translate, I find they're protective: telling Sebi to be careful, get some rest, don't drink too much. His last name steals my breath and hits me with a tsunami of questions. Godwulf. Robert

Godwulf. Seb must have a strong connection to him and a wave of dread threatens to carry me off. This stranger talks to Seb like I talk to my wife. I wonder what, exactly, is their relationship and visions of bigamy flash through my mind.

I look more closely at Robert's page and it's full of beautiful, expensive cars, handsome jewelry and—this seems out of place: security-related items. He has a lot of friends too—mostly people with the last name Godwulf.

This whole thing is beginning to freak me out and I feel anxiety prickling at my neck.

I pick up the phone to call Kevin but then put it down. I don't want to bother him with this. We had just reconnected and even though we picked up right where we'd left off and we could skip past all the small talk and go deep immediately, this feels too high school. I need to figure out what to do about this on my own.

Something else occurs to me. I type the name Sebi Godwulf into Google. Sebi has posted dozens of videos. Now I feel voyeuristic looking through them. Like I shouldn't have stumbled upon them. I scroll down a list of monologues. Some of this looks years old. Some are plays or bits from high school and college. In some, Seb looks very young. There are those recorded in a classroom or on stage. Shakespeare 1 is from *Midsummer Night's Dream*, Shakespeare 2 from *Hamlet*. Twelve other Shakespeare monologues are listed.

Others are from *Wall Street*, *Our Town*, *Mr. Holland's Opus* and *Good Will Hunting*. I love that last one so I click on it and it's good. I watch more. He was right about his acting abilities being a strength. Whether it was due to practice from a young age, or a natural gift is up for debate. I'd call it a gift. But all the monologues are male parts. It makes sense in one way but watching it, it seems odd.

I come across another one with no title other than Sebi G.- WTF??? with a smiley face next to it. Looks interesting, so I click on it. Filmed in a basement, Sophie is sitting in a chair with her hands bound behind her. I'm immediately disturbed by this. She looks to be very young—barely a teenager.

A toned boy with a baby face, a shock of thick dark hair and blue eyes sits across from her, taunting her, standing up to threaten her directly, explaining to her how she's about to be tortured. It's the most disturbing monologue I've ever encountered. The boy is saying cruel and sadistic things while Sophie cries, pleading for him to stop. It's completely freaking me out—not only because of the content and their ages, but because I *know* this boy. I could *swear* I've seen him somewhere. I'm simultaneously horrified and can't stop laughing at it. I don't understand why I'm laughing. I'm embarrassed even seeing it. I notice there are over 38,000 views and I want to erase this from the web and from everyone's memory. I'm terrified for Sophie—is this one of the videos that someone put out there that she doesn't know about? Or worse, did she post it?

I hear the garage go up and I freeze. I can feel myself flush beet red as Seb comes into the room. It's too late to hide this, though that's my instinct. I pause it.

"Hey," he says in cheerful contrast to what I've just witnessed.

I don't answer.

"You okay? You look like you're kinda losing it."

I feel like someone who has just uncovered a roommate's secret drug stash—a big one.

He approaches me with concern. "Hey—you okay?" He squeezes my shoulder. "Jesus, Steve, what's going on?"

"I'm...not...sure," I stutter.

He looks at the screen for clues.

"Oh, *that* one," he says, "What do you think of it?" I look at him and can't read anything. I have no idea what he's feeling.

There are those situations where there's *so much wrong*, you have no idea where to start. "From an acting standpoint, it's… convincing. Technically, flawless. Subject matter? Holy SHIT!"

"Yeah, it's pretty intense. We hear a lot of different reactions to it," he says casually, moving to the kitchen to put the groceries away. "Looks like it gave you hives."

"It's disturbing."

He pops back into the living room and nods his head once and squints at me. "Sort of what we were going for."

"Do you get how wrong this is?"

"That's the point, Steve. People are supposed to get that it's wrong. Turn it off. Let's get some dinner." He's acting like this is no big deal, but I sense something else—embarrassment maybe, or relief? That makes no sense. I try to shake it off but I can't.

It unnerves me to the point I toss and turn all night. The next day I'm like a zombie. There are entire universes around us that we never see, but a doorway to one has just opened in front of me and I don't like what I see.

March 6, 2011

I don't see Seb for a few days after that. Sophie's around, but mostly reading books and sleeping. She seems disoriented and tells me she's missing large chunks of time. This time of year seems especially difficult for them and I suspect it's because of her birthday, which she refuses to celebrate. I don't even know the exact date. She's clearly much weaker and I don't feel I can ask her about the video. In college, she'd been so full of life and so much fun. Since then, she'd gradually moved towards being more serious, more cautious. Fun had become more of a stranger until it finally gave up and left her to herself.

An art festival finally brings Seb out. We sleep in late, eat a big breakfast and head over just a couple hours before the festival closes. It's just a few blocks away and Rachel wants to walk. I hold her hand and we enjoy the crisp, perfect, sunny day.

As we walk, Rachel points out the birds and stops to pet the dogs out for a walk with our neighbors.

When we arrive, people are still coming and going at the indoor festival and we can hear the buzz of fun and excitement. We cross the street into the bustle. The instant Sebi comes forward, his hand drops away from mine. He's pointing at some raku pottery he found and I'm sad Rachel has slipped away, but I'm looking forward to having it out with Seb about his Facebook page. The video had overwhelmed me and we never got to address his pictures with Liz and Laura. I had a lot of questions.

As soon as we finish at the art festival and we're walking home, I tell him, "I found your Facebook page." I'm still furious about it and I want him to feel guilty about being caught.

"You did? Cool. I'll friend you."

I hate it when he refuses to read my mood and respond accordingly. "Sebi, seriously? I'm *pissed*. Do you *GET* that?"

"Well, now I do. I take it you don't like my pictures."

"No, I don't. *I don't like the pictures, Sebi.* And I'm terrified to ask but I need to know the story. What's the deal with these women? And the others? Over 1,000 friends? Who are all these people?"

The old smirk he'd worn when we'd broached the subject before is gone. "You're opening a can of worms that you might not like. Do you really want to know?" Sebi seems anxious to talk about it, but, at the same time, the look of "ouch" on his face tells me he doesn't want to hurt me.

I reassure him insistently, "Yeah, I *need* to know. Should we get some coffee?"

"Yeah."

Coffee is normally a topic that will bring out a playfulness in Sebi. But not this time. He seems ready for a serious conversation.

As we head there, Seb sees someone on the street and even though he looks away immediately, I can tell the guy recognizes him. The man, probably in his 30's, is fit and attractive. He yells out, "Sebi G!" as he approaches fast. Sebi smiles and laughs tensely as he shakes the guy's hand. "Good to see you..."

"Josh," the guy fills in his name.

"Josh," Sebi says. An awkward moment passes and Seb then says, "I'm gonna grab a cup of coffee now." I try to interpret the look, but I can't tell if this is a guy who has bothered Sophie in the past, who bought some of Sebi's art, or what. The guy walks away smiling and laughing.

I'd seen this before. Men would approach Sophie with a strange familiarity. She always looked uncomfortable. I'm uneasy too, now that I understand how they might know her. It was strange before, but this video adds a layer of fear.

"Seb? Where do you know that guy from?"

"I don't know. People recognize me from whatever—art shows or ads. I never know if I've met them so I just say it's nice to see you. An old trick my grandmother taught me."

"Do you think he's seen the video?"

"Who knows?' he asks, the irritation growing in his voice. "Why does it matter?"

It was like this with Seb. I'd think something was pretty significant but he'd dismiss it like it was nothing. Made me question reality.

We arrive at Starbuck's as it's getting dark, but caffeine never keeps Sebi up, so he gets a double espresso with cream. I get tea. I head to a table by the window, but Sebi heads in the opposite direction—to the back corner.

"Steve, over here."

"You always like sitting by the window."

He walks over and, wrapping an arm around my waist, leads me to a back table. "Not tonight."

We sit down in a quiet corner and he's pensive, but ready to share. "I met Laura first—freshman orientation, actually. Then we had some classes together and lived in the same dorm. We just kept running into each other and I thought she was beautiful. If you're looking at types, she's definitely my type. She's just flawlessly stunning and a fun person to be around. She can be serious, too, but mostly she's just a riot. She cares so much about people—always volunteering with kids. She's also smart, Steve. Brilliant. And she makes everyone around her feel smart and popular."

"She's like you," I couldn't help adding.

Sebi gives me an embarrassed half smile as he continues, "We started hanging out after class and one night, it just happened. We were laughing about some stupid something, our hands brushed and she grabbed me and pulled me in for a kiss. It was quick, just a peck between friends in case I didn't reciprocate. But I did. And it kinda went from there."

I had to shift gears from Sophie's husband to Sebi's roommate. If my wife was talking about cheating on me it'd be a very different discussion than if my roommate was talking about the love of his life.

"Were you guys dating or was it more casual than that?"

"Yeah, we were dating but I didn't want to get serious, so she wound up with Carla. They've been together ever since. But she didn't want to lose me, so we kept seeing each other when we could."

"She know about you?"

"Does who know what?"

"Does Laura know you're not Sophie? Does Carla know that you guys still see each other?"

Sebi seems to go inside for a minute. When he comes back, he says, "I don't know."

"Don't lie to me, Sebi."

"I'm not lying. I *honestly* don't know. I can guess. I'm pretty sure Laura knows it's me. And Carla knows about us. I don't know what sort of agreements they have. That's between them. When Laura first got together with Carla, we didn't see each other for about a year, but we were both pretty miserable without each other, so we went back to being friends—and then more than that."

"And Liz?"

"I actually met Liz right after Laura sort of broke things off with me and got together with Carla. I was feeling like crap and just wanted to get hammered so I stopped by the bar. Laura was angry at me for not wanting more, for not wanting to settle down. She was pretty clear that if we weren't getting serious, we were done.

"Liz was working at the bar that night and the place was quiet, so she kept me company. We talked for hours. She was flirting with me, I flirted back. She's like me. She flirts with everyone. It's just who she is.

"I got smashed, blacked out and woke up in her bed. Apparently, she had Chuck drive me home. He wasn't too happy with me—flirting with his girlfriend."

He's pensive, but also confused—trying to put something together that seemed just out of reach. I can see fear behind his eyes, too. When he looks this way, he wanted to be pulled away from it, so I change the subject.

"Seb, I try not to push, but I need to know—why are you here?"

"What do you mean? I'm here because I'm a coffee addict and because we needed to talk," he chuckles lightly.

"No. Why are you *here*? How did you come into existence?"

Sebi sets his jaw and looks as if I'd just insulted him. He glances at me and then away. "I don't know."

"That's not good enough, Seb. You're here for a reason. You're a big part of my life and you have been for years. You always put on a brave face and we like to focus on having fun, but I know there's more to you."

I'd read that some alters honestly don't know where they'd come from or why, but it's clear he knows his history and his origins because while he's looking down, tear drops began hitting the table.

"Oh God, I'm sorry. We don't need to talk about it if you don't want to."

"No. It's okay. I'm here because Sophie needs me."

"Can you tell me more?"

Sebi sits up, wipes his face, closes his eyes and then softly hits his head against the wall a few times before quietly stating, "No, I can't. Not yet." He gets up, not waiting for me to follow, and makes a beeline for the door.

I expected our walk home to be solemn and quiet. It wasn't. And I got more answers.

That night had been a typical cool one on the cusp of spring—the streets crazy with people heading out to do whatever you do in Denver when you're emerging from hibernation. After our coffee, I caught up with Seb outside. He was already vaping pot to calm down. As we walked, he was talkative and physical—slapping me on the back for emphasis as he spoke, putting his arm around me.

It felt like we were back to being old friends.

Seb began— "So...Liz. Yeah. Well, she was just always there for me. From that first night. She listened to me whine about Laura, even brought me doughnuts the next morning. She was a mom before she was a mom—always taking care of everyone."

I thought about Liz. Two hours ago, I'd hated this woman. Now that I knew she had cared for Sophie when she barely knew her, and that she had cared ever since, my entire opinion was shifting.

"We started spending more time together and, at some point, the affection we had for each other went from hugging to holding hands to more than that. Her husband doesn't know. I mean, he knows that she and Sophie are best friends, but he doesn't know what we do. It's really not about screwing him over. That's just a perk."

"Sounds like you don't like him."

"She's married to Chuck. Chuck Lansing."

"H O L Y *crap*. The same guy who screwed every freshman girl he could pin down?"

"Well, he preferred them younger, but yeah. Same guy."

"Can I admit something?" I ask. "I looked up Liz and Laura from your Facebook page. I totally didn't recognize Chuck in the pictures."

Sebi lets out one of his roaring laughs.

"I know, right? What the hell happened there? God, I HATE that guy! And can you say plastic surgery? I mean, I guess he gets it on the house but, still. A little overkill if you ask me."

"Looked like a perfume ad, am I right?" I comment.

"Well, yeah. He's a plastic surgeon so I imagine he's had a lot of work done. Those guys do each other for free."

And suddenly we're both laughing. It's hard to keep things serious with Sebi, but that's not his job. I could respect that. I also understood how much it took for him to tell me as much as he did.

We had more to discuss, but when we get home, we are both emotionally exhausted.

"I'm crashing here," Sebi says, pointing to the couch.

"You okay?"

"Yeah, I just want to have some time with Napoleon. I know it makes you crazy to have him in bed."

Seb was right. That dog takes up the entire space and then kicks in his sleep. No one ever gets any actual rest.

"You upset?" I ask.

"No, I'm not upset," he starts, but he is thoughtful and there's more..."I hate what I told you tonight. Feeling exposed. I just need some time."

———

The next morning, I come downstairs to find Sophie asleep on the floor, head resting on Napoleon. Toys are everywhere and cartoons are playing on her iPad.

The kids have told me they love to wake up hearing me fixing breakfast, so I start my usual routine. Since it's the kids, I skip the waffles and make monkey bread—a simple, doughy cinnamon thing. I get the dough started and then turn on the coffee maker and put some bacon in the cast iron pan.

Sophie hears me rattling around and comes into the kitchen with a doll in her arms. Her hair is a mess but it just adds to her charm.

"What's for breakfast?" she asks as a huge yawn scrunches up her nose. She's adorable.

"I thought bacon and I thought...*monkey bread*!"

She squeals and jumps up and down. "Can I help? Please?"

Rachel likes to roll the dough into balls and toss them into the pan. We'd been working with Dr. Newman for months now and I was getting familiar with each alter and knew a good deal about each. I was also feeling more comfortable interacting with them.

———

Whenever I share with anyone about Sophie, the question I find people asking me the most is "Why do you stay? How can you be so patient?"

I guess somebody else might leave, but for me, it's not just that I love Sophie. I love all the other parts as well. Yes, there are a lot of challenges and, no, this isn't the way I thought my life would go. But there are at least as many positives as negatives and I want to be with her. It's not just the hope that some day we can have a normal life. *That* will probably never happen. It's the hope that I can help her be healthier and that we can find some happiness together. What we have is stressful, but I do have hope. Besides, *everyone* is fighting their own demons.

Rachel is bubbling over with excitement now. I have to slow her down and tell her, "Wash your hands first." Like any 5 year old, Rachel has been hugging the dog, crawling around on the floor, digging in the couch for hidden treasure and probably picking her nose.

Rachel squirts too much dish soap onto her hands and begins rinsing them. "OUCH!" she screams.

With anyone else in The Timeshare, I'd just ask what was wrong. With this alter, I'm on top of it. I fly across the kitchen and grab the lever for the faucet and quickly twist it from hot to almost cold. "Remember the red means hot. Be careful, Rachel." I'd turned down the water heater, but she could still hurt herself.

When we first married, this alter would cry and sit in the closet and rock. As she felt more comfortable, and safer, she'd become more outgoing and happier.

I'm guessing Rachel's here today because Sebi still needs some time and Sophie probably feels pretty wrung out after yesterday's talk. The kids come out when everyone in The Timeshare is exhausted. They give the adults a break to regroup and recharge.

I help her dry her hands, get her situated at the table, and set the dough down along with a greased pan. She ditches the chair to sit on the table. I pour the hot cinnamon, butter, and brown sugar into the pan. Then Rachel makes dough balls and tosses them in. She claps when she's done and we put it in the oven. As we wait, we munch on bacon. Rachel has spread a blanket out on the floor in front of the stove so she can watch the bread rise and brown. The gift in this little one is that she reminds me to take in all the simple joys we tend to lose sight of as adults.

She loves to eat, but she eats like a little kid. A piece of bacon and two bites of cinnamon bread is about her limit. And that's only when she can sit still long enough for a meal.

"And what are we drinking today, Miss Rachel? Orange juice or milk?" I ask.

"Milk, milk, milk, milk!"

"Sebi's or yours?" I had learned to give Rachel just two choices or it was too overwhelming for her.

She giggles. I buy 2% for her. Sebi gets whole milk. Sometimes Rachel likes to "steal" Sebi's. I think it makes her feel closer to him. It's a theme I find playing out over and over in The Timeshare. When Sophie needs to feel stronger, she'll wear his cologne. The kids seem to use his watch as some sort of talisman. I even see Jamie in Seb's sweater from time to time.

Rachel points to the fridge and proclaims, "Sebi's today!" I pour the whole milk into a tiny pitcher shaped like a cow and set it on the table.

Pulling the bread out of the oven, I flip it over, cinnamon and butter trickling down the sides and soaking in. I set it on the table and Rachel climbs up onto a chair. I pull off a bit of bread and put it on her plate along with a couple strips of bacon. She sloshes milk partly into her glass and partly onto the table and giggles about it.

"My mom used to make me monkey bread," Rachel offers.

"Your *mom*?" I ask. It didn't sound like something her grand-mother would do.

"My *real* mom. When I stayed with her in San Francisco that one time."

"I haven't heard about that. Can you tell me?"

Rachel sits and considers for a moment, scrunching up her mouth and looking up. "Nope!" she chimes. "That's not my story."

Then she shudders and a moment later, her posture is completely different and Richard, quickly assessing the situation, is helping himself to bacon and monkey bread as he shakes out a cigarette. I hate it when he smokes at breakfast, but I'm not about to confront him.

"So you want to know about San Francisco? I gotta tell ya, it's not a story I like to tell. Sort of makes me look like an ass. And it was the biggest mistake I've ever made. Also one of the most painful memories I have."

Sebi might have cracked a joke right about now, but Richard was not a funny guy.

"I had a chance to save The Timeshare and I blew it. I had a chance to get them out and, if I had, I think life would have been very different for all of us. But I fucked it all up."

I grab a chair and sit down to listen to him.

Richard pushes the plate aside and gets up for a beer. "I've been around since forever and usually do a pretty good job. But sometimes I get it wrong and when I do, things go south pretty quick.

"When Sophie was 12, she was sort of past her best-by date for Papa's purposes. Plus, she was starting to get to be too much trouble. We were pretty feisty and would challenge him all the time—and that made her harder to handle. So, Papa called Todd and Becky, her biological parents, and told them he was putting her on a plane and they needed to pick her up from the airport.

"Sophie's little sister, Alison, was 6. Sophie was in heaven there. Her parents are really pretty cool people. They took the kids to the zoo, out to dinner, to concerts. It was peaceful. Normal, I guess. Her parents get along great and they treated the kids really well. But it was also a culture shock for Sophie.

"One day, they sent her out to play with Alison and told her that there was a boy who'd been bugging Alison and to "look out for her." That brought me out," Richard continues.

"The kid was maybe 10 or 11 and, sure enough, he came out of his house when he saw Alison and pushed her off her tricycle. Her knee got scraped up and she was crying. I told the kid to knock it off after making sure Alison was okay.

"That night, I thought about how I could protect Ali. The kid was younger than me, but bigger. I couldn't take him in a fight. Anything I did had to be fast—a one and done sort of thing. So I literally sharpened my nails. And when the kid came back the next day and tried to kick Ali off her trike, I swiped him with my claws and scratched the shit out of him. This was my way of 'looking out' for Ali.

"I get that what I did was wrong, but I don't suffer fools. If someone is a clear threat, I will knock them on their ass.

"A meeting was convened," Richard continues, "and it was determined that Sophie was just a bad kid that had to go. She was sent back to the grandparents because of *me. Because I screwed up*. I'm supposed to protect her and I did exactly the opposite.

"Getting sent back just about shattered her. Multiples break, but they're redeemable. It's like dropping a puzzle. The pieces can be put back together. But when they shatter, it's game over. They wind up losing their marbles. Ellyn helps everyone stay on an even keel. That's what she does."

"So is this when Ellyn was created?" I ask.

"Oh God, no, she came out a long time ago." Richard looks like he was listening to another conversation when he says, "Rachel can tell you more about that. But I had to try to see some hope and the only good thing was that we were back with Seb. Grandpa loved him, so they were going to separate us—they'd keep Seb and send Sophie to San Francisco permanently. He was pretty pissed when she came back."

I was confused by this and wondered if Seb was an actual person, but it seemed the wrong direction to go right now.

"Okay," I answered, my heart breaking. A 12-year-old child blaming themselves for this? I'd have broken, too. Richard knew what I was thinking because I was tearing up. For Sophie to feel like she had a chance to get out and then feel like she screwed it up would be devastating. It would be even worse for a protector alter. This was not a mistake she could take ownership of without tearing herself apart.

I'm not sure what to say. On the one hand, I can see how getting a break from all the horrible things at home was good. On the other hand, the back and forth must have been its own kind of torture.

"Steve," Richard says now, "I don't know if you want to hear about what brought Ellyn out. Rachel's an amazing little kid, but she'll tell ya the unvarnished truth. It's pretty intense."

Richard has access to some feelings so he has an awareness of the impact stories can have. Rachel doesn't. But if Rachel was willing to talk, I was willing to listen. I feel like the more information I had, the better I could help them. And I feel that if they could tell their story, maybe it would lighten the load a bit for them—maybe I could share the burden.

"I'd like to hear about it if she wants to tell me."

"Okay," Richard says with a warning in his voice, taking another swig of beer and stamping out his cigarette before going back inside.

Just then Rachel pops out and wipes her mouth with a napkin. "Ew! That's *disgusting!*" She thought beer tasted like vomit, she'd once said. I tell her to eat some monkey bread and that would help. She does and then launches into the story—no emotion on her end, but I thought I was going to throw up...

"...When we were little, Papa made Sebi tie me on the bed before he hurt me. Papa was mad at us because we hid the pill he gave us that would make us not fight and I pulled too much on the ties and my wrist got broken. Then, he had Sebi untie me and it hurt even more. I felt like lightning hit my wrist. Papa wanted me punished for not taking the pill."

She takes another bite of monkey bread and a big gulp of milk.

Her mouth full, she continues, "So, Papa flipped me over and told Sebi to tie me up again. Sebi said, 'No! I won't do it!' and Papa kicked him in his knee really hard and told him to do it. He said no again and Papa said that he'd kill me in front of Sebi if he didn't. Sebi kept saying to me he was so, so, so sorry as he tied me up, but my wrist hurt so bad that I saw stars and then everything was black and that's all I know."

Now, munching on monkey bread, she tells me matter-of-factly, "That's when Ellyn came out."

Rachel sees her teddy bear across the room and hops down to get it. Then she's back in her chair, happily nibbling on breakfast as I try to pull myself together. I want to just grab her and hold her—to rock her, to try to make all of this not have happened, but I knew it didn't even register to her how bad it was. Rachel would get really upset over a movie not working, or being out of licorice, but this? No emotion at all. And I know there are details she left out that are likely more horrific than I'm capable of hearing.

My only defense is to tell myself *there is no way this happened.* She has to be making it up. Sebi is an alter—not a real person. And even if he was a real person, it makes no sense that an alter would be formed around someone like that. Still, I know that even now Sophie has to see the physical therapist for her left thumb and wrist, and at times the pain wakes her up at night, and she sometimes has flashbacks. The physical therapist had said it was from a very old, complex break that hadn't been treated properly. It was hard to put this in the fiction category.

I feel like I'm losing my mind. I find cartoons for Rachel to watch and go upstairs to catch my breath. I'm feeling panicky. Just knowing this sort of evil even exists is too much. Thinking it touched Sophie is unbearable. Believing that she lived with it was beyond my ability to comprehend. I keep telling myself this is not real, reminding myself to breathe.

My head is starting to throb and I look for an Advil. Instead, I find the Klonopin. It's for anxiety, after all. I take a couple of those and then go in search of pain relief.

I focus on something else to get through it. Sebi was obviously a real person who'd been brought into The Timeshare. I try to focus on the mystery rather than the details of what I'd just heard.

I have to tell myself that hearing the stories helps Sophie somehow, yet I wonder if I can go on. I realize what a luxury just doing that is. I could *choose* to hear more—or not. Sophie never had that option. Something in me pushes to hear more—to hear everything the alters wanted to tell me. Maybe, if I could take some of her pain away, it would bring her back. I feel so powerless and doing this seems like the only way I could help.

I come back downstairs and see that Rachel has found a box of cookies. She's so entranced with her cartoon that she's mindlessly nibbling.

"Rachel, is it okay if I talk to Richard for a minute?"

Rachel snags another cookie and closes her eyes. A moment later, Richard is back. He notices the cookie in his hand, grimaces and sets it down, brushing his fingers against his leg to remove the residue.

"Twice in one morning. I should feel honored," he says. "Why did you call me out?" He sounds suspicious and annoyed. He knew the rules about calling out different alters and knew I'd violated them.

"I have a couple of questions." I plow ahead without waiting for his approval. I've learned that he responds better when I'm assertive.

"I don't understand Ellyn's role," I start.

Richard says, "Like why she came to be in that moment? Seb was our lifeline, our sanity—and Papa was threatening to take him away from us. He was trying to turn him into an enemy rather than a protector. Ellyn's job was to see him as good—to hold him in that place of protector. She needed to remember all the good stuff to remind him when he'd start to go dark."

I press on. "Rachel told me about the wrist, but she said there was a pill her grandfather would give her. What's that about? And what's up with Sebi? Was he a real person at one time?"

Richard looks panicked and pissed—like he had shared more than he should have—like he's not sure he can trust me.

"Who Sebi is is none of your fucking business. And the drug is a sedative. It knocks you out, relaxes the muscles to the point where you really can't fight back. It's a type of date rape drug. But it made Sophie feel sick and confused, so she hid it that day. Papa gave it to her to cloud her memory and so she couldn't fight back. When you fight back, you wind up with damaged goods. No one wants to rent a broken kid."

Hearing that, I run to the bathroom and get sick. Then I sit there trying to sort everything out.

How she'd endured all of this—even with the alters to help, I couldn't imagine. And how the hell did this go on for so long with so many clues and yet no one said anything? Her grandmother obviously tried to get her out of the house as much as she could with all the lessons and classes she had, but, *dear God, how did no one notice?*

Then I thought about how I was making it through this. I had to tell myself it wasn't real. The fact is that we don't *want* to know this is going on. It's too horrible. The worse it is, the more we dissociate it as a society, leaving these kids to fend for themselves.

I come back downstairs, shaky and weak, and Richard is still there eating bacon and drinking beer. "Sorry about that, man," he says. "You okay?"

"Yeah. I think so. I wanted to know. I needed to know."

I'd gotten sick, but Sophie had suffered far more than that. I wanted to hear it all today. It didn't matter if I got sick or passed out or lost my mind. There are no words—the feeling was too strong. It had a Romeo and Juliet feel to it. She had died in a way. I wanted to die too, metaphorically. I had to get Sophie back and if I couldn't, I wanted to go where she was going.

"So, let me ask you, Richard—how did you come to be?"

"I was wondering when this would come up." Richard purses his lips and narrows his eyes. I could tell this was not easy for him to discuss, but I couldn't back away from it at this point.

He looks sideways at me as he takes long drinks of beer. I know he can read it on my face...I wasn't ready to hear his story.

"I'm not telling you. And honestly it pisses me off—you wanting to know these details. They're private for a reason. I don't get the fascination."

"I want to understand better."

"That's bullshit. It's morbid curiosity. I'm not telling you my story, but I can tell you that I handle the physical stuff. I don't register pain in the same way the others do, so I stood in front of them. I'm also willing to fight. I can tell you that when Papa figured out that he couldn't hurt us physically, he hurt people and animals we cared about—in front of us. But now we're getting into Sebi's territory. I handle the pain. Seb handles the mind games. People think I'm tough but there are two people I've got nothing on—Elizabeth and Seb."

True, I hadn't heard details and I didn't know the whole truth and that was probably a good thing. I realize Richard wasn't telling me his story—not because he couldn't handle sharing it but because he was sure I couldn't handle hearing it. He was protecting me. That was his job—protecting people.

I realize that what little I had heard was day-to-day life for Sophie. I know she must have had hundreds of these experiences. Just one wouldn't have created The Timeshare. I'd just lifted up a tiny corner and barely peeked underneath, but I feel carried away by the anger rising in me and I still feel a sense of life and death panic.

I'm not sure what to do now. Do I call Dr. Newman? I really want to talk with Kevin, but this isn't his wheelhouse and I don't want to traumatize him. I finally settle on calling someone from my partners' group. He's not home, so I leave a message and get to work cleaning up dishes.

Dr. Newman had told me, when I was getting this sort of out of body experience, to do something mundane and everyday. It can help you get grounded. I'm working on it, but these stories are impossible to endure. I wonder how other people handle it and I make a mental note to ask about it in group next time.

Halfway through the dishes, I hear screaming and find Rachel fighting Napoleon for her doll. She likely had been showing it to him and he mistook it for an offer to play. I hurriedly wipe my wet hands off on my pants and rush into the living room to rescue the doll and put Napoleon outside. Rachel is sobbing and the doll has been partially decapitated. I rock with her and tell her I can fix it.

The wonderful thing about Rachel is that most of her day to day problems are easily remedied. I often feel like a hero when I'm around her.

She spends the rest of the morning watching TV and napping, rocking her newly repaired doll and telling it that everything is okay now. I'm unsettled. I can't get these disturbing images out of my mind and my heart is still racing. I want to find her grandfather and beat the shit out of him. I have got to do *something* and think about going for a run, but I can't leave Rachel alone.

"Rach," I tell her, "I'm going to go upstairs to make a quick call. You good?"

She nods absently, focusing on her cartoons and munching on the marshmallows she's picked out of a box of cereal.

I kiss her on the head and smile, then go to our bedroom and close the door. Then to the bathroom and close that door. I'm shaking— too upset to cry. I don't even know who to call. I scroll through my contacts. I stop at Kevin's name and feel a spark of hope as I hit call.

Relief begins to wash through me the second he picks up. "Kev, I haven't told you the whole truth. Sophie does have anxiety, but she also has multiple personalities."

I hadn't wanted to share this with Kevin, but I don't know who else to talk to. It all tumbles out. I'm not even sure I said hello when he answered, I just launched in.

My admission is met by silence and I'm not sure if Kevin is angry with me for not telling him earlier, or if he's freaked out by this news. I wait.

"You have got to be kidding me."

"What?"

"They say Shannon is depressed because of abuse, that she's dissociative. No other personalities though—just depersonalization. They tell me she never feels like she's in her own body and it's awful for her."

"Sophie has had that before. It's pretty much hell. So here we are again. It's unreal how we're always going through the same thing at the same time."

"I think there's a reason for that. It'd be too hard to go through this alone. I hadn't wanted to tell you because I was afraid it'd freak you out."

Kevin asks if Sophie is in therapy for it and I tell him about Dr. Newman, and how just hearing about the abuse is taking me down. I'm worried I'm going to get depressed again. Worried that the frequent panic attacks I had battled away as a kid will pop up again after years of being dormant. I feel like I'm not strong enough now.

Kevin tells me he feels the same way—he can't abandon Shannon, but he's not sure he's strong enough to survive this.

I'm still scared, but after our talk, I feel stronger.

———

At Dr. Newman's that day, I'm already tense and feeling like this visit would be momentous. Questions are swarming around in my head. I really want to get to the root of the issue with Chuck. I know there is *something* there and it's bugging me—like a mystery that keeps you up at night. But I feel it's even more important now to address the video. And I need to know more about Seb's origins.

The more I think about it, the more concerned I am about Seb, after hearing Rachel and Richard's revelations of being forced to watch their Papa hurt people he loved. And I now understand why Sophie has to see Dr. Newman twice a week even after years of therapy. There's still too much ground to cover.

As soon as we sit down on Dr. Newman's couch, I bring up the video. I feel like all the mysteries are now piling up—one on top of the other—and I want to reduce that pile by one today rather than adding to it.

I pull up the video on my phone and show it to Dr. Newman. I ask, "Have you seen this?"

"Yes, I have," he says.

"And it doesn't bother you? Because it surprised the hell out of me to find this out there for anyone to see."

I can tell Dr. Newman didn't want to say anything else but he looks unaffected by the video. Like it isn't a big deal. Instead, he looks to Sebi and raises his eyebrows, inviting him to speak up.

"This is not an avenue I want to wander too far down with you right now," is all Sebi says.

I swallow hard against the lump in my throat, feeling I'd entered an unfamiliar and terrifying area. If I didn't know more, I'd worry. If I did learn the truth, it would likely haunt me.

"Sophie looked like a kid in that video, Seb," I start out.

"A teenager."

"How old?"

"I don't remember."

"But it sounded like that kid understood the subject. He was so cruel. It was incredibly dark. Honestly, it was horrifying."

He breathes out a laugh, "Yeah."

"How the hell is this funny to you? I work with teenagers, Seb. They're babies! They shouldn't even know this sort of thing exists! I'm freaking OUT. Do you GET that??"

"What do you want me to say, Steve? We come from different places."

"Were you guys involved in this sort of thing—hurting people?"

Seb considers this. He lifts his head and scratches his neck as he thinks. He doesn't look trapped by my question but, rather, he needed time to consider the answer.

"I'm not sure how much of this you can hear, Steve. So let me say this: Richard took the physical stuff. Elizabeth, the emotional stuff. I handled the mind games. That included seeing other people getting hurt, but no—I didn't hurt anyone who didn't want to be hurt. They gave me the option to hurt myself badly or hurt someone else just a little bit. That's how they get you started. That's where these burns come from."

He shows me the back of his hand. I'd seen the white spots and always wondered where they came from.

"Acid burns, Steve. They made me burn myself—and before it was healed, they made me burn myself again. So no, I couldn't hurt other people. Even if it meant I'd be hurt instead."

"Unless they wanted to be hurt."

"Occupational hazard when it comes to this line of work. Some people want to be hurt—not badly, but a bite or superficial cuts during knife play. Shit like that. I think only one guy had to go to the ER for a tetanus shot and stitches, but he did tell me to bite him as hard as I could, so..."

"When you were a kid."

"Yes."

"Who is 'they?'" I ask.

"What do you mean?"

"You said that they gave you a choice to hurt yourself or someone else. Who's they?"

"That's something I won't talk about and it's something I will never discuss with you—ever. So, drop it."

I look to Dr. Newman wondering if this is just melodrama. He just takes a deep breath and looks very serious.

I'm speechless. It strikes me how real this all is and I feel like I'm clawing my way out of a grave. I stand up and ask Dr. Newman if I could have a minute.

He nods but, for the first time, I see serious concern on his face. "Sebi, will you excuse us for a minute?" he asks, getting up from his chair and inviting me out into the empty waiting room.

"Sure," Seb says, relaxing, pulling his hat over his eyes and spreading out on the couch.

I apologize for losing it. I tell Dr. Newman I can't catch my breath and may need to go to the hospital. We sit down on the floor, and he tells me to feel the ground under me, to notice the chairs, the books.

Notice the scent of the flowers on the table, hear the clock ticking on the wall. "Now," he says, with both of his hands on my knees, "Take a deep breath. Let it go...take another one...let it go...."

After a while, I feel a *little* better, but still feel like I have to run. Dr. Newman hands me the trash can in case I get sick. Standard procedure apparently.

"Everything we've talked about in there is over. It happened a long time ago," he says. "It's done. It can't hurt you. And it can't hurt Sophie."

I scoff. "It may be in the past, but it's not over. It's still messing with us."

"I get that," he offers gently. "The effects are still hurting both of you. But the abuse has stopped. The decisions she makes now can be impacted by the past, but it's over. For Sebi and the others, this was their reality. It's where they come from, the lens through which they see the world. It's dark and it's skewed. And we're working on it, but when we brush up against that place, it's mind-blowing."

"Just knowing things like that are out in the world is too much. How can you listen to this day after day and not lose it?" I say.

"Because someone helped *me* out of that world. I have to go in after other people going through the same thing to get them out. Sophie will get out, too."

"You're multiple?"

"I was. When I went through treatment decades ago, the standard was to integrate people. It was harsh and, in my opinion, unnecessary. The belief was that in integration, any bad stuff would be burned off while skills would be retained. That was not my experience. But I was treated a long time ago and we know better now."

"And that's why you don't believe in integration."

"That's one reason, but there are some more clinical reasons as well. Because these systems are dynamic, we're seeing people who had been integrated coming back with another layer of alters. It doesn't always happen, but my philosophy is that I want to teach my patients to work within this reality they've created. We can get into more of that later. For right now, let's focus on getting you through today. What do you need?"

"No idea," I say, calming but still feeling my heart pounding.

"Remember what we discussed before—when you're freaking out like this, one of the things that can help is doing normal day to day things. Bathe your senses in normalcy. Go for a run, take a shower, have a burger. Do all of those things you love to do—anything that feels normal and positive. It sounds too simple, but it works. All I did with you out here was suggest taking a couple of breaths. You'll be okay."

Something else occurs to me and I have to know because I feel like something is horribly wrong with me: "Why did I laugh?"

"When?"

"When I saw the video. I couldn't stop laughing and my face felt like it was on fire."

"Sounds like overwhelming shame."

"Why would I feel shame?"

"I don't know, but it's okay. I wouldn't focus on it too much and don't beat yourself up. Something in you got triggered." Dr. Newman knew I was a worrier and I'd just been given a plate full.

"Try not to worry about it, Steve. I see it as a good thing. You knew it was incredibly wrong for a child to talk that way."

I think about that for a minute, then say, "I have another question for you." I want to take my mind off my feelings of panic and, at the same time, I need to prove I can handle this.

"Of course."

"Okay, this whole dark origin thing. I thought Sebi was a protector, but Rachel told me that he was forced to participate in hurting Sophie."

"He is. He is a protector. Remember that book I gave you that talked about how some alters identify with the abuser? They're persecutor alters. That's how Sebi was forced to start out. When he came online, he tried to protect the others by hurting them. He thought if he hurt the body, Papa wouldn't. But he's got a lot of shame around that, so we don't tend to get into it too much.

"That's where the video came from. He was still in that place. They weren't teenagers. They were 12. As teens, they had started to turn things around with Dr. Ziegal. That video—let me just tell you that he gets it. He knows the exact date that video was made. And he knows how upsetting it is. I can't say much more, but I want you to hear this: in therapy, we help patients understand how everything changes when you realize that the persecutors in a system are actually trying their best to keep you safe. Once you understand that, everything changes. Once they get that, we can help them shift persecutors into protector roles. Persecutors are protectors who got bad information, so they're doing it in a way that's consistent with the insanity of the situation. Am I making sense?"

"To be honest, not even a little bit. I just can't get my head around it. I'm not sure I want to, either. That book helped me understand some things, but it freaked me out, too. Dr. Herman talks about 'coexisting with the knowledge of the capacity for evil.' That they have to live with the image of themselves 'as an accomplice to the perpetrator.' It makes sense, but in a really terrible way.

"It's really complex, but yes. Trauma changes the way you think about yourself. It actually changes the structure of the brain. This sort of thing is hard for people who haven't been through it to understand. It's simply what Sophie knew. It was her world. A draw of abusive men is that they tell women they'll protect them. They'll get into fights with anyone who mistreats 'their lady.' But then they go home and beat the crap out of her. The line between protector and persecutor is pretty thin. A lot of men understand their role to be a protector but some have a pretty unhealthy idea of what that means."

"Still feeling off in the woods here."

"Okay. Let's come at this from another angle. Keep in mind that this is a monologue. It's theater. It's still disturbing, but this is not an episode of actual abuse being filmed. It's a script that the boy in the video found online. I can't say anything else but I think you'll be learning more from Seb at some point."

I was still shaking but I let it go for now. Sometimes things made sense after I let them sit for awhile. And then something occurred to me. "What happened to confidentiality?"

"I have signed permission on this particular topic, so it's all good. We thought it might come up. Do you feel like you can go on?"

"Well, I don't feel like I'm over this. Definitely something I need to keep unpeeling, but, yeah, I wondered about the Chuck thing."

As Dr. Newman and I reenter the office, it looks like we're interrupting Seb's nap. He wakes up and asks, "You okay?"

"I think so. That video was hard to see, Seb. Does that register for you?

"Hey, I don't write the shit. It was just a monologue I found online."

"But you read it. You selected it when you were just 12 years old. That's disturbing to me."

"What do you want me to say?"

"I want to know that you get how it might be disturbing."

"Of course I do, but to me that's a draw. That's why we did it."

"I don't get it. A draw? And who was the boy in the video?"

I see Seb and Dr. Newman exchange an uneasy look.

"It's a draw because I get a *ton* of traffic. That's my most watched video. It's controversial. Different sites keep taking it down so I have to keep editing bits out and moving it around. But it's compelling."

"Dr. Newman told me the boy in the video found the monologue. But just a second ago you said you found it. What the hell is going on? Who found the monologue? Who's the boy in the video?"

Seb looks afraid but Dr. Newman nods to him, encouraging him to continue.

"His name is Sebastian."

"Is that who you're named after, Seb?"

"Yeah."

I knew that sometimes real people were integrated into a system. I'd read about that.

"So, who is he?"

"I'm not getting into that today. Steve, I know there's stuff you want to know right now, but I have to protect The Timeshare and I need to look out for you, too. We can't just throw it all out there. It'd be too much—for all of us."

I'm feeling exasperated. "Fine. But this is exploitative—of you and that other kid. I don't understand why the hell you'd record something like that—let alone post it online."

"You like living in the house we have? Driving a car instead of taking the bus?"

"Seb, what does that have to do with anything?"

"How do you think we pay for all of that?"

"My job pays pretty well."

"Not well enough to cover everything. A lot of the money we have comes from my work at the agency. And social media funnels people in."

"The agency? Do you mean the modeling agency?" I ask, confused. Something isn't adding up. "What the hell does this have to do with modeling?"

Seb doesn't answer.

"How does this funnel people into a modeling agency, Seb? How is it connected?" I press.

I'm too horrified to wait for an answer. I feel like every avenue I choose is a dark alley. And now it's beginning to seem like the mysteries were being untangled but I no longer wanted the answers. Apparently, there was a lot more than what I'd seen or even suspected.

"Dr. Newman, I'm sorry. I just can't. I gotta head home," I say, tossing the car keys to Seb. "I'll uber."

I had the car drop me off at a restaurant near our house, took a couple valium and got smashed while talking with Kevin on the phone. I don't even remember walking home, but I got there, and passed out face-down on the couch.

Over the next few days, I'm so lost in thought that I'm leaving my car keys in the freezer and the milk in the microwave. That video has been such an assault on my senses that I can't even think straight. The fact that Sophie's work was paying for things made me feel involved— like I was benefiting from her abuse. And I had no idea how far her work went.

A few days later we're back with Dr. Newman to try and untangle everything around this new development.

"Seb, I need to understand how that video is connected to the agency."

"We have actors as well as models. This highlights what we can do in terms of acting." He notes the disgust on my face. "Crazy, controversial videos pull people in."

"I'm sorry, but that sounds like total BS."

"It's not. Look at the website—they have actors. But we use social media to direct people back to it."

"I don't even want to know who would be looking for children that talk the way you did in that video. What you're saying makes no sense at all. Am I going to get any truth today?"

"I feel like you want me to admit something. What do you need me to say to make you happy?"

"Don't do that, Seb. I want the truth and I feel like I'm not getting it."

"What are you so worried about?"

"I'm worried that you're going to get hurt. I'm worried that you're going to do something dangerous."

"I'm not being hurt, Steve. The people I work with treat me really well."

"Do you still do acting jobs?"

"I don't."

"See, this is where I get confused. You lead me down the wrong path and then totally shut down the conversation when I need answers. What work, exactly, are you doing?"

"I do modeling...and I fill in with other things when Mark needs me."

I'm ready to lose it again. "What does that mean?"

"Whatever you're worried about, it's not that. Look, it's just—I do the modeling and then I'll attend events sometimes."

"Well, that sounds divertingly harmless. What sort of events?"

"Galas, big parties, business meetings, sports stuff. It's nothing."

With Seb, I'm learning that I have to ask the right questions to get anywhere. It occurs to me that I was looking at this from the wrong angle. "Who do you go with, Seb?"

"Whoever is paying the bill."

An aha moment washes over me and I feel momentarily victorious that I nailed him down with the right question. Then I'm left with the recognition of what he was saying.

"*Oh my God*, Seb. Are you telling me you're working as an escort?"

He sighs and tilts his head. "I guess you could call it that."

"What the hell would you call it?" I demand.

"You need to calm down. Think of it this way—if you didn't have Sophie, but you wanted to attend some big event and were expected to bring someone, what would you do?"

"I don't know, Seb." I don't want him explaining this away and I'm frustrated that he couldn't understand my concerns.

"Well, if you don't want to freak yourself out, think about it. You'd call Mark—or someone like him—and ask for someone to go with you. That's it. That's all this is."

"I shouldn't worry because my wife is just dating other people for money. Is that it?"

Seb gives me a disgusted look. "You can think of this however you want to think of it, but it pays the bills."

I feel like I'm trying to fight a raging fire with a squirt gun. "Regardless, this needs to stop. It's not safe and it's not healthy. It's also going to kill our marriage."

"Think about it before you tell me to quit. It pays really well and I'm not doing anything I don't want to do."

Dr. Newman can see that I'm about to have another panic attack so he steps in. "Steve, I'm going to suggest that we set this aside for right now. We have a lot of other issues we need to resolve and I'm thinking we need to unpack those first and then move on to all of this a little later."

"We need to deal with this now," I demand.

Dr. Newman sighs and gestures to go on.

Seb is reluctant to start, but he feels pushed. "There's more to this and I can't tell you the more."

"That does *not* make me feel better. It makes me want to hear the whole story."

"I can't tell you, Steve—and I won't."

"Can I ask you to at least take down that video?"

"I'll look into it. I can tell you that once something is on the internet it's out of my hands, but I'll see what I can do."

"Thank you. I think that's a step in the right direction. And I want you to quit with attending the 'special events' with whoever is paying the bill."

"I'll do my best."

Dr. Newman quietly offers, "Seb, would I be right in saying that you understand how upsetting the video is to Steve?"

"Yeah, I get that. That was the whole point, but I don't want to talk about it," Seb says, unable to look at me.

"I think Steve just needs to know that you understand where he's coming from."

Seb is struggling now. "I do."

"Okay. So, does this feel settled enough for now?"

I feel like it's far from settled. I'm getting bits and pieces and I want to see the whole picture. "As long as it can be taken down. I don't want it out in the world," I say.

Seb looks up with tears in his eyes and he seems more contemplative than I've ever seen him. Now he says, "I don't want it out there either, to be honest." There's a hitch in his voice backed by fear. "We put it out there to try and get help, but no one got it. They just thought it was edgy and showed it to their friends. I'll take it down—along with some other things. I needed to have it out there until someone got it. And you did. It's going to feel good to take it down."

His mood is hard to read, but I detect a feeling of deep gratitude from him. I feel like we're making some progress now—moving in the right direction.

"Good. Okay. What else do we need to look at today?"

Seb seems emboldened. "I'd like to find out how I can get other stuff down too—from other websites—that I don't own."

I don't want to sound alarmed, but I am. "Seb, is there something else we need to worry about?"

"I probably shouldn't have said anything. It's just—the internet kind of takes on a life of its own. I don't know what all is out there. When you model, you never know how your work will be used or where it'll end up."

Dr. Newman adds, "That's true. We don't know what's out there, so let's focus on what we can control."

"I just need to make sure Sophie is safe in whatever work she's doing. I don't care about the money."

"There may be a way for me to quit the part you don't like and still not have our income drop. I've been offered another position at the agency."

"What would you be doing?"

"Recruiting. Finding talent."

"Why does that make me uneasy?"

"I don't know. I think it's going to be a challenge—and it's a promotion."

"I worry, Seb. I worry that you won't know when you're about to cross a line. I'm worried you'll get into a very dangerous situation and have no awareness. I know that you've not wanted to let other alters know what's going on-you've resisted being co-conscious, but I think doing that would be a good idea. Checks and balances."

"Are you scolding me now? Like I'm a little kid? Someone needs to keep an eye on me?"

"No, Seb. I just want you to be able to share what's going on so you can get different perspectives—keep everyone safe."

"I don't need a babysitter, Steve. I know what I'm doing."

"I just think there's more to consider. Everyone shares the body, so everyone should get a vote in what you all are doing. I think you'll be stronger for it."

Seb doesn't answer, but it looks like the wheels are turning.

October 24, 2011

As the weeks rolled into months, things with Seb remained unresolved, but as with all marriages, at some point you have to drop it or end it. I chose to drop it. Summer slipped by quickly and the long warm days crept back towards shorter, cooler ones. We found ourselves feeling more tired, heading to bed earlier. Jamie especially enjoyed cooking this time of year—hearty Romanian stews, German breads, French breakfasts. We enjoyed fires in the fire pit out back, toasting marshmallows.

Yet, every time I saw Seb, I wondered about that video. I wanted to know the story, but I knew not to ask. Sophie had so few positive memories of her childhood and certain times of year seemed to be triggers for her. I couldn't bring myself to ask why.

For me, as a kid, fall was my favorite time of year. We'd go to a pumpkin patch and each of us would pick out a pumpkin to carve. My brother David was super picky and would take hours to find just the right one. The corn maze, pie-eating contests, baking competitions...it was such a fun time. Then trick or treating with David and Rebecca— we usually coordinated our costumes, which got lots of oooh's and awww's from neighbors—and lots of treats.

Now, I wanted to pull Sophie out of the gloom that descends on her this time of year, so I find a local pumpkin patch with a petting zoo and maze. Rachel comes out the instant we pull into the lot—a dog running alongside our car brings her out. It bowls us over with kisses as we step onto the dirt parking lot.

Rachel runs over to the horses first, climbing up on the fence to pet them. Chickens were pecking around and she gets distracted, hopping down and running after them. I'd heard a variety of reactions to this sort of thing in my partners' group. Some people were embarrassed when their partners were child alters in front of other people. I didn't mind it. People in our neighborhood tended not to ask too many questions and everyone would keep to themselves. There's a certain freedom in that.

I corral Sophie in by telling her to come over and see the dog again. She runs over and is rolling on the ground with it. I ask if she wants to look at pumpkins and we head to the fields in a hayride wagon pulled by a tractor. She spots her pumpkin and we stop. Of course, one pumpkin leads to another and, before we're done, we have a dozen in various shapes and sizes.

The gentleman running the tractor is kind, and, as I've surmised from other outings, he is probably thinking Sophie is a special needs adult. As we're heading back, I ask him if we'd be able to ride the horses. He looks at Sophie and asks, "Will she be okay with that?"

I tell him that she will be, but he suggests we come back another day when they can give us more individual attention. I agree—it's crowded and I'm uncertain how Rachel will react. Petting a horse and riding one are two different things.

We arrive at the corn maze and the farmer asks if we'd like to go inside. Rachel looks fearful and I tell her we don't need to go. Relief fills her face and we head back to buy our pumpkins. She sees pumpkin bread and pumpkin butter, so we get those as well as a couple caramel apples.

On the way home, Rachel eats both apples and starts on the pumpkin bread. I never know when to stop her when she's eating junk. The day had gotten chilly, so we build a fire when we get home and then watch fun Halloween movies while we paint pumpkins.

Later in the evening, Seb comes out and acts sluggish. "Why did you let Rachel eat all that crap?" he says. "Oh my God. I need something more solid, but first I need a run. You wanna go with me?"

As we take a slow jog, I hear him having a conversation under his breath, telling Rachel she can't eat like that because she takes off and whoever is left has to deal with the consequences. I smile at this.

We turn the corner and arrive home. Jamie comes out to make salmon with dill sauce and pea pods. We eat dinner on the deck, but it's getting darker earlier and it's really too cold to be eating outside.

December 10, 2011

I love winter in Colorado—the snow drifts down in tiny flakes before hitting the ground and within 24 hours, it's melted.

December is a busy time for us. Seb has a ton of art shows and we have a bunch of parties to go to. We also have a lot of fundraisers to attend.

One of Seb's friends invites him to a Gala to celebrate emerging Colorado artists. At the time it seemed like a good idea to say yes but now that the day is here, I'm dragging my feet. It's a formal dinner and Sophie is acutely uncomfortable in these situations, but Seb loves them. Today, dressed in a dark gray suit with a purple shirt and blue tie, gray vest with silver paisley design, hair pulled into a high knot, wingtip shoes with no socks, Seb clips down the stairs and asks if I'm ready.

It's an hour until the event starts and I'm starving, so I make myself a grilled cheese.

"Dude, they'll have dinner there!" Sebi laughingly scolds me.

He fixes himself a scotch on the rocks, lights a cigarette and pulls out the Amandine Prajitura Jamie's made for the auction. He places the cake on a beautiful porcelain plate he made and covers it in plastic wrap. Then he sits across from me at the table.

"Sebi, I've been wanting to ask you something."

"Oh God. What?" I can tell he just wants to go out and enjoy the night and he had sensed I wanted to go down some dark alley.

"I've been wanting to ask you about this for years and I'd really like an answer. Tell me why it's so important for you to get back at Chuck."

"Because the guy goes after high school girls. It's not right. My family taught me that."

Sebi senses my confusion—"No, not my mom's side of the family. They're nuts. My dad's side. They helped me understand what was happening to me was wrong—kind of anchored me in reality. Obviously, they didn't know the extent of my abuse, but they did know Papa had a temper and seemed really off.

"They're amazing people. We'd go there every Thanksgiving and just hang out. They'd open their doors to everyone and have a feast. Schupfnudeln and goose, cabbage rolls and bean soup. And the *papanași cu brânză de vaci și affine* was to die for. Sort of like a donut with blueberries and cheese. Ask Jamie to make it for you sometime. Anyway, it's where Jamie learned to cook. He always had a natural affinity for it. They started teaching him in Kindergarten! But that was before he was a part of The Timeshare."

This was Sebi's way of deflecting—lead me down a more pleasant path or tell me something that would make me curious. Dangling a little mystery about Jamie in front of me was brilliant, but I wasn't having it today.

"So you hate Chuck with a firey passion because he was having sex with 17 year olds when he was 19? I'm going to call bullshit on this one, Sebi. There's more to the story."

"There is more to the story, but it's not mine to tell."

"I'd like to hear it."

"Tonight? *Really*? Can't we have just *one* normal evening? *Please*?"

"I would love that, too," I laugh, noting the irony. Seb has a remarkable sense of humor, so I appeal to it. "But seeing as how the body of my beautiful 29-year-old wife is currently inhabited by a very creative and intelligent 19-year-old young man who has just wrapped up an incredible looking cake made by a talented chef—who also inhabits the same body—it seems unlikely that *normal* is going to be on our menu anytime soon."

Seb laughs wryly, appreciating the humor, but not happy about having to get into anything serious tonight.

"Hang on." He sets down the cigarette, takes his phone from his jacket pocket and pulls up a song about survival, sung by a woman whose voice breaks but remains strong.

I know during these times to just be quiet and wait. This is likely someone else's story and The Timeshare had rules. The music means this person was deep inside, perhaps someone who is very private and doesn't want to share their story.

Sebi closes his eyes and takes deep breaths as he moves almost imperceptibly to the music.

The music fades and Seb shakes briefly and jerks his head before the eyes open and I know someone else is here. Hopefully someone with answers. The eyes are still blue, but have a different quality—softer, lighter, and they look around, taking in the room and me.

This alter's eyes close and s/he smiles while letting down the hair and running his/her fingers through it. "Such a simple pleasure—isn't it? Clean hair? It feels so good."

S/he has a slight southern accent. S/he opens her eyes and sees the cigarette, picks up the plate and delicately but firmly states, "This is not acceptable," and extinguishes it.

I nod in agreement—"I know, right?" I tried not to be fascinated by the way The Timeshare would switch personalities, but sometimes, like tonight, I couldn't help it.

A sad but resigned smile creeps over their face. "Pain management," this insightful one says. "I'm here to answer a question, but I'm sorry, I don't know what you asked."

"I wanted to know what you have against Chuck."

"Oh. Chuck." S/he nods and looks at the floor, letting the hair cover the face.

I'm not sure who's speaking, "Do you mind if I ask..."

"Oh, that's right. Ellyn. I'm Ellyn. I was in college with you guys." Then she offers, "I'm in a relationship with Liz as well. When you're a multiple, the only real option is polyamory—to have many loves.

Each alter deserves to experience a loving relationship, but as different people, we're going to be attracted to different things, have different needs. But I digress.

"Chuck is a complicated subject. Liz is also a complicated subject. I'm not sure how much of this I want to discuss. To be honest, I'm not able to entirely grasp the whole thing. I'm still working through it myself. I'll tell you about Chuck, but I need to put this in context, so please excuse what may seem superfluous. And you can't tell anyone about it. Not Dr. Newman and not Liz or Laura. Seb suspects something happened that night, but no memory. Sophie doesn't know, I don't think."

"Absolutely. I promise."

Ellyn smiles lightly "For me, it was a love at first sight sort of thing with Liz. You've seen her right?"

"Yes, I get how that could happen," I easily admit. "She's very attractive."

She smiles and seems to be grounding herself in a memory. "I know that you're angry with Seb about his relationship with Liz, but that's not him. That's me. I mean, the being in love with Liz part. He and Liz are very close, but it truly is a friendship. I respect your relationship with Sophie, so it hasn't gone very far. But there is love there. I think it's the classic thing of a lesbian in love with a straight girl. It appeals to my tragic nature."

She's joking, but her humor holds a sad kernel of truth, I think.

Tears gather in her eyes, briefly pooling and then flowing. She's not sobbing. It's more like when you get punched hard in the gut and you don't want to show you're hurt, but you can't stop the tears.

"Something always seemed off to me about Chuck and Liz. They seemed mis-matched. Liz was dating Chuck when I met her. I should have respected their relationship, but one night at the bar, Liz and I were flirting. I had too much to drink and I passed out. Liz had to keep working, but she was worried about me so she asked Chuck to take me back to her apartment. She'd be home later to keep an eye on me."

She takes a drink from Sebi's glass and swallows hard.

"It didn't end well."

"Oh my God, El. I'm so sorry."

"I only remember flashes of it. For the longest time, I went over it and over it in my head to try to get some control over it. If I hadn't been drinking—if I hadn't flirted with Liz—if I'd gone with a friend. I even told myself that maybe I imagined the whole thing.

"Can I have some more scotch, please?" she asks, handing me Sebi's empty glass.

"Sure." I hastily pour her another drink and hand it to her.

"I wanted to tell Liz, but she was so crazy about him and I didn't want to hurt her. Then the longer it went on, the more I *couldn't* tell her. She'd blame herself. Then, because of the timing, I was worried I could be pregnant so I had to go to the doctor on campus. She's the one who nailed us on the multiplicity."

She pauses for a moment to catch her breath and sip more scotch.

"You know what's odd?"

"What's that?" I ask as gently as I can.

"At the time, I didn't cry. I just got *pissed*. Like, *radically pissed*. I got connected with the rape crisis place—not as a client, but as a leader. I organized marches, worked for tougher convictions. I wanted to become a lawyer. I was able to take a few classes, but I didn't have control of the body for enough time. I didn't cry about it until years later."

"Thank you for telling me. I'm sorry for what happened to you. And I'm sorry it's still so painful to talk about. It sounds like you did a lot of good for a lot of people. You made things safer."

As remarkable as it seems, this is real progress. Ellyn experienced both the memory and the emotion. She had to take long pauses and needed time to pull herself together as she went, but she told her story and felt her feelings.

I promise her I wouldn't say anything about the rape, but I wonder now, *if* we had told each other the whole truth about our lives, if things would be better. I think we'd have greater compassion anyway.

She thanks me for listening and tells me she has to go back inside.

A minute later, Richard comes out saying, "Remember how that little asshole got the shit kicked out of him?"

"I do actually." I vaguely remember hearing something about it. He was supposed to go to Canada with the ski club over winter break, but he had to cancel because he was beaten up so badly. The rumor was that he got his ass handed to him by a girl.

"Yeah, that was me," he said smiling and giving me a wink.

Note to self: Do *not* piss Richard off.

Richard blinks and Seb steps forward, wiping his face and looking around like he was just waking up. Richard's hazel brown eye color shifts out to make room for Sebi's blue. He takes a deep breath, checks his watch and asks, "Ready to go?"

I understand the superpower thing now. They had just told me about something very traumatic, and within a few minutes, by switching into another person, she could be ready for a fun evening with friends. I'm not so skilled and need a few minutes. I excuse myself, order an uber and find Sebi's pipe.

I'm gone too long and Seb comes looking for me, "Hey," he says, opening the door and catching me mid-toke.

"Ah, yeah." I say, not bothering to hide the pipe but feeling embarrassed.

"A little overwhelming, right? Sorry about that," he says. "You okay?"

"Yup. I just need to lighten the load a little. This seems to help."

We smoke together until the uber arrives and then head to the fundraiser. No one notices that we'd started celebrating a little early—or maybe they assume we started drinking at another party. They're one after another this time of year.

The evening is fun after all and the dessert Jamie made is a huge hit at the auction. Seb, as I knew he would be, is in his element—perfectly comfortable as the center of attention, but effortlessly sharing the spotlight, too. Everyone loves how he's dressed and his enthusiasm for art and genuine appreciation of others pulls people in. Seb knows how to charm people and feels right at home among the other artists.

Eventually I call for a car and, on the way home, show him what we won at the auction—a weekend in Winter Park, dinner at The Grill, a gift certificate for craft beer and a six-week drawing class offered by Pete.

"Oh, Jesus, you're kidding me! You didn't! So I guess that's for me?"

"Yup. And I'm starting handball. It's time. We're jumping off this cliff together!"

———

We were both even more anxious than we'd anticipated. I decide to take some lessons before starting the handball league. Sebi is braver, willing to try drawing, but unconvinced he'd move beyond stick figures. He leaves the first class early.

"God, I *hate* this!" he moans, "I feel like there's an ability locked up inside and I can't access it. It's not just that I can't seem to get past it, I'm worried about letting Pete down. Everyone in there is getting it— except me. I *hate* feeling this way."

This was his pattern. He'd show up for the first class, feel like crap, and quit. A couple times he made it through class two, but nothing after that. He felt he should be better able to translate what he saw onto paper. He could do that with clay, his visions immediately taking shape.

Pete told his students to look at shapes, light, and shadow rather than trying to draw a person or an apple or a duck. No pressure to get it right or for things to look a certain way. Just *see the lines. See the shadow. Work with your eraser to draw out the light. Then couple it with strong lines for contrast.*

Sebi would sit in class and watch Pete do the demo. To Seb, it was some sort of magic and it fascinated him. Everyone else would begin to work on their drawings, but Sebi would just observe—trying to take it all in so that his work would be perfect from the first stroke. Then he'd start and it wouldn't look right. He'd erase and try again, erase, try again. And he'd get more and more frustrated.

But Pete wouldn't let him give up. He would come over and say, "That's a great start. Now, let's look at *this* line. Try and hold your pencil up so you can see the angle better." Pete was endlessly encouraging, which is exactly what Seb needed.

After the second class, Pete could sense that Seb was still struggling and approached him. "I'll make a deal with you—if you agree to keep coming and give me a chance to figure out how I can teach drawing to you in a way that you can best learn it, I assure you that you'll be amazed at what you can do."

Seb was still skeptical, but agreed to stick with it for six weeks—and then gladly accepted Pete's offer to come in an hour early each week for extra help. The goal was not to be a great artist—or even to have the drawing match what he saw in his head. The goal was just to stay in the class.

Sebi attended class three, which was a true milestone. At the end of class, Pete told him, "I have a theory about how you learn. You okay if we test it out next week?"

Sebi nodded in agreement. He appreciated Pete's playful attitude and his commitment to teaching. More than that—the trust he engendered felt truly healing.

"I'm going to show a different technique next time and I guarantee something will click for you," Pete said.

Seb liked to earn his accomplishments but he could get discouraged quickly. At the start of class four, he was trailing behind the other students—unable to translate things spatially. He was obsessive in his work, wanting me to be able to see how he saw himself and the others in The Timeshare, but he couldn't get it right and it was really making him nuts.

That next week, after everyone settled in, Pete said, "We're going to try something different tonight. Grab a piece of paper and just scribble. Don't try to make anything. I just want you to scribble."

Seb was scribbling away while the other students looked a little confused.

"No, seriously," Pete told them, "Just scribble."

"Now, grab your eraser and pull out the pattern. What do you see in your scribbles? Use your eraser like a pencil and pull out the picture."

As the other students struggled to see *something*, Seb immediately knew what Pete meant and pulled the pattern from the negative space—a group of birds that made a man's face. It was obvious to him. It was like the right key to the lock had finally been found and, suddenly, it all made sense.

Feeling confident at that point, he stayed after class to finish it. Pete sat with him and asked, "Do you happen to have dyslexia?"

"Yeah, I do but I never really thought that much about it," he said.

"Leonardo da Vinci, Pablo Picasso, Jackson Pollock, Andy Warhol. You're in good company. Their dyslexia helped them to see the world differently and you have that gift, too. We just need to come at this a different way. Did you notice you were the best at this? It came easy to you. Thanks to your dyslexia, you have a powerful ability to identify patterns."

Then he adds, "I know something about this because I'm dyslexic, too." He winks at Sebi and helps him pack up.

Seb is hooked. He's unable to stop drawing. From week four to week five his art goes from looking like a 3rd grader's doodles to a middle school level. We celebrate with dinner out at a French Bistro in Boulder we love—Brasserie Ten Ten—Trout Almondine for him, Cassoulet for me.

After that, every night I'd come home to him working with a light box or holding a big board in his lap, spinning it around to see a different angle, looking at it in the mirror, tracing images so he could learn shapes, then working on paper, finding patterns, pulling them out with an eraser.

He worked at drawing with a driving passion. It was more than the love he had for his pottery. He enjoyed that, but could always stop for the night. With drawing, he wanted to be able to translate exactly what he saw in his mind and would completely lose track of time.

But, although he was getting better, the accomplishments were incremental and he was growing frustrated. He'd taken a leap from his childlike drawings but now felt stuck again. However, he didn't quit.

I thought about how Seb rarely trusted anyone. Whenever he had trusted as a child, he was not only disappointed, he was hurt badly. Over the years, he would relentlessly question experts on everything. He wasn't trying to be difficult. He just had to be in control of things that impacted him. It made sense. The true miracle was that Sebi trusted this teacher enough to do what he said.

May 17, 2016

Sophie and I really needed a break and were considering how to get one when Sophie received an invitation to Laura and Carla's wedding. They'd been together since college, and were finally going to make it official.

We debated about going because travel was so hard for Sophie. Also, Sebi had been a big point of contention between Laura and Carla. In the end, though, it seemed like the right thing to do. Seb loved Laura and this was an important day for her.

Packing for seven alters is tricky. Everyone has their own stuff they'd like to bring. We go online for ideas and some kind woman from a chat board suggests each alter get the same amount of reasonable space. They can pack whatever, but it has to fit into—basically—about a backpack. That plan actually works well. Rachel has a couple extra stuffed animals, but that's okay.

We drive out and arrive early enough to go to the pier and visit the sea lions, check out the wax museum and do all the other touristy things Rachel loves to do. Seb is ready to let loose and our quiet stroll down the beach turns into a run culminating in an impromptu wading and splashing party that leaves us thoroughly soaked. After lying in the sand to dry off, we stop in to the Ferry Building for coffee and granola. We wander a bit more, gape at a bunch of living statues, eat an amazing lunch of salmon carpaccio and head back to our hotel.

While traveling anywhere is generally a nightmare, Rachel loves hotels. She loves the views, the TV, the comforters, the little soaps and shampoos, the stationery and pens. This day, as we pass through the lobby, she spots the swimming pool. She points at it and asks with a sense of wonder, "Can we go in there?"

We've had a really fun day and I'm thinking a swim would feel great before bed, so I agree. We dig our swimsuits out of the luggage and hit the pool. After we splash around a bit, we settle into floating around on the pool noodles.

"Did you know I had a swimming teacher?" Rachel asks.

"You did? What was he like?"

"He was so fun! But some of the lessons were really hard. I had to go underwater and it was *really* scary."

"It sounds scary!" I agree.

"Yup, it was. So he put coins on the bottom and then he held my hand and told me to take a deep breath and then he helped me so it wasn't so bad. He was nice."

I'm glad she'd had him in her life.

We order a pizza for dinner and then burrow into Rachel's bed. She's brought a teddy bear, doll, and stuffed rabbit that all need to be tucked in with her. When we traveled, we'd usually get a room with two queen beds. At home we'd sleep in separate rooms because some alters, particularly fragments, would come out and not know who I was. I also had a hard time getting any rest in a bed populated by dozens of stuffed animals and dolls. We had tried some suggestions other people had posted online and we asked Dr. Newman about it, but ultimately, separate rooms seemed like the right avenue.

As I'm reading a story to her, she spots one of Sebi's rudimentary drawings. He's not proud of his work yet, but he's proud that he's stuck with it. Rachel smiles, pointing to it and saying, "He figured it out!"

"What did he figure out, sweetie?" I ask her.

"He can draw again."

"Yes, he's doing really good with his drawing class, isn't he?"

"Yup. Grandma didn't win."

"What do you mean?"

"Remember he told you about that drawing he did in 6th grade? The one he won a ribbon for?"

"Yeah," I cautiously say, remembering how he'd talked about how it had been such a great day.

"Well, when he got home from school and he showed the picture and ribbon to Grandma, she told him he only won it because none of the good artists entered the contest and that they only gave him the ribbon because they felt sorry for him. And then she ripped up his drawing and threw everything away."

She considered my reaction for a minute. I was boiling angry. "Bitch," Rachel adds.

It's funny to hear such a little voice say that word with such conviction, but it was accurate. I couldn't agree more. Elizabeth would retain the feelings while all Sebi remembered was winning and how great that felt. But something was working to protect him and that part kept him from drawing. Something about his teacher changed all of that and I was grateful. Sebi had won, but I was furious with his grandmother.

"Yes, Rachel, that was a horrible thing to do."

Rachel giggled at my agreement.

"But now he can draw again. Now he can get really good. She can't tear up his drawings anymore."

I kiss Rachel's forehead, read a few more children's books to her and then tuck her in.

I take a few minutes to look at Sophie as she rests. She's stunning and I want to be in bed next to her all night. I miss my wife. I want to hold her and make love with her. But I also don't know who she is right now—Sophie, Rachel, Seb? And I knew from experience that waking her up with a kiss never went where I wanted it to go.

While I was starving for my wife, I knew there were alters I couldn't be with—it'd be inappropriate and harmful for Sophie. I shut everything down for the night and then crawl into my bed alone. The cold sheets seem to echo the consuming loneliness I feel.

I begin to drift off, thinking of the times when we were first together and how beautifully intense our physical relationship was.

Being in Berkeley had brought it all back. I'm dreaming about all the times we'd be in my apartment, order a pizza and pop in a movie, never making it to the end before we were too consumed with making out to pay attention to it.

In my dream, I'm back in grad school. I'm in bed with Sophie. She brushes her lips against my ear, then lets her hair spill over me as she's kissing my chest, biting my neck.

I become aware that my dream feels remarkably real—but that's not unusual. My sexual dreams always are. I'm becoming extremely aroused and roll over to my back, half awake. I'm unaware of doing it, but I feel my hand slowly moving down my chest, to my abs, beginning to move under my waistband. And then, I'm suddenly aware this is not my hand and I jerk awake.

"Oh, Jesus!" I say, startled, opening my eyes to see Sophie practically on top of me.

"You were moaning in your sleep. Sounds like you were having fun without me over here," she says, a pout on her face.

I'm starting to wake up but still feel like I'm in my dream. It's not Sophie, but whoever this is, she's pretty aggressive and I submit, sinking deeper into the bed and pulling her closer to me. She's kissing me more passionately than she has in years. And she's kissing me everywhere. My mind is racing, but my body shuts it down hard. I need this.

I know I've been with her in the past, but it had been years ago— before I knew there were different personalities. I'd been with her at college, and a lot of times, early in our marriage.

It's not Anna...she was reserved and submissive. Whoever this is, she's more dominant and directive, which I like. I feel like this is an unexpected bonus of traveling and I'm happy to go with it. With this alter, there's a very long prequel to making love.

She tells me to turn over and she's scratching my back, kissing me, biting and sucking on my neck, telling me that I taste good. I can tell

I'll have bruises tomorrow and I don't care. Then she directs me to do the same with her, asking me to hold her arms behind her back.

I'm not sure how comfortable I am with that, so I'm gentle. She can pull her arms away if she wants. With my other hand, I start at her neck and scratch in little circles, kissing her as I scratch the next area. As I'm biting her neck, she moans in a way that makes my body feel things it hasn't felt in years.

She pulls her arms away from me, turns over and is running her tongue along my neck as her hand rests, teasingly, just above my waistband.

And then, my mind comes back online for a split second and I know I need to ask. I pull her away and she fights me. "Stop!" I laugh. "What's your name? I want to be able to say it while we're making love."

She moans in a sort of deep growl. "Mmm. I would love that. I'm Chelsea," she says without reservation.

"Chelsea," I say and the kissing continues. I really don't want to stop, but something feels off.

"Chelsea. Chelsea, stop for a second. I need to know how old you are."

"It doesn't matter. I hate that people make a big thing of it."

Red flag.

"I can't keep going until I know."

"You know me. We were in college together. Don't you remember me?"

"Of course I remember. But I need to know—how old are you? Chelsea? Tell me."

"I'm 19."

She continues to try to kiss me and it's killing me. I want her so much. Not Sophie. Not Anna. I want Chelsea. I remember her from college and the sex *was* amazing. She has said she's 19, and I want to leave it there. If she's lying, that's on her, right? But I know there would be fallout for both of us if she's younger.

"I have to stop until I know the truth. How old are you, honey?"

She's moving her hips against me, grabbing my arm to be as close as possible.

"Don't freak out. I'm 16, but it's okay. Really. It's not like it's our first time. It was okay before, so it's okay now. And you have no idea how much I *need* you tonight." She knows everything that I like, the intensity I respond to, what I can't resist. And she does that. She's kissing and biting my neck again, which she knows is my on-button.

I hate these situations because I have no idea how to handle them. I'm desperate for sex and I have to try to think of a way I can make this okay. *She is 16.* Isn't that the age of consent *somewhere*? And she's my wife, for God's sake. That *has* to make it okay.

But the answer is obvious to me. There is no way this is acceptable. For all intents and purposes, I'd be a 37-year-old man making love with a 16-year-old girl. I try to think of some compromise.

"I can kiss you. But that's it. Is that enough or will it just make you feel worse?" I ask her, pretty sure it's going to make me feel worse.

We spend the next twenty minutes locked in this weird sort of combat of the wills. Both of us wanting more, but me stopping anytime she tries to take it from making out to foreplay. She doesn't make it easy to draw that line, and at times we start to cross it. I'm telling myself we've already been kissing and if it went further, it wouldn't be that big of an issue, but I have to think for both of us and I know that it would be.

And then she threatens me.

"I don't know what your problem is. If you don't want me, I bet I can find someone who does. I've done it before. Do you remember how *that* felt?"

I *did* remember and it stung all over again. We were supposed to go to a party during her senior year and I got called into work. She went without me. When I called to check on her, she told me to get there within the hour or she'd sleep with someone else. I called her bluff. That was not a good night for our relationship.

Now, I shut everything down and tell her that threatening me is a complete turn off and I couldn't make love with her at this point even if I wanted to. She punches me in the arm, hard, and goes back to her own bed where she cries as she's kicking the sheets around. There is a low, guttural, quiet growl going on that's really weird.

I hit the bathroom, lock the door and take a very long shower, admittedly thinking of Chelsea the entire time. I finally get back to bed about 4am. I set the alarm for 11, knowing it will come too early.

In the morning, I'm feeling pretty rough. Seb doesn't remember anything, but wonders why *he's* so tired. It doesn't seem like the time to bring it up, so I drop it for now, telling him it's hard to sleep in a strange place.

We get out of our respective beds—both sitting on the edge facing each other. We laugh about how sleepy we are. Then Seb looks at me and squints. He moves over to sit next to me and runs his finger over my collarbone and neck.

"Dude, what's this about?"

"What?"

"Is that a hickie or did you burn yourself with a curling iron?" he laughs.

"Oh shit," I rush to the mirror to look. I have three small bruises along my lower neck and collarbone. I try to covertly check Sophie for the same marks. She has one running down the side of her neck as well. Seb sees me looking and runs to the mirror.

"What the hell, dude?" he asks, no longer laughing. "What happened? I always know when Anna is out and she wasn't here last night. Wanna tell me what's going on?"

"I had a visitor last night. Chelsea sort of ambushed me."

"*Who* is Chelsea?"

I was not in the mood to go nine rounds with Seb after last night. "Seb, I swear to God, I can't talk about it right now. Chelsea is an alter in The Timeshare and we can cover it later, but can we please shelve this until we get back home?"

And then there is a leap of faith that takes me by surprise. "This scares me to death, Steve. I don't know who she is." He pauses to consider what to do.

"But I trust you," he finally says, "so yes, we can shelve it for now."

We stand at the mirror, each inspecting our necks. Seb grabs some make up and we're able to cover up the bruises with that and our collars.

"Laura is going to *kill* me if she sees this," I hear him mutter and I feel myself silently fuming.

Fortunately, our hotel is near the wedding venue. This is our old stomping ground and there are a lot of memories here. I wonder if that's why Chelsea came out last night. They seem to come out based on what's going on, but also the context can do it. And the context here is college. We're right on the edge of campus.

As we head downstairs, the sun feels invasive but at least it's cool enough to be comfortable. We're so close, we decide to walk and, although we're both quiet, there's a lot to take in. Students are grabbing their morning coffee while families are on their way to lunch. I catch Seb smiling at me as we both remember our time here.

We don't even make it into the lobby before Laura spots us and runs over squealing and laughing. She kisses Sebi on the lips and then hugs him before acknowledging me with a nod. Then she grabs Sebi's hand and tells him she has a surprise for him.

I follow, feeling like a third wheel, and stand in the doorway of the dressing room as she points to an expensive black suit with gray shirt and silver tie.

"You're my best man!" she says with a big smile on her face. Then she's suddenly serious, "I mean, if you're okay with that."

"I love it, Sunshine," Sebi says, smiling. She kisses him again and tells him to get dressed.

The small wedding is understated but elegant. Seb walks Laura down the aisle, holding her hand until they get to Carla, at which point, Seb takes her hand as well, gives her a brief kiss on the cheek and then joins their hands, taking their bouquets and standing to the side.

The wedding is brief, but beautiful. The vows strike me as exceptional. There's nothing about staying together forever, about faithfulness. This is not about locking the other person in, forcing them to stay even when they want to leave. Instead, they promise to always consider the other and encourage each other's dreams. They vow to stay together as long as they could make one another happy and to willingly release the other should they ever want to leave. It's the most unusual wedding I've ever attended.

We stay through the reception, but I can tell Seb's completely exhausted. I need some sleep myself. Carla and Laura hand out little favors at the door as people leave. When Seb reaches for Carla's hand to congratulate her, she rejects it, instead pulling him in for a hug as she thanks him for coming.

Then Laura envelopes him in her arms for a hug that lasts much longer than I'm comfortable with. She gives him a brief kiss on the lips, then brushes her fingers lightly against them to remove her lipstick. I look at Carla and she's smiling and rolling her eyes.

Carla hands me a small package of wedding favors and Laura whispers something to Seb. He smiles and kisses her cheek. "Love you, Sunshine. And I'm so happy for you."

As we walk back to the hotel, Sebi seems down.

"I'm so glad that she asked me to be here. And I'm glad we came. Thank you. We know it's a hassle to travel with us and we really appreciate it."

"It was fun to be back. A lot of memories."

"Yeah. There's a lot of that."

"What's bothering you?"

"Regrets," Seb says. "I don't want to talk about it." He pulls out a joint and asks, "Do you mind?"

"Where did you get that?"

"Laura. She left a couple in the coat pocket. Wedding favors. She knew today would be a suckfest for me."

"Honestly, no I don't mind. As long as you share."

We smoke along the way and instinctively wind up at our favorite brew pub and eat way too much food. But it's so good and we won't be back for a long time. The walk back to the hotel helps. And Seb opens up.

"I don't know what I want, Steve. I want to be with Laura, but I don't want to marry her. And it's not fair for me to tell her she can't be married just so we can be together part time. Sorry. I know this can't be easy for you to hear."

"No, it's not, Seb. I'm sorry you're feeling so crappy, but I don't think I can handle this conversation right now."

———

It's early, but we're tired, so both of us crash as soon as we hit the hotel. I sleep hard until 4 the next morning. I look over to see that Sophie isn't in her bed. My first thought is that Chelsea has woken up and, still angry about my rejecting her, has snuck out to hook up with some random stranger.

I bolt from bed and then I see the light in the bathroom and hear the sound of quiet crying.

"Now what?" is all I can think to myself. I just want a simple vacation with my damned wife. Why can't I catch a break?

I walk across the room and try talking with her through the door. Elizabeth, it seems, has woken up in a strange place and is terrified. She's trying to get over her agoraphobia, but "flooding," once considered the gold standard, was not the best way to go about it. In flooding, the patient is thrown into whatever terrifies them until they're over it. It's now recognized as cruel, traumatizing, and ineffective. And we had accidentally flooded Elizabeth.

I acquiesce and allow her to stay locked in the bathroom as long as necessary, but at 7 am, I was resorting to bribery. "Elizabeth, I don't think you realize that there are cookies out here. They left them last night, but we were too tired to notice. You can't say no to chocolate chip. I mean, that would be totally wrong."

"Slide one under the door?"

"Of the bathroom? Ew, gross!" I say in a teasing voice. "I can't do that. That's disgusting. No, if you want a cookie, you'll just have to come out here."

Elizabeth opens the door a crack and for the first time ever I see a relaxed smile of relief on her face—relief for being understood and heard and loved. The door swings open and she hugs me without pulling away. When she let's go, she asks playfully, "Now, where's my cookie?"

———

We return home from the wedding and I realize how stressed I am trying to help Sophie stay on an even keel. I feel like I'm forced to be on high alert and I need some time to unwind and just relax. I'm relieved to have business that takes me away to San Diego for a few days. Kevin's able to meet me. He's had a rough few months as well.

We find a hotel in the Gaslamp Quarter and stay out late every night, something we hadn't done since high school. It's crowded and crazy, but the late May evening is cool and comfortable. Everywhere we go, people seem to be in a good mood. Craft beer, burgers, the Irish pub, great Italian food. Just what we both needed.

Kevin, however, is feeling incredible remorse and perhaps even greater relief. He'd found a place for Shannon where she would be safe and well cared for. He visits her religiously every week and does all he can to ensure her comfort.

In contrast, I feel less settled about my situation with Sophie and have little hope of resolving things. I'm exhausted, frustrated, and feeling hopeless. I wonder if I'm delusional, hanging on to something that's doomed to fail. In many ways I feel like I've moved into the role of her caretaker, and it isn't what I signed up for. I know how awful that sounds and, when people marry, we agree to this as one of our vows, but the situation has become a full-time thing with no end in sight and I'm just tired. I have no interest in any other woman, nor does Kevin, I know. We want our wives back, but they are, for all intents and purposes, gone.

"You know, Sophie and I were back in Berkeley last week for a wedding," I tell Kevin. "It was a weird trip and I had a pretty rough night."

"Oh yeah, what happened?"

"At college, Sophie and I had a pretty crazy sex life. After we got married, it was good until a couple years in and then, when I found out about the multiplicity, things slowed way down. One of the alters told me that Sophie is asexual. Long story, but we're still having sex from time to time, but it feels more like an obligation on her part."

"I get that. I had the same thing with Shannon. I mean, since the depression got so bad, we haven't had sex at all. It's been at least a year."

"So you know how it feels. At home, we sleep in separate rooms, so it's not easy for anything to happen anyway. But in Berkeley, we were in separate beds, same room. I'm sound asleep and dreaming when Sophie gets in bed with me and she's voracious. It's like we were back in college."

Kevin can hear the pain in my voice. "You make it sound like that was a bad thing."

"I had to ask who it was. Turns out this alter is 16, under-age, and I had to keep pulling her off me. While I feel like I'm dying for sex. I'm ready to lose my mind with this bullshit."

"Oh my God. It's a special kind of hell, isn't it?" he says and we both know our situations are simply unsustainable.

And suddenly things become crystal clear for me and a fragile sense of hope begins to emerge from the sadness that had been swallowing me up. I need to get on with life—*with or without Sophie.* I can see that Kevin is coming to the same conclusion about Shannon. We're both profoundly sad and that sadness can't help but create the foundation for a deeper connection.

It's late afternoon when I get home from that weekend with Kevin and, walking through the door, dinner smells amazing. I immediately know Jamie is out. I have to smile.

The radio is blasting French music. I come up the stairs and announce that I'm back. Jamie pokes his head out of the kitchen, "Hey! How was the trip? We're having ribeye tonight with those little purple potatoes and mustard greens you like. Hungry?"

I am. But I also feel a tremendous amount of guilt. Kevin had moved into some other more important role in my life and I needed to talk with Sophie about it. But now I didn't know how to bring it up and I wasn't even sure that the discussion would help anything.

In the kitchen I see Jamie finishing the preparation, tossing bits of meat to Napoleon as he goes along. I'm glad to see The Timeshare back on track after last month's autopilot episode. Each time it happened, they were bouncing back more quickly.

Jamie is great with the kids—directive enough for them to feel safe, yet kind. Of course, his real passion is cooking, so when he's out, we eat the most amazing things. He expected me to pitch in, too. I admit, I had grown to like this guy.

He expertly juliennes an onion and crafts his own version of beurre blanc with capers for the mustard greens. "Try this demi glace for the steak," he orders. And as my eyes roll at the flavor, he proudly proclaims, "Am I right?"

Then he directs, "Help me with the *mise en place.*"

"Mise en what?"

"Prep em!" he directs, pointing to a cutting board and knife surrounded with veggies. "Dice those onions, carrots and celery—the mirepoix for my base. I'm making a stew for you guys for next week. And did you smell that brioche? It's going to be amazing! I've got like ten things going at once here!" Jamie says, clearly enjoying being in his element.

Between the French terms and the speed at which he moves, I can't keep up. I frustrate him to no end until he blows up—"Never mind. I'll do it." He spins the knife easily and I realize he's left-handed. Jamie starts chopping vegetables while assigning me to something less taxing, and more appropriate to my skill level.

"Stir the roux. And keep stirring or you'll burn it. Without it, your stew is gonna be crap," he says. There's a warmth in the commands, but you could easily miss it.

"You know the secret to a good roux?" he asks. "Clarified butter. And a little bacon grease doesn't hurt." He winks at me and then is back to giving orders.

He dips his pinkie into the roux and tastes it, giving it another grind of salt, another stir and setting it off the burner.

"Throw that salad on the table—oh wait, sprinkle this dill over it first," he says, coarsely chopping the fresh herb from our garden. I sprinkle and then put the salad in the middle of the simply set table.

Beer in the bottle, a jar of horseradish for our steak, plates with no placemats or napkins, forks, and big, wood-handled steak knives. Jamie's table.

We sit down and catch up as we eat. "How was your week?" I ask.

"Status quo. You know, Sebi did his art stuff, Elizabeth helped me keep things cleaned up, Rachel was inside—reading. Anna had some work stuff to do. I checked in on everyone. Yeah, it was good. Laura was here for a couple days, so Sebi's in a good mood. You'd think Laura would be on her honeymoon with Carla, but she comes out here. Do you get anything about this whole situation because I am *totally* lost."

I don't get it, but I don't want to get into it. I change the subject.

"I have a question for you," I start.

"Shoot!" Jamie says, helping himself to more salad, easily accommodating the change of topic.

"I was told your grandparents taught you to cook—the nice ones. But aren't they German and Romanian?"

"Sure are," he says, not registering my confusion.

"But most of your stuff is French."

"Look," he takes a sip of his soda as he's thinking, then leans toward me. "They taught me to *appreciate* food and to love cooking. My great grandfather is Romanian and he didn't always have food growing up, so he taught Grandpa that food is always a privilege. It's a reason to celebrate. Romanian food is so incredible—really heavy and comforting with very distinct flavors. German food has these amazing textures and there's so much tradition around it. It shows up in my cooking.

"Mustard greens, dill, horseradish. That's my grandma. She was always passing on recipes given to her by her great grandmother and we learned to make it the same way they did generations ago. It's such an immersive experience. It's like your ancestors are right there with you. So, yeah, they taught me to love it. Not only that, they taught me to love cooking for others. Thanksgiving they invited *everyone* in. Did you know that my grandmother used to cook up huge pots of potato soup and bake Bauernbrot bread and hand it out to homeless people? She loved to feed folks."

"That's amazing. They sound like very cool people. But Jaim, French food?"

"Oh, right. Well, you know that I spent that summer in Germany, right?"

"Yeah. Between Sophomore and Junior year."

"Well, I spent a couple weeks in Paris at a cooking school. It was just a few hours away from where I was living in Germany. I studied pastries and soup bases and emulsions. We had a whole class just on *beurre blanc*. But I learned a *lot* and it sort of kicked off an obsession for me."

"You went to Paris to study French cooking? But you don't speak French."

"Ah, mais je fais. Assez pour se débrouiller."

(Ah, but I do. Enough to get by.)

He raises an eyebrow and chuckles, "I told you I couldn't stand that French teacher in high school. Never said she didn't teach me nothing."

We both take a moment to laugh. Any opportunity for humor saved us. I realize Jamie had never told me his story. I never knew of his origins. I felt like his telling me might help him move through healing faster. It's a way of taking action when there doesn't seem to be anything I can do to make it better.

I press on. "Jamie, I never asked you where you came from. I didn't know if you wanted to tell me. I know it was probably bad."

He takes a moment to evaluate me, holding me in his gaze for a long minute that feels uncomfortable.

"I *don't* like to talk about it, Steve. I haven't even told Dr. Newman, but I trust you." He takes a moment, blinking and then closing his eyes. A deep breath later, his eyes flutter open and he starts. "When we were little, we had a best friend at preschool named Jamie. We met him the very first day. We were really scared to be there, so we went into this little fort they had in the corner. Little Jamie came right over and asked Sophie to play. She wouldn't come out, so he got in there with her and stayed all day, just rocking with her. At snack time, he brought her graham crackers and chocolate milk. The next day, too, but finally, Sophie did come out and Jamie was always by her side."

He continues. "Before coming to America, before meeting Sophie at preschool, he had been in a Romanian orphanage—he was sent there when his parents couldn't be found. I guess he was just wandering around on the streets.

He'd only been there for a few months—just a toddler—when he caught the eye of a news crew. He was so beautiful, but needed a life-saving surgery. It would repair his heart and he'd be at 100%. They offered to do it for free at a hospital here in the U.S.—if they could get him here. It took another few months of negotiating and getting money together and preparing documentation because everything was in such chaos, but they managed to arrange it."

I had seen on the news that those orphanages were hell on earth. Overcrowding, not enough food, no attention, lots of abuse and sexual assaults. You can imagine, after losing your parents and then being thrown into that situation, it messes with your head.

"When Jamie got here, he stayed with a nurse from the hospital— a single woman. She was great, but she was not in a good place financially.

"Sophie would pack an extra sandwich for him at lunch and would sneak him toys. There was a connection there. They had both lost their parents in some way, both been neglected and abused."

Hearing all this, I remembered going through Sophie's old scrapbooks and seeing pictures of them together. Sophie on one side, a dark-haired boy with blue eyes on the other, Jamie between them—full of life, laughing in every picture. An ever-present gray scarf around his neck that was too big for a child. At the time, I didn't know who he was. But the scarf looked familiar.

"Jamie was a great kid, but he had problems. He'd bite himself, break stuff, steal things. He was an angry little guy. The surgery when he was 3 went well, but he needed another one. Halfway through Kindergarten, they did the next surgery and he was gone. They couldn't get his heart restarted.

"For a child to lose her best friend in the world is too much to bear and she had no one to help her make sense of it but her Kindergarten teacher, Mrs. Johnson. She was an older woman, very large and every ounce of her packed with this unconditional love. It was just what Sophie needed.

"Mrs. Johnson went to the funeral and agreed to take Sophie. Her grandparents felt like that would put a lid on the grief and she'd shut up about him. The funeral was at a Catholic church and the priest spoke with Sophie afterwards. He was immensely kind and gentle and she hung on his every word. That conversation helped her move through her grief—not only about Jamie, but about every loss she ever had. He told her that Jamie was safe now. He was held and he knew he was loved. He held her hand and told her to please remember that. I think Sophie understood and really connected with that."

He smiles as he continues. "At the funeral, the nurse who took care of Jamie sat next to Sophie and they cried together. People filed past the casket and I think I started to emerge when she stopped for just a second, touched it, and whispered, 'Don't worry. I've got you.' It was literal in a way—like she took on Jamie's soul. After the funeral, the nurse gave Sophie Jamie's scarf to remember him by. It was the only thing he had from his parents. He was wearing it when they found him.

"Sophie's parents were matter-of-fact about it and told her to find a new friend. Jamie wasn't anything special and it had been a ridiculous waste of resources to bring him over in the first place. They approached it with the same compassion they had when her cat got hit by a car, telling her it was just skin and bones now and tossing it in the garbage can, not caring that Sophie would see it when she took the trash out after dinner.

"Someone in The Timeshare was trying to comfort her and they told her that because she knew Jamie and because she would never forget him, he was really a part of her.

"And that cemented it in Sophie. She couldn't lose Jamie, so she made him a part of her. And it made perfect sense that he matured and grew up. I'm who Jamie would be if he had lived," he concludes.

"So that's you. You're Jamie."

"Yes. This part of The Timeshare lives in his honor. If he'd never had a heart condition and had never been in the orphanage, I'm who he would have been."

I wasn't sure I quite understood how that worked, but I could untangle that knot later.

"The scarf. Is that the same one Seb wears now?"

Jamie smiles at me and nods and I feel brought even closer into his world. "It's become sort of a security blanket. But it's falling apart."

I'm wondering if all of this is real and am starting to feel nuts. Jamie notices my expression and closes his eyes and Elizabeth comes forward. "I'm sorry. It must be hard to hear all our stories. Can I show you something?"

"Yes, of course," I say.

She sits down at the piano and plays a simple, upbeat tune. She smiles at me after playing but I couldn't manage to smile back.

———

The next morning, Sophie trips over the piano bench and tells me we should get rid of the thing. She *hated* that piano. More than making her sad, it infuriates her.

I always wondered what that was about and I ask again. When I'd brought it up before, Sophie told me it took up too much space, it was in the way and she hated tripping over it. Then she made a strange comment: "Pianos belong in the basement."

"Why's that?" I had asked.

And she simply responded under her breath, "Because they do. Everybody knows that."

I'd never seen a piano in a basement. In my house growing up, our basement was pretty damp and dark. We just used it for storage. I imagine Sophie's was about the same. Every piano I'd ever seen was in the living room.

This time I press her a bit and she snaps back, telling me I had 30 days to move it out or she'd sell it. I tell her that she has some alters who could play piano well and who enjoy it, so we'd discuss it at Dr. Newman's next time. She looks perplexed—like she is trying to remember, but finally she just gives a frustrated sigh and agrees.

At Dr. Newman's a few days later, Sophie is there with me to find a solution to the piano situation. She doesn't feel great and when she shifts positions, she grunts and grimaces a bit. Sebi had been out yesterday and had eaten an enormous amount of food so her stomach likely is upset. Add to that the fact that he put in his average three mile run and weight-lifting and Sophie is feeling the pain.

"I hear we're looking at a piano," Dr. Newman starts, taking a loud sip of his coffee. I could tell this topic is something that would take some time to get through because he's being directive, not letting us meander down various paths until we find our way.

I interrupt. "Dr. Newman, sorry. I have something I think may be more pressing. While we were in Berkeley, I ran into an alter named Chelsea. Seb says he doesn't know who she is, but he's worried about it, too. I think maybe we need to address that first."

"We can do that. Seb?"

"I agree. The piano can wait."

"Okay. Tell me what happened." All eyes are on me. Seb doesn't remember and Chelsea certainly isn't going to come forward to explain it.

"So, I guess that's me. Umm. Well, I tucked Rachel in and went to bed. I was asleep when Chelsea got in bed with me and started kissing me. We messed around a bit but I felt like something was off, so I stopped and found out she's 16. I slept with her a lot in college, before I knew. This time, she was not happy we stopped and threatened to find someone else to have sex with."

"Jesus," Seb said, looking to Dr. Newman. "I hope this isn't what I think it is. Do you think...?"

"I don't know, Seb. But regardless of where she came from, we need to bring her in and figure out how to handle this. Are you okay discussing this in front of Steve?"

"What's going on?" I ask.

Dr. Newman looks to Seb, who shakes his head no. "Seb isn't comfortable getting into this, but I'm glad you mentioned it, Steve. It's important that I work with The Timeshare on this. I'm sorry, I can't say anything else."

"So where do we go from here?" I ask.

"Well, you're here and we need to deal with the piano issue. Seb, if you're okay waiting to talk about Chelsea...?"

Seb nods, "If you think it's okay."

"Well, this happened when you were in Berkeley where she was out a good deal of the time before. Sounds like she was brought out by the familiar surroundings. Now you're back here. You're the only one who can judge it, but we have an appointment in a few days."

"Yeah, let's talk about the piano. I think it's okay."

I'm feeling side-lined and I need some answers. "Okay, I get that you don't want to deal with this, but what the hell do I do when she blind-sides me at 2 in the morning?"

From their reaction, it seems there's no easy answer. "It's complex," Seb says. "Basically, there's no way to win with these types of alters. I'm going to say that, at this point, it's probably safer for The Timeshare if you have sex with her. She doesn't have the best judgment and she'll go out and find a stranger to have sex with. Just think of her as pure id. She has intense desires and will do whatever she feels is necessary to fulfill them."

I'm jolted from wanting her desperately to feeling terrified I'll have some sort of equipment failure and she'll wind up at some dive looking for sex.

"Okay then," I say, hoping Chelsea doesn't make another appearance.

"Let's take a breath and move on to something that's hopefully a little less charged," Dr. Newman says, inviting us to take a reprieve. I feel like I can't take a deep breath and need a lighter topic, even if it'll involve a conflict.

"Tell me about the piano, Steve."

"Well, my parents wanted to keep it in the family and my brother David wouldn't take it and Rebecca's house isn't big enough." I tried to be generic enough now that the door was opened, but so that Sophie could take the conversation wherever she wanted it to go.

"Soph?" Dr. Newman invites her into the discussion.

"What? You *know* I hate that thing. And you know that I can't even stand to *hear* a piano. It's like fingernails on a chalkboard. The thing is a pain in the ass to dust, it takes up a whole corner of the living room. There are a million reasons to get rid of it."

"You want to go through those point by point, we can. I have a couple kids I need to get through college, so take all the time you need. Or did you want to tell Steve the real reason?"

Sophie shifted, grimaced, scratched her neck, and looked to the side, clenching her teeth.

"Fine, *I'll* tell him!" Sebi had jumped out. "Look, personally, I love the piano. My grandmother taught me to play and as far as I'm concerned, it builds discipline and it brought me and her closer." Sebi always tried to put a positive spin on things. If he could give someone the benefit of the doubt, he would. Then he rather ominously adds, "But I wasn't out at night."

I found he would do this when there was more to the story, but it wasn't his to tell. It was a way for him to not violate boundaries, but still let me know there was something that should be shared.

"*What the hell?*" I whisper under my breath. *What happened with the piano?* Jamie had mentioned it, too. Said that it was connected to something horrible. And after wondering what the hang-up was, now I suddenly found myself back-tracking, uncertain whether or not I really wanted to hear this. It felt like we'd jumped from an impossible topic to a terrifying one.

"Sophie just has a bad association with the piano. Can we *please* just leave it at that?" Sebi is curt in his plea.

"Let's *not* just leave it, Sebi. This needs to be discussed." Dr. Newman is gentler now but still firm with resolve.

Sebi holds his breath for a second and then lets it out in a blast. "I don't see the point. I can talk with you about all this, Dr. Newman, but Steve doesn't need to know every detail. Look what it did to us," Sebi indicates his head and then splays his fist out into an open hand like an explosion. "What would knowing do to him? How's it going to help anything?"

I'm coming into greater awareness of Sebi's role. He has a lot of them, but one is serving as a sort of screen to protect people from too much information. He had taken me into The Timeshare, in a way, and wanted to protect me, too.

Dr. Newman assures Seb, "He wouldn't be here if he didn't want to know."

If I was going to be honest, after all this, I wasn't sure I *did* want to know. I was feeling more and more unsettled and anxious about the whole thing. I want to know if I can help, *if* I can fix things. But I'm not sure I want to know if there's nothing I can do. And this sounded like one of those things.

We have a good fifteen minutes of negotiating going on now. Different people are popping out and back in. It looks like a struggle.

Finally Elizabeth is out again, shaking and crying. She had to be the one to tell me, because this was her pain, her secret. It was a rule of The Timeshare, so that trust is kept.

Even though she loved the piano and loved playing it, the origins were horrendous.

Dr. Newman reaches for the trash bin in case Elizabeth needs it and takes his position on the floor, ready to have his hand grabbed.

She speaks so quietly and, between her sobbing and whisper of a voice, I have to really tune in to hear her.

"She doesn't like the piano," Elizabeth whispers, "because at night when Papa would hurt me, Grandma would go down to the basement to play it so she didn't have to hear what was going on. We felt like the only person who could help us had abandoned us. And Papa used it to torture Sebi. Seb knew what was coming next for us when he heard the piano."

This is part of Elizabeth's story and I can't imagine how she could tolerate even telling me. But I understand Sophie's hate now.

Elizabeth, now feeling exposed and vulnerable, gets up from the couch and goes behind a screen in the office. I get up to follow but Dr. Newman shakes his head and tells me to give her some time. She wants to be invisible, he says. It's the only gift we could give her that she could receive right now.

I want to help my wife but I'm also becoming educated about her particular manifestations of multiplicity. So I ask him why Sophie hated the piano if this happened to Elizabeth—and why was Elizabeth okay with it?

"I'll answer the first part and then we'll ask Elizabeth about the second part." Dr. Newman is big on making sure each alter is able to speak for himself or herself. He felt it was the best way to get accurate information and not violate the trust. Probably wise.

"This is something we've been working on and Sophie gave me permission to talk with you about it if it ever came up. The Timeshare has diffused this memory and the feelings associated with it. Elizabeth was the one being abused the most at night. Sophie left and was not co-conscious at the time. Now we're integrating the experience and the first step is asking Elizabeth to share it with the others. That's the diffusing part. Then the memory and feelings are integrated—with everyone who is willing to share in it to help Elizabeth."

"Let me ask you this," Dr. Newman inquires, "How did Sophie feel about the piano when you first got it?"

"I don't know. She wasn't thrilled about the space it'd take up, but she was happy to help my parents and thought maybe she'd have time to learn how to play at some point."

"Right. But as we've been working and parts have been coming forward and Sophie has become more co-conscious and they're sharing the experiences, we're seeing her hatred of the piano growing because she's seeing that it hurt Elizabeth. If you saw someone you loved being hurt, you'd want to get rid of the thing that's hurting them, right?"

"Of course."

"That's where we are."

"So do we put the piano in storage or something?"

And from behind the screen we hear a quiet sob and Elizabeth comes out asking that we keep it.

"I like it too, Elizabeth," I say, smiling, "especially when you play."

Elizabeth blushes and hides her face. She pulls a braid to her mouth and begins chewing on her hair. She has a lot of these habits. She bites her lip until it bleeds, pulls out her eyebrows, chews on her hair.

Dr. Newman waits and then asks, "Can you tell us more about why you feel you want to keep the piano, Elizabeth?"

"I like it. I like playing it," she says, starting to pull on her eyebrow, ripping out one hair at a time. I want to grab her hand and tell her to stop, but I don't.

"That might feel confusing to Steve because, to him, it seems like something that you would want to avoid. Can you explain a little bit more?"

Elizabeth grows quiet. I can tell she knows the answer but is debating whether or not to share it with me. I have a feeling Dr. Newman knows, too.

"Don't you get it?" Sophie's back and exhausted, but she's more angry. "She likes playing the damned thing because she feels like it takes power away from Papa."

"How?"

"Because it's the one thing she loved that he couldn't destroy. One of his greatest joys was to rip her favorite things from her. Breaking her dolls, taking her stuffed animals and putting them out of reach on a top shelf of the closet where she could see them but not get to them, hiding her security blanket before she left for camp when she was terrified. Moving the piano to the creepiest part of the basement. But her love of piano was her way of being defiant."

"I have to say that I kinda love that about her."

We could hear low muttering and I look at Dr. Newman to ask him if I should be worried when she did that. She's asking and answering her own questions out loud. I can hear different intonations, pauses, accents and pace in her speech but can't pick out exactly what's being said. She sounds like a crazy person and it's *freaking* me out.

"No, not at all. We've just had a parade of alters today. She's pulling herself together."

I wanted to know how Elizabeth had come to be but I knew she'd been through a lot today so instead I ask Dr. Newman what direction to go.

"It's not up to me, Steve. I think it's okay to ask. If she doesn't want to tell you, she doesn't have to, and doing it here may be the best way."

I ask for Elizabeth to come out when she's ready and a few minutes later she emerges.

"Elizabeth, can you tell me about how you came to The Timeshare?"

She brings a braid of hair to her teeth and begins chewing on it as she briefly thinks it over. "I don't remember, but it was bad. Maybe it was around the time that lady brought me the doll?"

"Can you tell me about that?"

"I'm tired. Can Rachel?"

"Sure—as long as you're okay with that."

Rachel boldly steps forward and looks around. She scolds Dr. Newman saying, "Hey, you said you'd get toys. Where are they?"

"I know Rachel, I'm working on it. I just haven't had time to get to it yet. Plus, I'm not a toy expert. Maybe you can give me some ideas sometime?"

Dr. Newman looks to me.

"Rachel, can you tell me about the doll?" Rachel looks confused and squints at us. I clarify, "...the lady who brought Elizabeth a doll."

"Oh, yeah."

"Was that when Elizabeth came online?"

"No. She was here before that but she didn't have a name."

This seems odd to me. I assumed that would be the first thing that would happen—an alter would be created and say, "Hey my name is..." "She didn't have a name?"

"None of us had names in the beginning. We don't need them inside. We didn't have names until we started working with a therapist and he needed to have a handle for things. We didn't know how to do that—how to name everyone. So he said to find people in real life that reminded us of our inside people. And that's what we did. But we knew what Elizabeth's name would be because of that doll."

I become aware, again, of how little I understand this thing.

"So, when did she come online?"

Rachel seems to go inside for a moment and then quickly returns. "I don't know. No one knows that. But the doll is how she got her name."

"Can you please tell me about that?"

"Sure. So, this nice lady who knew our family came over at Christmas time with a doll for us. It was the Beth doll from Little Women. She had said she wanted us to have it because it reminded her so much of us. She said that we were well-behaved, smart, sweet, and pretty. We were so excited and gave her a big hug and just sat and stared at it. I wish you could have seen it. It was the prettiest doll!"

"Well, after she left, Papa snatched it away from us because he was so mad we didn't say thank you to the lady. He said that Beth was kind and polite and generous and we were stupid, selfish, and spoiled and he crushed the doll's head and threw us in the basement. It's scary down there. It's dark and there's mice. And I hate the sound the lock makes on the door." She shivers.

Rachel pauses and closes her eyes, squinting and pursing her lips as she tunes into The Timeshare. "I *know* that. I'm not saying it!"

"Anyway, that's when she got her name because she *is* like Beth. She's really nice and she helps a lot and she's a good girl."

For as quiet and obedient as Elizabeth is, she's a little spitfire. She has real guts. Like stand in front of a tank guts. I want to nurture this part, to help her see what I see in her. Not only is she a spunky little girl, she stands her ground even though she knows what will come next.

Richard comes forward and I'm concerned he'll be angry that I'd asked, but I needn't have been concerned, he just had information to share. "You know how I was a bad ass—standing in front of the others and taking the physical punishment? I've got nothing on this little one. She is tough! She drove Grandpa nuts because she was very *turn the other cheek*. I'm not going to say anymore, but thought you should know."

Dr. Newman offers to help her bring Jamie forward and Elizabeth tells him, no, she'd like to try getting home and knows how to ask for help. I was glad to see this revelation had emboldened her.

On the way home, Elizabeth asks if we can stop for ice cream. This is huge for a number of reasons. First, Elizabeth rarely asks for anything. This is a sign of huge healing. Second, she usually wants to get home immediately after a session because her anxiety builds more and more the longer we're away.

We stop by Little Man Ice Cream for one of our favorite treats—16th Street Chocolate. Elizabeth is a kid, but she'd been thrown into an adult role long before she should have been. I thought about the things I liked as a kid and wanted to do more of that with her.

As we pull into the driveway, Elizabeth asks, "You said the garage is making you crazy. Should we clean it up?"

I had mentioned that a couple weeks ago, but I hadn't gotten to it yet. Elizabeth jumps right in and I find she has incredible spatial abilities. She's a master at organizing and, two hours later, the garage is immaculate.

We throw together a quick dinner and tuck in under the table. I tell her that Richard had come forward to let us know how much he admired her—and how I did, too. I told her I was impressed with her. I asked her how she ever got so brave and she told me, "Jesus."

That caught me off guard and I couldn't see how this figured in. "Tell me more. I don't get it."

"Turn the other cheek. That story in the Bible isn't about allowing people to treat you badly. It's about turning your cheek when someone does that so others can see that person's true colors. Don't take it personally. When people treat you badly, it's coming from what's inside them, not anything you've done. By allowing that guard to strike him twice, Jesus was allowing him to reveal himself to everyone—to show that he was not a nice man. So he couldn't hit Jesus a second time without showing who he was. A minister told me that once."

I could see why Elizabeth had chosen to take a religious route. The church Sophie grew up in sounded amazing. Like me, she had been raised Episcopal and often told me about pancake breakfasts, singing in the choir, serving as an acolyte, devouring lessons on religion and even teaching a class on different faiths when she was in high school. She taught vacation bible school in the summers and did a lot of volunteer work at the church. She credits them with giving her a safe place to be and teaching her values that served her well.

Elizabeth tells me shyly, but with a glint of pride in her eye, "I was the one who did all the stuff at church growing up. Because of my religion, I know I'm never alone. I may go through hell, but I'm not walking through it by myself. One night when awful things were happening and the piano was playing in the basement, I felt so sick. Papa had sprayed something up my nose and it was making the room spin and the music sound eerily slow. I felt so alone. Then Papa left and I just felt this flutter of wings surrounding me. I felt like I was on fire, but the wings were cool and gentle and I felt someone tell me they would keep me safe and I could sleep. I know, it sounds like it was because of the drugs, but I don't think so. I think it was a God thing."

I'm speechless. People had known they couldn't get her out when she was a child. But they also knew they could throw her a lifeline and I was impressed with how she was able to grab onto those. It was a miracle she could trust enough to reach out. And when there were no lifelines left, she still reached out. Whether you believe God reached back or she created that in her mind, she was such a strong child.

I asked her why she slept sitting up and curled into a ball. Her answer about broke me. She was so proud of her ability to innovate. I was heartsick that she needed to be...

"I don't like being surprised. If I sleep that way, they have to wake me up before they can hurt me. At least I'm awake. I don't have a lot of choices, but I can choose that."

———

Over the next few weeks I spend more time with Elizabeth. Her revelations had made her bolder, healthier, and more present. Something had shifted within her and it seemed to me her language and behavior were that of an older girl. She was growing up, and that was a very good sign. She felt safer and was more able to trust me.

"Elizabeth, I have a question for you."

She looks at me expectantly without saying anything.

"I wonder if the way you're sleeping might be causing some pain for you. And eating under the table—when I try that, it really hurts my back. Do you think you can tell Burt about it?"

"Can you tell him? I'm too embarrassed."

"If that'd be easier, yes. I can tell him."

Sophie feels the pain, but has little awareness of what causes it. I often serve as translator.

Sophie sees her physical therapist Burt twice a week when her pain level is bad. Before Sophie's session, I take him aside and explain that he may not know that she eats off the floor and sleeps sitting cross legged, but hunched over.

Burt never judges, but I can tell he's surprised. He looks like he's having an aha moment. He tells me it was consistent with what he was seeing.

"I wish I would have known to ask," he says, "This explains so much. I have some ideas. It's not all of it, of course, but anything we can do to reduce her pain helps. Thanks for trusting me enough to tell me."

Burt is great because he's willing to roll with whatever. As for sleeping, he doesn't ask why—that's a question for Dr. Newman. Instead, he asks if she could try sleeping sitting up but not curled over. I agree to try and help her to do that, but admit I thought she felt safer curled up. He asks if we might work up to that then...for now, perhaps she could curl over on a big pillow rather than sleeping completely collapsed over her arms. We'd give it a try, I say.

As for her habit of eating on the floor, he suggests getting a little breakfast table with fold out legs. It would allow her to eat less hunched over.

Elizabeth panics when I first suggest the breakfast table, telling me her plate *has* to be on the floor or Papa would find out. She seemed to believe Papa was the same age he was when Sophie was young. She didn't know her childhood home had gone into foreclosure and her grandparents lived in a retirement home.

We still needed to do a bit of work with Dr. Newman, but when she was able to use the tray, and the pillow at night, she started feeling better. Fewer migraines and her neck didn't hurt all the time. As a bonus, Elizabeth felt understood and cared for. And she was willing to work with me on this, which demonstrated an enormous amount of trust on her part. I was proud of her. When she reported to Burt, she said her pain level was better.

———

During my time with Elizabeth, Seb seems more distant. One morning, I come downstairs to find him smoking and looking out the window. He doesn't notice my presence and as I approach, I see he's crying. Very un-Sebi like.

"What's up?" I ask, keeping it light in case he wants to be pulled away from his pain.

"I'm thinking about Elizabeth. I love her like a sister, you know?"

I know that anything I say at this point will hurt. As gently as I can, I tell him, "I know that, Seb. I'm sure she loves you, too."

"I don't think so."

"Why don't you tell her how you feel?"

"I can't. She'll hate me for abandoning her."

"When did you abandon her?"

"We couldn't handle the feelings. Richard handled the immediate pain. Sophie, the long-term pain. Jamie kept the kids as safe as he could. I handled the mind games. But Elizabeth was left to deal with all the feelings on her own. And then, when I was 13, I couldn't handle it anymore and I just checked out. I thought we'd all go together, but it didn't work out that way. She must hate us."

"You don't know that. You did everything you could."

"No, I didn't. None of us did. If we were stronger, we'd have split less. We wouldn't have checked out."

I don't know what to say. To be honest, I really don't understand all of this. So often, I feel he's speaking in riddles. And all I can do it sit with him as he cries.

June 13, 2016

Summer in Colorado is huge for art festivals. Sebi loves them—it's a good place to get ideas, connect with kindred spirits and learn new techniques.

At the festival, I'm standing in the shade, admiring someone's paintings and, when I look over to see where Sebi is, I can't find him at first.

I scan the crowd and see him sitting at one of the potter's wheels—the artist is showing him a different way to center—something Seb has always struggled with. Sebi's white polo shirt and plaid golf shorts are covered in clay and he's laughing with a small crowd that's gathered.

Then I notice a 30-something guy approaching Sebi. He's well-dressed in a suit and tie with shorts and expensive gray shoes. Unusual for such a warm day. Seb had told me once about a guy who dressed like this. He said he was pretentious and cruel. I wondered if this is that guy.

Sebi has his back to me and I'm not sure I like the way this guy looks. With bulging blue eyes and no chin, he looks like that guy in high school who's always trying too hard to fit in. They're unpredictable and do stupid things trying to be popular, not realizing it has more to do with character than what you wear or acting like you're better than everyone else.

As Sebi catches the guy's eye, his smile fades and he excuses himself from the potter. He gets up to confront the guy head on and I wonder if Richard might make an appearance. I imagine a brawl in the middle of this nice little art festival and I run over, just in case.

I'm close enough to hear their conversation, but neither of them notices me. The guy is emphatic with Seb, trying to make a point. And I start to get a creepy vibe from him.

He's pleading, "I've called the agency and they say you're booked. Look, I'm sorry about last time. It was a complete misunderstanding. We've known each other so long. Let's figure this out. Just...call me, okay?" He grabs Seb's hand and presses his business card into it.

He looks like he wants to hug Sebi, but can't decide if it would help or hurt his case, so he touches his arm and then turns and walks away.

Just then a very attractive guy in a cream-colored linen suit rounds the corner. Tan, fit, in his 50's and graying in that way that's so sophisticated it's annoying. He approaches, and puts his hand on Seb's shoulder. He whispers something in Seb's ear and Seb looks embarrassed, shaking his head no.

I approach, staring at this guy and asking Seb if he's okay. As he answers, I see a glint of brown in the eyes. Richard's close but Seb is still in charge.

"Yes, of course. Steve, I don't think you've met Mark. He owns the agency."

Mark reaches out for my hand and I notice he even smells good. This is the guy who used to find dates for my wife—the guy she still models for. I don't trust him and I don't like him. I hesitate but then shake his hand for Seb's sake.

He looks back to Sebi and smiles, "If you're good, I'm going to catch up to my wife. Try not to worry. We'll handle this. Take care, and, Steve? Nice to meet you."

"What was that about?" I ask after he leaves.

"Nothing. Mark was just checking in with me. Craig's a photographer that I've known forever...since grade school. I did some work with him a couple months ago. We had a weird session and Mark told him I wouldn't work with him again and now he's freaking out about it."

"Should I be worried?"

"No, not at all. He's harmless. Let's go."

I've learned to drop things when he does. It's not worth a big fight and it gets me nowhere anyway.

"Hungry? I'm kinda starving and I saw a Greek place back there."

"I could eat," Seb says and we begin to make our way to the restaurant.

As we sit down with our gyros, Sebi asks, "Know why we love these things?"

"Gyros?"

"No, art festivals."

"Tell me."

"When I was growing up, there was a big art festival in town and every year, we'd volunteer. I loved being around all the artists.

"We not only put together the tables and boards for artists to display their work, we got to help them problem solve, to sit and chat and learn from creative people who were doing a lot of innovative things. The art center was a refuge for us and we loved it there.

"After they got everything put together for the artists, it was time to prepare the food. This was one of my favorite parts. At my grandparent's house, I learned how to cook German and Romanian food. At the festival, I learned to cook everything else.

"People of all nationalities came together to prepare these amazing ethnic dishes: Indian, Asian, Italian, French, German, African, Mexican, Greek, and Eastern European. Casseroles, soups, pastas, desserts. Jamie was their sous chef. He'd chop onions, peel garlic, mix Tabbouleh, stir, stuff, and bake.

"At home, my diet was pretty restricted because of my job. But at the festival? Food was celebrated and it was such a different feel. We really felt welcomed as a part of the team.

"I loved watching the people the next day. I'd helped to create something they were enjoying. And to see them eating food I'd helped prepare? I felt like I was feeding the whole town. It was such an accomplishment and one I felt so good about. Did I tell you I wanted to be a chef at one point?"

I know this is the Jamie part. Sometimes a switch is sudden, sometimes subtle. When it's sudden, they like to be recognized. When it's subtle, they prefer not to be noticed until they've completely settled in to the body. I'd learned that, fairly often, a personality would just pass through to make a comment and leave.

I know Jamie can hear me, so I tell him, "You are an incredible chef."

A smile of acknowledgment and he's gone. But I'm grateful to understand why they love art festivals so much.

—

I'm curious and somewhat suspicious, so after Sophie falls asleep that night, I dig out the guy's card. He's a photographer she has worked with in the past—I recognize the name. But I wonder about the misunderstanding and I have more questions.

I look him up online and see that his work includes some fashion photos, but also some racier stuff and then some stuff that's way beyond my comfort level. Models in bondage, some made up so they look like they have black eyes, cuts and bruises, some looking way out of it—drugged.

One picture catches my eye. It's a woman in leather lingerie and very high heels with red soles and long dark hair falling over her face. She's leaning forward—not in a sexy way, but in an "I've been beaten" way.

A tear in the lingerie shows dark bruises along her ribcage. A charm dangles from her necklace and catches the light. She's sitting in a chair that's angled so the model is in profile. Her hands are tied behind her with plastic or...? It's some sort of film and her wrists are sliced up and bloody. I enlarge the picture and recognize that *this is Sophie* and my heart sinks. It wasn't twine that had cut up Sebi's wrists. It wasn't an allergic reaction. *It was film.* And this is the day that it happened. That's why he winced and favored his left side. I press my eyes shut to cut off the tears.

I zoom in on her wrists. The film looks weird to me. There's something different about it. It's thin. I pick up the phone to call my friend Jeremy who's a photographer and we arrange to have lunch.

A few days later, I show him the picture I found online. He looks at it and raises his eyebrows in shock, "Dude, I'd've *never* guessed this was *your* thing."

"It's not," I say firmly, feeling irritated and fiercely protective of Sophie.

Jeremy knew some of our story and I knew I could trust him. He didn't know all of it, of course, but I had told him enough. "What's up with this picture? Do you notice anything wrong about it?"

"Well, I mean, it's pretty intense"...so let my eyes adjust for a second. Is this...is this Sophie? I knew she did modeling, but I didn't know she was doing this sort of edgy stuff."

"Yes, it's Sophie. And no, I'm not happy about it."

"I wouldn't be either. Look how she's sitting. It looks like she's been drugged. Or beaten. Maybe both. I hope I'm not telling you anything that's blowing your mind, but I think I know who the photographer is and, if I'm right, anything is possible."

"Who are you thinking it is?"

"Well, this looks like Craig Bishop. Is it Craig Bishop's work?" he says, scrolling through other photos in the series.

"It is."

"That guy. You know, he uses shock value to cover the fact that he really has no talent. It's not good that she's working with him. And the film he's got her tied up with..." He squints, looking closer. "Is it…?" Jeremy blows up the picture so he can see it better. He turns white and gets a very serious look on his face as he says. "That's 8 millimeter film."

"Okay."

"You don't understand, Steve. That could be a reference to something that's very bad news."

"What does that mean?"

"It's a whole industry and if you're curious, look up the movie "8mm" online. Even if he's not into it, he's alluding that he *is*. I'm not sure you want to know, but I would just suggest you get Sophie out of whatever connection she has with him. It could get far worse."

———

I feel the need to run away, so Sophie and I head west up to Winter Park along with about 300,000 other people. Traffic is a bitch, but we finally get there and feel the usual relief. We stop for dinner before heading to the resort.

I get up to pay the bill and when I come back, a beautiful, polished-looking guy in his 60's has taken my place at the table. Silver strands accent his dark brown hair. His green eyes seem to dance as he smiles at Sophie. It's the same guy I'd seen up here before but I could never place him. He looks kind, and Sophie seems comfortable. I hear her laughing as she's touching the guy's hand and holding it for a moment. I can't hear what they're saying, but as I approach, I hear he's speaking another language. "Bitte sei vorsichtig. Du weißt, wie wichtig du für mich bist, wie sehr du liebst. Pass auf dich auf." (Please just be careful. You know how important you are to me, how loved, dear one. Take good care.) As he gets up and leans over to her, a charm on a chain falls out of his shirt and dangles between them.

He takes her hand and brushes her cheek with his lips as he whispers something to her. I stare another minute and then it clicks. Robert. Robert Godwulf from Facebook.

As he walks away, I put my hand on Sophie's shoulder so she knows I saw everything. I'm hoping this will elicit a confession.

She puts her hand on mine. She's not feeling caught. And this doesn't feel like Sophie. I can feel stronger muscles in the shoulder and the hand is warm—it doesn't land gently on mine. This feels like Sebi.

I select my tone carefully. I want him to know I've heard enough to be angry. "Who was that?"

"That's Robert...Godwulf.

"Godwulf. Is he why you chose the name?"

"He is. He's a great guy. I really look up to him." Sebi says. Then he pulls out his St Christopher charm. "See this?"

"Yeah." I say, worry in my voice.

"Robert is part of a line of ancestors I very much admire. The St. Christopher charms were handed down through the Godwulf line. It goes back generations. Robert gave it to me when he told me about the Godwulfs.

"Remember I went to Germany that summer instead of returning home? I was there with him, learning about the family. I met a lot of them and learned about their—our—history. And I made the choice to claim my family name."

"I remember that summer. As I recall, you came back with a broken ankle. So, what you're telling me doesn't sound like the whole story."

"Yeah. There's a little more to it."

"Care to share?"

"What do you want to know?"

"Who is Robert? What does he do?"

"He's a jeweler."

"How do you know him? Should I be concerned about your relationship with him?"

Seb laughs. "It's not what you think, Steve. He's my uncle."

"If he's your uncle, wouldn't that mean that your dad's name would be Godwulf, too?

"Godwulf was my grandmother's maiden name—the nice grandma. Robert took her name. My dad kept his dad's name, Luca. I see Robert a lot because we both work with the agency."

"He's a model?"

"He does some of that, yes, but he works at another company that contracts with Mark."

"So he provides jewelry—for the models."

"Yesss..." Seb says in a way that tells me there's much more to this that he's not going to tell me today.

If I asked, we'd just go in circles. I'm so frustrated with all the lies and secrets that I can't take one more second of it. I feel like I need to get away from Sophie but at the same time I have to take care of her.

Back in the room, I rummage through my things for something... *anything*. But we packed in a hurry and I don't have any alcohol with me, nor do I have any pot. I find a bottle of Klonopin in Seb's drawer. Dangerous ground. It had been my drug of choice years ago, giving me a longer, more mellow buzz than Xanax. I convince myself I don't have any other option, so I pop a couple and within a few minutes I'm there but not there.

———

Our next appointment with Dr. Newman, I bring up our encounter with Robert. I explain that I'm concerned about what Seb is into and how he and Anna keep themselves hidden.

"This again, Steve?," Seb says. "Can you please just leave it alone? It's just modeling."

"So why do you need to be hidden from The Timeshare?"

"Because my job is to keep them safe. They don't need to worry about work stuff."

"Why would it worry them? If it's just modeling, why stay hidden?"

"Steve, you know about that world. There's some other work involved, particularly if you want to make any decent amount of money."

"Oh God, Sophie, are you still escorting?"

"I have some long-term commitments I need to keep, Steve. It's not a lot. I'm down to just a few clients at this point.

"Shit. That's why you're still getting STI tests every few months."

"Protocol," he says, expressionless. "Plus, it keeps you safe."

I'm stunned, and then I learn that Dr. Newman knew from the start and now *I'm pissed* that he hadn't tried to stop it. I wonder how much more he knew that I didn't. I feel desperate to know how deep this pit is.

This work is destroying my wife. *And* saving her. It gives her a sense of worth and power. She has her own money so she feels less "owned" by me, more able to be self-sufficient. The problem—and this is something she doesn't understand-is that in doing this work, she's risking our marriage.

As much as I hate it, it's easy to see how she got to this place. From what I'm learning, she'd always been exploited sexually one way or another. By the time she made the video that freaked me out, her life was hell. It made sense that this is where she wound up. There was never a time she wasn't working in that world.

Sebi begins to fill in some of the blanks and answer my questions. He provides details I didn't want to know to questions I couldn't stop myself from asking...

"Steve, this is just a job. It's really no different than being a chef or cleaning someone's house."

"It's significantly different, Seb."

"Am I going to get a lecture now?"

"No, I'll drop it, but seriously? Being a chef or cleaning someone's house isn't illegal. It's not unethical. It doesn't hurt you as a person. Let me ask something else—the weird cuts and marks on your wrists, the ones I saw that night we were getting ready for your art sale? You said those were an allergic reaction to the twine you used on those bracelets. What *was* it from?"

Sebi shivers and jerks his head. The eyes began to change and whoever is here is looking around. S/he closes the eyes and looks deep in thought. A minute later, s/he nods, then opens the eyes to reveal the emerald green of Sophie.

"Sounds like you've already figured that out," she says. "It was from Craig, the photographer? Sebi didn't know. But that's why Mark won't let me work with him again," she continues, rubbing her wrists. "He tied me up with film. It chafes like a son of a bitch.

"The driver saw it and reported it to Mark and took me to the doctor that Mark keeps on staff. He'll tell Craig I'm booked up for now but I have a feeling he'll be black-balled from the agency," Sophie adds.

"I need to tell you that I already knew," I say. "I looked up his website. There's a picture of you on there. And the film didn't just chafe. It *sliced up* your wrists. In the picture it also looks like you had a huge bruise on your ribcage. You never told me. It broke my heart to see that."

She looks away from me as she rubs her left side reflectively. Everything is coming out now and it seems like it's just too much. Sophie did the modeling. Sebi and Anna did the escort work. But it all went hand in hand.

I realize now *this* is what Sebi was worried about when he asked about how to get stuff off other people's sites. He *can* take down the stuff he put up, but other people have things on their websites as well, and he has no control over them. Now that he's healing and coming into greater awareness, he must feel exploited.

My words are catching in my throat. "Jesus, Sophie. Did you tell him he was hurting you?"

"I'm not sure he'd care. He's a bit of a sadist," she says. "Besides, it's easier not to say anything than to say something and have them tell you they know it hurts and they don't care. They're paying $300/hour. They own me for that time. They can do whatever they want."

"No, they *can't!*" I never knew whether to be more angry at Sophie herself or at her lack of understanding around how things in the real world worked. Dr. Newman had said that because of her abuse, she had absolutely no self-preservation instinct. But why didn't Ellyn educate her? Were they that compartmentalized?

Granted, the things she did are not things that people routinely discuss, so that's why it never came up. She honestly thought this was the way the world worked. This seemed normal to her.

"Sophie, think about it! If someone rents a *U-Haul*, they can't trash it. If someone rents *anything*, they can't abuse it. Why on *earth* would you believe it's okay for people to treat you that way?"

Sophie thinks about it for a minute and looks confused and ashamed—like she *should* know this. It's that regret you get when you find out you've been doing it wrong your whole life, and then discover how different your entire world would look if you'd had that information earlier.

"There's something else you should know," I add. "I spoke with Jeremy. I didn't tell him the picture was you, but he knows you model and he recognized you. He told me this guy is dangerous, Sophie, and he seemed really, really worried. He told me I had to get you away from him and he made it sound like this guy might hurt you worse next time."

"Jeremy is a drama queen," Sophie says. "Craig likes to make people think he's some hard core guy, but he's really harmless. I've known him my whole life. I went to school with him. He was a creep then and he's a creep now. He's the little pervert that hurt me playing doctor from the time we were in Kindergarten together. But I don't think he's ever seriously hurt anyone. Besides, there's something satisfying about having him pay me to model for him."

I was shocked that she felt what he did to her wasn't serious. "Sophie, that is a very dangerous game of cat and mouse."

Every time I think I understand the depths of this thing, another sinkhole opens up under me. While she doesn't seem to be worried about Craig, alarms are going off in my head and I'm terrified for her. I have a recurring nightmare about this—Sophie is walking towards the edge of a cliff, laughing and teasing me as I'm desperately screaming and trying to warn her. She won't stop and eventually slips over the edge. This feels a lot like that.

I knew Sophie would be in a bad place after all of this, but I wasn't in a great place either. This was why I was glad to be in the group for partners. When I felt like I was about to lose it, I had someone to call.

Sophie and I have both been put through the wringer by all the revelations. Yes, we came from different places, but we both felt like the reality we'd been living in was tearing us apart and all that we could see beneath it was more darkness.

———

We forced normalcy for the weekend. I'd either have to ignore the subject for now or get out. I dropped any talk about the agency. We purposely avoided *anything* having to do with multiplicity. Instead, we went through the motions: we ate breakfast in bed, went to a movie, cooked dinner together and laughed. We needed this reprieve desperately and it felt like the noose had been loosened for those few days.

June 23, 2016

On Monday, neither of us wants to go in to see Dr. Newman. I think we both feel like we've done so much work and need to rest for awhile. The problem is that we are in the middle of things that need to be resolved. So we decide we'd go to therapy but then treat ourselves to something fun afterwards. How we defined that depended on who was out at the end of our time today with Dr. Newman. We just never seemed to reach a stopping point with therapy.

Anna is with me. As soon as we sit down on Dr. Newman's couch, I start in. "I've had a lot of time to think about what you said last time and something is eating away at me. Sophie had once said that sex is just work to her. I need to know if she feels that way with me."

Over this time of knowing Sophie, I'd learned that, while most people find sex as a way to connect with their partner, for these parts of her, sex is no different than cleaning the toilet or vacuuming. It's something that needs to be done and it's easier to do it if you're paid for the work.

Now, I see Anna take in a sharp breath, yawn, and shiver and I know she's no longer in charge. For a brief moment, it looks to me like The Timeshare is going on autopilot. It's the oddest feeling—like no one is in the body. And then someone else is there, but I could feel there's a reluctance to come out. I don't know who it is.

In answer to my questions, I hear, "Sex isn't how we connect with you. No one in The Timeshare connects to you in that way. We can have sex, but it's no different than watching TV or sharing a meal."

I feel a consuming sadness. Sex, for me, is when I feel closest to Sophie. It's sacred and complicated, but to me it's the deepest point of connection I feel I can have with anyone and I realize, in that moment, that's what's missing with her. There's no real connection sexually—physically yes, but she was never really there with me.

"The only person," she says now, "I've ever connected with sexually is Laura. Other than that, sex is a job for me. It's just work."

I feel my heart crumble and try to remind myself that this is one aspect of my wife, just the opinion of one personality.

I recognize the posture, tone and accent of Sebi, but today he sounds so earnest, with no trace of the usual playfulness in his voice. He sounds vulnerable and I know this was his truth. It's rare for him to share at this level.

There's a pause and Sebi looks like he's searching, trying to decide if he could say what he needs to say next. I lean in and hold him in my gaze.

"I have to take a leap of faith," Sebi says now, but his voice is shaking. I'd never seen him this tentative or fearful. He pauses, leaving room for Dr. Newman or me to give him permission...or perhaps just to talk himself out of it.

I had learned to wait, so I just look at him without staring, trying to be as encouraging as possible. He looks back at me in a way that makes me wonder what's going to happen next.

"Steve," he says, pausing to be sure I'm tuned in. "I've wanted to tell you something that's really hard for me to say." He takes a drink of water and jokes, "It'd make my life a lot easier if this was vodka."

My heart races as I brace myself for more bad news.

Seb closes his eyes and takes another deep breath. He sits up and hits his head against the wall a few times and, with his eyes still closed, says, "God, this is hard."

Now I'm really worried. I'm not sure I can handle another betrayal. I feel a surge of panic as fight or flight kicks in. In my mind, I race through what might come next and wonder if the next thing he'd say is going to rip out my heart.

Instead, he gets up and starts pacing. Then, as he finally speaks, it sounds like he's thinking out loud.

"This is a struggle for me. I'm in such a weird place. I need to say this, but I need to be clear. I don't want to be defined by what I'm about to say and I don't want to hurt you." He consciously avoids my gaze.

"I don't even know if you want what I want," he continues. "I'm worried about jumping into something with you and then feeling like I'm at work, which would mess everything up. I'm having a hard time making that leap." He takes a moment to pull himself together and to take a breath.

"I couldn't have sex with you before because it felt like an assignment, like it was a job. It has to flow naturally from wanting it and the timing was never right. I didn't know if I should talk to you about it, just see if it happens or what, but...the bottom line is that I'm starting to have feelings for you and I want to try and connect with you...the way I connect with Laura."

He takes a shaky breath and it sounds like he's struggling with either panic or perhaps excitement. I can't read which. Then he's in front of me, crouching down and looking right into my eyes.

"When I play piano for you, when we play music together, that's how I connect with you. There's an intimacy to it." He takes my hands and his voice is intense. Like he really needs me to get this.

"That, to me," he continues, searching my eyes with his, "is like making love for other people. It's a connection in a safe place. I don't do that with very many people. Music sustains me. It gives me courage, confidence, peace of mind. It connects me to other people like sex connects you to people you're making love with. Music was where I hid. It's sacred. And I share that space with one person—you."

"I know you feel like I have a deeper bond with Liz and Laura," he continues, "but it's different. I want you to know playing music with you is huge."

I can tell he's struggling, but I'm still not clear on where he's going. I have an idea, but I don't want to guess at it. This is too vulnerable an area for both of us.

Sebi still can't look at me and, again, he closes his eyes and takes a deep breath before going on. As he continues, he fixes his gaze on the carpet. "It's just that...the music isn't enough anymore."

His heart is pounding so hard now, I can see the charm from his necklace dancing on his chest. "I feel like I want something more from you." He's crying now but the tears seem like they're coming from fear in the face of such vulnerability. "I need something more—with you. But it's been very confusing for me. It's taken me a long time to pull this apart and figure it out."

I don't understand what he's saying and I can't quite grasp the concept of connecting sexually through music. I don't feel that. So much of this I don't understand. I know sex means different things to different people. I know some people who just go through the motions after years of being married. Sex had little meaning to them. But I'd never heard of this idea that some other conduit like music can provide sexual satisfaction.

Then more registers—I think he's saying what I *had hoped* he'd say since I met him—that he wanted me, that he wanted us to be together and to be more than roommates.

He saw the hope in my eyes.

"Oh God, I was afraid you'd get *that* look. Steve, I don't know what this all means yet. I don't know if it *will* happen or when. And I can't give up Laura. I'm still straight. It's just that I've developed feelings for you, too."

Dr. Newman sits silently watching, available if we need help, but mostly just providing a safe place for us to talk. It feels so strange to be discussing such private matters with someone else present.

"I do have hope, Seb, and it's really nice. There's no pressure of an "if or a when." For me, it's enough to know that you have feelings for me. If it goes further, that's fine. But if not, I just feel grateful you want more of a connection. Remember, you have never owed me a thing. That's still true."

We skip the idea of doing something fun after our session. Instead, we both know we need time to think. Sebi seems embarrassed and I don't want to make it worse. We grab dinner and then he heads out to the shed to work—and he doesn't invite me to hang out with him as he often does. He just needs time. This realization represents progress for me. In the past I simply would have felt rejected.

Later, as I head to bed, I'm tempted to go out and tell him he's welcome to join me, but that might feel like pressure, so I stick with, "I'm heading up. Good night."

I hear, "Night" drift back to me from the shed.

―――――

The next morning, he's asleep on the couch, sprawled out with his arms stretched above his head. His face looks different from Sophie's—even when he's asleep. But I get the same feeling looking at him that I get when I see Sophie sleeping. I see an innocence come through that makes me feel like I'd do anything for them. I can almost imagine him as a little boy trying to protect Sophie. What a brave soul. I still wonder where he had come from, but I'm gaining a deeper appreciation and, if I was honest with myself, a stronger affection for Sebi.

I also notice a shift within myself. I'd always thought Sebi and I could be intimate because I saw him as Sophie. Now I don't. I see him as Sebi—a man, at least in spirit. He's been struggling with the idea that if we were intimate that would define him as bisexual, and that created a huge conflict. I was having my own struggles in that department as well. And while Sebi simply seemed confused by it, it scared me to death.

―――――

Early July is hit or miss weather wise. Today I'm grateful Dr. Newman's office is air conditioned.

"How did things go after you got home last time?" Dr. Newman asks as we walk into the office for our next session.

I'd been doing a lot of thinking. I'm happy that Seb's considering a change in our relationship, but furious that Dr. Newman knew about the escort work and hadn't tried to put a stop to it. I'm a mix of emotions and I don't handle it very well.

I have a chip on my shoulder. I feel like I've been lied to and I want an apology. I also want to hear Dr. Newman denounce the whole escort thing. It's clearly unhealthy and I'm ready to fire him if he doesn't.

I know therapy is about helping Sophie, but I'm feeling pissed off. "You know," I say, "in my partners' group I hear about people who have wives that prostitute, but I never thought I'd be in the same boat. I guess I thought Sophie was better than that. Smarter." It's one of those things you say in anger that you think is just you expressing your feelings and letting off some steam. But the instant you say it, you recognize that you've completely slammed someone you love. Then you spend the next few minutes trying to justify your own feelings while digging yourself out of the hole you're in, but you just wind up deeper in the ground. It never ends well.

Dr. Newman looks like he's deep in thought, but as I finish my diatribe, takes a breath, and says, "Steve, we spend a great deal of time talking about Sebi's indiscretions and, sometimes, judging them. But we've never really explored *your* history."

He had expertly turned the tables on me and I'm feeling extremely uncomfortable.

"I'm asking because sometimes what happens is we completely focus on one person and the other person feels ignored. And sometimes they have secrets they need to talk about, too. If both people aren't honest, it's not really fair. The Timeshare has put in a lot of work. Now it's your turn."

Dr. Newman leaves the door open to the discussion. I can pick up the conversation and run with it or I can leave it there.

"I think my stuff is pretty standard," I say. "Boring, to be honest. My parents had their own hang-ups around sex. My dad was really conservative and never discussed it, but he seemed happy with my mom. Mom was a feminist and she didn't hate men, but she did feel a lot of them exploited women. I felt like if I even *had* a sex drive, it was wrong. I never saw my dad even look at another woman. Porn wasn't allowed in the house. Obviously. We heard about sex from the time we were young, but it was more about consent than how to handle our own drives.

"Umm...my mom found a lingerie catalog in my room when I was a teenager and lectured me on objectifying women. My brother David unexpectedly came home from college and walked in on me having sex. I think I was 16. David is not a very compassionate guy and he held that over my head for a few months and then told my mom. She flipped out, worried I'd coerced my girlfriend into having sex. I explained it was the other way around, actually. I was fine waiting. She wasn't. She was a lot older than me—our student math teacher. Didn't end well for her."

"Anything else?" Dr. Newman asks, sounding a little bored.

"I think that's really it. We had sex ed in school so there was a lot of giggling. Oh, one time I was making out with one of my friends, Kibbie, on the bus when I was in 6th grade—it was dark, night time, on the way home from a field trip. Seemed like the right thing to do at the time, but I got sent to the principal's office for that. Maybe there's more there, but I can't think of anything else," I lie.

Now I feel like a coward. I finally appreciate how brave Sebi is to be so vulnerable, to bring up so many memories and feelings, to share his story in order to heal. The whole Timeshare is brave. But I'm afraid if I say more, it will give me away. I'm afraid of being judged, of being abandoned. I rationalize lying by telling myself it would be wrong to betray a long-held confidence. I'm afraid that if I say it out loud, it will begin to define me. No, I can't tell them. This is such a fragile and precious thing and I don't want anything to disturb it. I can't risk the things that are holding me together.

Dr. Newman looks at me for a long moment. Then he looks at Sebi and back at me. I feel like I'm under a hot interrogation light. "It's interesting that you have such a bland sexual history and yet something in you chose to be with Sophie, who has a very different history. Usually there's more there. You don't need to tell me. I'm not the one who needs to know. But if you want your marriage to have any sort of chance, I'd suggest you tell someone in The Timeshare. And I suggest you do it soon. We're done for today."

Dr. Newman gets up, opens the door and waits for us to leave.

I'm shocked the session ended so abruptly after only 15 minutes. Sebi puts his hands on my shoulders and steers me out of the office waving to Dr. Newman on the way out and telling me, "You'll get used to it. If you say something that pisses him off, he cuts your time short. I once told him I was beyond repair and I was sure he was going to kick my ass. Don't worry about it."

I'm touched by Sebi's generosity after I had basically just called him an idiot. I guess we're both getting better at not taking things personally.

———

I try to keep my problems to myself, but everything is piling up and I'm feeling buried. I was having a little pity party that I couldn't just let loose on Dr. Newman and have him do the work of translating it into something that made sense. I hadn't grasped how hard Sophie was working in therapy.

On top of problems at work and therapy weighing on me, my mom is continuing to get worse. It's hard to think of my parents growing older. I know my concern for her was weighing on my mind, covering my whole life with a veil of gray.

People like to think of a man as the rock, the solid one, no emotions. But I feel near the breaking point. In fact, with very few exceptions, I feel like my whole life has been unraveling ever since I'd learned about Sophie's multiplicity.

I didn't really need to talk about it again. There was nothing anyone could do, so talking seems pointless. It feels like everything is about to change and I just wanted to get back to solid land.

Seb is concerned. That night, we can't find our usual conversational rhythm. I'm in my head and Sebi's charisma isn't able to reach me. He can feel it, too, but, as usual, he never pries. If I wanted to talk, I would.

He starts rooting around in the kitchen and I can tell Jamie is out. He likes to use food to take care of people and when he senses things are bad, he cooks. He goes outside and grills steaks and onions for us as well as making some amazing flatbread and hummus with diced tomatoes and basil. We enjoy our meal with a little too much beer.

After dinner, Sebi's back out. He lies down on the couch and clicks on the movie *Dr. Strange*. Sebi and the others have a habit of watching the same shows over and over again. They say it's soothing. Sebi watched *The Incredible Hulk* so much he wore out the disc and had to get another one.

I finish up the dishes and come into the living room, bringing him another beer. Not wanting to take my assigned seat on the recliner, I pause at the foot of the couch. Sebi looks at me expectantly—waiting for an answer as to why I was hovering there, staring at him.

I'm trying to decide if I have the courage to ask for what I need. I'm still furious and worried about the escort situation but, at the same time, encouraged by Seb's attraction to me—and I'm terrified about this photographer I'd just learned about. Seb wasn't taking the issue seriously, and I have no idea how to keep The Timeshare safe. But I can't calm myself. I'd taken a couple of Sophie's Klonopin, and was waiting for them to kick in.

Sebi's intuitive and can read anyone easily—me better than most. He shifts his legs, dropping one foot to the floor and opening his arms, welcoming me to join him on the couch. I curl up and rest my head on his chest. Sebi runs his fingers through my hair and I ask if we can sleep in the same bed—no expectations. I just need to be next to him.

We stay together on the couch until the movie is over. I fall asleep and Seb has to help me up the steps. He peels off my shirt and pants and pours me into bed. Then he crawls in behind me, arms encircling me as he reaches for my hand. I smile seeing that we're in matching tanks and boxer shorts.

My exhaustion, fear and shame wring tears out of me and, as I cry, he holds me. No questions or judgment or pity. I feel safe here. I want more, but can't risk asking. I drift off feeling his steady breath on my neck. It's reassuring and familiar.

Even in my sleep, there's an awareness that I need to tell someone in The Timeshare my secret before it's too late. But it's such a comforting night for both of us and I feel closer to Sebi than ever. I'm beginning to see hope for our relationship in a way that I hadn't for a long time.

———

The morning light is just starting to make the room glow. I'm feeling warm in Sebi's embrace, content. I take a deep breath and can smell the steak and smoke and beer from last night's dinner. The scent of Sebi's subtle cologne feels like home. I'm still asleep enough not to have dominion over my senses but awake enough to enjoy the feeling of being held. Sebi's waking up and shifts his arm under me. It feels like he might be pulling away and an aching sadness is triggered in me that spreads over my whole body.

In my half-sleep, I'm still in my dream, still in a tent by the lake over a dozen years ago. I lace Sebi's fingers into mine, take a deep breath, and pull him back to me as I plead, "Please don't let go yet, Kibbie." It's a memory, not meant to be a confession, but I couldn't unsay it.

Sebi pushes out a laugh of disbelief and says softly, "What did you just say?"

I'm suddenly wide awake but disoriented. I don't know what I said. I'm just waking up and only have a vague feeling of saying something I shouldn't have. I begin to remember my dream and realize I let my secret surface while my guard was down. I'm not ready for this discussion.

"Who's Kibbie?" Sebi asks softly. There's curiosity in his voice but no judgment.

I can feel panic rising in my throat. I feel caught.

"I don't know what you're talking about. I didn't say anything," I blurt out.

Sebi's voice is playful—"You did, actually. You grabbed my hand, pulled me in close and said, 'Please don't let go yet, Kibbie.' Who is she? Is that the girl you were making out with on the bus in 6th grade?"

For a moment, I wonder if I can get away with telling him I was mumbling and he misunderstood—that I had said Sebi. Or perhaps I could just spin this so it felt safer. But I remember Seb's honesty and I want to respect that. I have to tell the truth—all of it—even if it means anger and rejection for me.

Seb hasn't pushed me away. He still has his arm around me and is holding my hand. He isn't angry and the question isn't accusing. I need to tell him.

He teases me, saying, "Tell me the story. It sounds like a good one."

"I would so prefer not to get into this right now."

Sebi laughs out loud, "I hear ya. That's the story of my whole fucking life. But you can't drop something like that and then not tell me the story."

I can't catch my breath. My stomach is churning and my heart racing, but I know I have to tell him if I want to save my marriage. I know sharing this sort of story could be uncomfortable and even hurtful. But it's also important.

"Okay, I'll tell you. Get comfortable. But promise not to judge me."

Sebi's smiling, eager to hear the story. "I *promise*," he says earnestly as he pulls me closer and holds my hand tighter.

"Remember how Dr. Newman told me I needed to tell you about my history—and I needed to do it soon? Well, here it is and, honestly, I'm pretty terrified to tell you this, so please be patient."

Seb's mood shifts with mine and he abandons his playful attitude for a more serious tone. "Of course."

"It was the end of my senior year of high school. Kibbie was one of my best friends. And yes, same person from the bus. We enjoyed a lot of the same things—we even double dated from time to time.

"Just before graduation, we went camping for the weekend. Our families camped together all the time and by high school, Kibbie and I would head for the lake any time things got too crazy. We both knew that this might be our last camping trip ever—we'd be starting our summer jobs soon and then would head to different colleges in the fall.

"There's a sense of finality your senior year of high school—lots of times you're doing fun things and a bitter sweetness creeps in because you know it may be your last time—your last dance, your last game, your last time walking down that hall, seeing that teacher, hanging out with friends...

"Anyway, we left Friday in the early afternoon and headed to the lake a few hours away. Before setting up our tent, we wandered around, reclaiming our old stomping ground. Pine trees growing out of rock outcroppings, blueberry bushes starting to sprout. The trail was familiar but new every time we camped. We went to the top of an outcropping to get a better view of the lake. It's the most peaceful place I've ever known.

"After re-acclimating, we settled down and pitched the tent and unloaded the car.

"My mom had made us foil dinners, cube steak with onions, carrots and potatoes with seasoned butter wrapped up in foil. We built a fire and while we waited for it to burn down to hot coals, we jumped in the water. It was a cool night, but the water still felt amazing. When it's cool out and you jump into a cooler lake, you feel alive in a different sort of way. It's like you come into awareness of every part of your body. Everything feels awake.

"We swam out to the raft a few yards from shore and then swam back. When my feet hit the shore, something jabbed me. Kibbie thought I was playing but then realized something was really wrong. I had stepped on something sharp like a piece of glass or something.

Kibbie helped me to shore. The water felt great, but this pain in my foot made me break into a cold sweat. I thought I might pass out. Having an arm around me—that warmth—felt like a life preserver, keeping me conscious. I was holding on for dear life and suddenly the attraction I'd felt for Kibbie for years became crystal clear to me. It wasn't just a friendship or playing around. I knew it was a love thing.

"My foot was bleeding, a fish hook hanging out of my heel. With a mom who's a nurse, Kibbie knew what to do. The hook had to be pushed through, the barb cut off and the other end pulled out. And then we poured some vodka over it and threw on a band aid.

"The fire had died down, so we tossed the foil packets in. We listened to them sizzle as the water lapped up on the shore. It was one of my favorite places to be and it was sad to think this might be my last time there.

"The sun was setting as we finished off dinner with some apple pie. That was followed with a few beers and some pot my brother got for us. Thinking back on it now, it was funny how nostalgic we were at only 18 years old. Our conversation covered a lot of ground that night—favorite teachers, past relationships, things we'll miss about high school, worries about college, politics, dreams.

"It was starting to get cold and we were feeling tired so we tossed some dirt on the fire and headed to the tent, thinking it'd be warmer.

"But it was unusually cool for late May and we hadn't anticipated that. We piled on the extra blankets that we found in the trunk, but they didn't help. After listening to one another's teeth chatter for a few hours, we debated about what to do—sleep in the car and run the heater? Unwise. We'd use up the gas and be stuck in the middle of nowhere with no phone service. Head home? No, neither of us wanted to give up our last camping trip.

"We agreed that body heat was the solution. When you've been friends for years and find yourself in this sort of situation, it's a weird area. Especially with my earlier revelation, I was trying to sort out how I could be essentially naked in a sleeping bag with Kibbie and not give myself away. We crawled in and made jokes to ease the awkwardness. It was a survival thing, so we didn't really have a choice. They say skin to skin is best, but that was just too weird. We took off our sweatshirts but kept on our T-shirts and sweatpants.

"We tried back to back but that didn't do much to keep us warm. We settled on Kibbie spooning me. It was ridiculous and several times we talked about going back. We were still too cold to sleep. But eventually, we gave in to exhaustion.

"We got a few hours of rest and, as the sun rose, the tent went from freezing to comfortable. Kibbie shifted and I don't know what it was, but something changed. Clearly still asleep, Kib's arm slipped away from my chest to my stomach. It felt strange so I grabbed it and pulled it back up, but our fingers laced and something sort of sparked.

"We'd been back to front for hours and the sun was making it warm enough that we were both sweating a little bit. The tent smelled like smoke and steak, cigarettes and beer, sunshine and cologne.

"I think that's what happened this morning...here. Our room reminded me of that night," I add.

"Steve..." Seb interrupts. "You're beating around the bush. I'm not going to judge you. I'm not going to be mad. This happened a long time ago. Ancient history. It's all good. Just tell me."

"I'm getting there. I told you to be patient, okay? This is tough for me. I had to work through a lot of my own crap to be able to get this far, you know?"

"Okay, I get it, but you're cooking breakfast after this."

"I'm gonna do that anyway. Just listen. I think what took me back there was that the tent smelled like our room this morning. Our family camped a lot, with a lot of friends. We'd been camping with Kibbie's family dozens of times. It was a place of comfort before heading into a completely unknown world that scared the shit out of me. I knew I had to go away to college. It was time. It was expected. But it was terrifying. And Kibbie stood between me and it. I felt safe..."

"I was groggy and Kibbie was sound asleep. I pulled in closer. It wasn't a sexual thing at all. It was...I don't know what it was. I felt like I just wanted to be held and if I'm honest about it, I wanted Kibbie to be holding me. I loved my girlfriend, but I was always the one protecting her, being strong, making her feel safe, killing the spiders, telling her it was going to be okay, shielding her from the scary movie. And I was glad to play that role in her life, but right then, in that tent, I wanted to feel safe and this was where I needed to be.

"Kibbie was still sleeping. He was totally out of it, probably thought I was his girlfriend because he just wrapped his arms around me tighter."

"Kibbie," Seb says. "Kibbie was a *guy*? Shit, Steve. I mean, I've always gotten a serious bi-vibe from you, but damn!"

I don't want to lose my courage and I'm terrified of Seb's reaction, but I have to get through this. "Can I finish the story, please?"

Seb shifts to get more comfortable, then pulls me back to him. I feel safe and don't feel any judgment. "Shoot," he says.

"Thank you. So," I continue, "I heard him take in a deep breath and wondered if he smelled the same comforting things I did. I wondered if he was feeling like he wanted to stop time for a couple of days. To be in this place between high school and the real world. To stay here a little longer, knowing we'd have to go soon and we could never come back.

"I felt his face move closer to my neck and he breathed in again. I still don't know if he was awake or asleep, but I felt his nose brush against my ear and there was this sort of pulse that ran through me. His arm moved from encircling me to a hand on my arm and as he pushed me away, I thought he'd woken up, discovered we were spooning and realized it was warm enough that we didn't need to be doing that anymore. And something in me felt tremendous relief and crushing disappointment. It was a strange mix. We'd be packing up to leave soon and I had to recognize something I wanted very much had come to an end before it even started. I begged him not to let go yet.

"The *instant* I said it, I regretted it. He didn't know how I felt—how I'd been feeling for a long time, but couldn't admit—even to myself. And now that he knew, I was sure that'd be it.

"When he pushed me away, I felt something inside me die. Then he was looking at me, taking me in like he'd never seen me before, his hand still on my arm. He looked wide awake now and I could tell he was trying to make a decision. I felt like he was trying to decide between punching me in the face or taking off without me.

"He swallowed hard, moved his hand to the back of my neck,

pulled me to him and kissed me on the lips. I was confused more than anything, wondering if I was still dreaming..."

I stop the story abruptly, feeling I've betrayed a confidence and that it might shatter that pure memory. I'm leaving the door wide open to Seb's judgment and I can't say any more until I know how he's going to react.

My voice cracking, I end with, "You can fill in the rest of the blanks. But he's married now. He's the only guy I've ever been with. Same for him."

I'm feeling I've opened my chest and laid my heart at Sebi's feet. I look at him, searching his face for a clue as to how he feels.

I don't want to get into this in therapy. If we do, I feel like my whole life will unravel. "*Please* don't tell Dr. Newman."

I'm worried that after this confession, Seb might—out of anger. After all, we'd brought in everything he had done, every wrong he'd committed in our marriage. He'd be justified in bringing it up.

Sebi's voice is deeper than I'd ever heard it, quiet and reassuring as he tells me the same thing I'd heard him say to the people of The Timeshare when anyone asked a question about someone else's pain: "Not my story to tell. If it's important, you'll bring it up."

Telling Sebi my secret was embarrassing and I feel exposed. It was such a relief to tell him but it's also terrifying because I didn't know how he'd react. And I miss Kibbie. Or really, I miss feeling like someone else is stronger. It was hard feeling like I had to carry everything on my own. I feel like I should tell Seb the rest of it, but I can't work up the courage. Not yet.

Sebi pushes me away to look in my face. I flush with shame and brace myself for what would happen next. Then he puts his hand behind my neck, pulls me to him and brushes his lips against mine as he softly asks, "Was it like this?" waiting a beat before kissing me with an intensity that steals my breath.

I close my eyes and feel a little dizzy, terrified and more turned on than I've felt in a very long time. I also feel afraid that if we go on, I could completely let go with him—more than I could with Sophie or anyone else in The Timeshare. It feels irresponsible. It also feels like something I very much need.

"Seb?" I ask, feeling confused. I don't know if he's so angry that he's trying to hurt me by mocking me, if he's turned on, or if he's just trying to understand.

"Shhh," he whispers, kissing me again. When Anna kissed me, it was a sort of unengaged sharing of the space. With Chelsea, there was a desperation. But I didn't feel any real engagement with them. It was like it didn't really matter who they were with. When Sebi kisses me, it's like he's drawing me in, like he wants to slowly merge with me.

I don't want to stop him, but I need to be sure this is okay. The last time we tried, it had been a disaster. I feared if it went badly again, it could destroy our relationship. I try to tell him this was a terrible idea. He totally Alpha-dogs me, just as Kibbie had years ago. After having to be the one to handle everything for so long, it actually feels amazing.

Whenever I try to ask if he's sure, he silences my objections with a kiss or gently covers my mouth with his hand or dances around my ear with his tongue or kisses my neck until I can't think straight. His skin is so soft and his scent pulls me further into the experience. He smells different than Sophie. It's more than the cologne. It's indescribable and lends itself more to evoking a feeling within me than a conscious recognition of any specific scent.

Once I'm able to begin letting go a little, we find the same flow that we have when we cook together, when we talk, when we work on his art together. We enjoy the same flow we have when we play music together. It was completely different than being with Anna or Chelsea or anyone else in The Timeshare.

As we touch each other, and kiss each other and move together, we're both pretty vocal. I look and listen for signs of other alters. I never feel I can really enjoy sex because I'm so on guard watching to be sure no one comes out who can be hurt by what we're doing. I have to be so tuned in to the cues, that I can't fully lose myself in the experience.

I begin my usual routine, I kiss the lips, move to the neck and then the chest. My mind isn't really engaged in what I'm doing. I know we might need to stop at any point, so I never allow my body to completely engage. This is just habit.

Sebi stops abruptly and I'm momentarily terrified someone else is coming forward—someone angry. But it's Sebi. He gently holds my face in his hands, looking unflinchingly into my eyes as he firmly instructs me, "You don't need to do that this time. Slow down." Then he flips me away, my hands suddenly in his as he straddles me and pins me to the mattress. "We have all day."

He sits back and holds me in his gaze. I feel like he's soaking me in. Then painfully slowly, he run his fingers down my chest, stopping at my navel. He looks at my face, cocks his head sideways and watches me, evaluating my reactions. I think I still look a little concerned and confused as to what's going to happen next.

Sebi smiles but it's not warm. It's wily. He begins kissing me and each time I try to touch him or rush, he silently and playfully pushes my hands away, laughing. Then he moves back to my neck, which feels like both punishment and reward. There's a fun to sex with him that I'd never experienced with anyone else.

No one in The Timeshare enjoyed oral sex. It had been so exploited for them...but I missed it—not that I'd experienced it very often. I think so many women who have had awful experiences with it.

But that morning, I learned this was not an experience that had been ruined for Sebi. I shudder in shock and pleasure when he takes me into his mouth and, as he continues, whenever he feels me tense, he would stop, put his hand on my stomach to calm me, wait for me to relax into it, and continue. As I get closer, he reaches for my hand. I'm certain he'll stop, but he doesn't.

I fell asleep with Sebi lying on my chest and I have never felt so relaxed and content. I didn't have to be on guard making love with him.

When I wake up a few hours later, I hear Sebi in the kitchen cooking. Or, *trying* to cook. I come down the steps and wrap my arms around him and he starts laughing, showing me a plate of burned bacon. "Hey, it's Cajun," he jokes. I'm doubled over laughing and when I stand up, he gives me a look like REALLY? and laughs with me before saying, "Help me out, would you? I can't work Jamie's damn stove."

I finish the bacon as Sebi works on the blueberry pancakes.

We sit down to our meal and I eat a bit and stop. I'm starving, but suddenly I feel concerned about my appearances. I want to look my best for him.

He looks across the table and tells me, "You better carb load. We have a lot of work to do this afternoon and you're going to need your strength." If we're heading to the art shed, it means a long day of heavy lifting, so I eat.

After breakfast, I get up to do dishes and Sebi grabs my hand, "Leave 'em." He leads me to the bathroom where we shower together—something I'd never done with any of them. I'm glad to have our intimacy extended a little longer. We dry each other off and as I begin to head for the closet to get my clothes, he playfully asks, "Where do you think you're going?"

"To the closet, to get dressed. You said we had a lot of work to do."

"Not that kind of work," he smiles at me and raises his eyebrow as he takes my hand again and leads me back to bed.

This time, we experiment to learn what we like, what we need from each other. It's relaxing, fun and honestly, educational...

"I'm not complaining," I say, "but why didn't we start with this?"

"Because you needed to relax first, to trust me. And I don't know how you could think straight with all that tension. Now, you've told me your secret and you've been in my mouth. That takes trust. So we can tell the truth about what we enjoy in bed. You know I'm open and you're not worried I'll learn some deep, dark secret."

"That's true. It feels like a weight's been lifted." It's a half truth, but true enough that I can honestly agree with him. I need to tell him the rest.

"Look, Seb, I need to tell you something before we do anything else."

"Uh huh. *Later.*" There's a playfulness in his voice but it's seductive.

I reason that I can tell him later. Like any guy, I had some ideas. I also know Sebi has a lot more ideas and far more knowledge in this area and it didn't bother me for him to be my teacher.

Sophie and I married fairly young and with the two other women I'd been with, doggie style was about as crazy as it got. And then Kibbie.

I joke that maybe we need the checklist from Dr. Newman.

He smiles back at me, "That's just a good starting point."

I realize that while I don't know what half of those things on Dr. Newman's list are, to Sebi they're just the basics.

Before each new experience, Sebi starts by asking if I had already tried it. That was generous of him, actually, knowing that I hadn't tried *anything*. He explains different techniques to me and then asks if it sounds interesting. We spend the next few hours experimenting with things he had kept hidden around the bedroom, laughing about safe words, trying things out and stopping when it's uncomfortable or we decide we didn't like it.

In the past, Anna had taken her cues from me. Chelsea did whatever she wanted to do and was really dominant. But with Seb, it feels like we're partnering. Some things we did I regretted not knowing about years ago because they were so amazing. Orgasm denial? Dear God, yes! Hottest thing on the entire planet. I wondered why I'd never heard of it before. Some things surprise the hell out of me. I'm not a fan of pain generally, but Seb finds some appealing and rather elementary options to try.

At one point, he pulls out a knife and raises his eyebrow in question. I laugh and tell him, "Oh, hell no."

Our morning session had involved an easy flow. But in the afternoon, there's a lot of stopping and starting and consent discussed. Seb puts on some music that I'd heard before and hadn't thought of as erotic then. This time, I do. I can see how all of this could build trust fast. And he was right. I am glad I'd carb loaded.

We sleep again and then call for pizza in the early evening.

———

Sebi is completely different than anyone I'd ever been with. Confident, in control, knowing exactly when to make things more intense and when to back off. He wanted to learn everything about me and when I'm not sure about something, he talks me through things. The attention feels incredible. Just for a moment, the gray veil lifts and I no longer feel even a hint of loneliness.

Sebi stays with me that entire night, the whole next day and another night. I'm grateful for that, but I also know that it indicates he's very likely sharing the role as host with Sophie. Alters rarely stay out for more than a few hours.

As we play, we also talk about other fantasies I had. I'm embarrassed that my most frequent one was being with two people at once—Sophie and someone else. Or maybe Sebi and someone. But Sebi just smiles and tells me it's okay. Most of us have similar fantasies.

"So when the girls are here, are you jealous of them or me?" he jokes.

"Probably all of you," I laugh back.

Through the entire day, he asks me what like, what I want and need. He's very present and patient and generous. With Anna, at times, I felt like she really just wanted me to get on with it so she could go to sleep.

No one else in The Timeshare felt this relaxed about sex. It was like they were somewhere else when we made love. But Sebi is there. He's able to relax into the moment and being present means that he's truly with me and feels everything intensely.

He makes me feel like a talented lover, which is something I had never experienced. He makes love like he eats food—gratefully, passionately. But there's something else. There's this patience that just makes the desire build. He forces me to take my time. He wants this to last as long as possible.

I was savoring it, too. I didn't want it to end. And I didn't know if this was a one-time thing or just the beginning.

When we finally get out of bed the next morning, I feel like a new person. I feel safe and loved. I feel fulfilled. And I feel satisfied in a way I never had with Sophie. I pushed away guilt and worry. I just wanted to enjoy the buzz.

I thought breakfast might be uncomfortable after launching into this new relationship so hardcore and so fast, but it isn't. It's like the morning after you finally make love with someone you know is going to be with you for a long time. You're basking in this stupid, pure joy—like it's a bubble surrounding your whole life. Everything feels brighter and you're relentlessly happy.

We had finally consummated this relationship and it feels like a new start. We hold hands at breakfast, share pecks on the cheek and long kisses.

At one point, I ask, "Seb, can I ask you about the music thing? How you connected to me through the piano? I've never really understood that. I thought the piano was a negative thing for The Timeshare. Is it sort of a defiance thing like it is for Elizabeth?"

"No, it's not defiance. I don't see it the same way as the others. Music saved me. Grandma taught me how to focus on it when I needed to zone out—to not see and hear the horrible things that were happening around me. It was my secret weapon, like a shield. I never saw her piano playing at night as impending doom. For me, it was like an early warning system. And so playing piano for you is a way of connecting with you on the most intimate level—a way of keeping you safe.

"Sophie has a special connection to music, too," he continues. "Before things went to shit that summer in San Francisco, her mom was teaching her to play guitar. I think that's why she loves it so much when you play. It means home to her. It feels like love."

Like Sophie, Seb had grabbed onto every scrap he could in order to survive. And when he played piano for me, it was sacred to him. A commitment. A connection. I got it now.

Sebi looks thoughtfully at me for a long moment. Then he squints his eyes, pulls out a cigarette and lights it.

I squint back at him—sort of a joking mental judo match. He knows I prefer he smoke outside and it isn't cold and snowy this time.

"You keep asking me where I came from. You've always deserved to know and I feel like I'm ready to tell you," he starts.

"Okay," I say slowly, feeling the guilt creeping back in. I still had secrets and I wasn't sure it was okay to keep them. Telling them feels like a betrayal of someone I cared about and keeping them to myself feels like a betrayal of The Timeshare. But now is not the time. Soon, though. I just needed time to think it through.

"I know that a lot of what you've heard hasn't made sense," Seb says. "I hope that what I tell you will help. I was a real person outside of Sophie, but I have always been with her. Since before she was born."

This sounds like more riddles.

He stops, realizing that, for me, this news might seem strange and unsettling. "I left my body when I was 13. I was ready to leave it, but Sophie couldn't let me go."

"What are you talking about—left your body? Who were you?"

"I'm Sophie's male half."

"What does *that* mean—male half?"

"Steve, I'm her twin brother. After that winter when she was sent to San Francisco, we promised we'd never be separated again. And the only way we could guarantee that we'd be together was to die together. We talked about heaven, what we'd heard about it. That children always go there and it's a place where you feel unconditional love, where you're held and always safe. Sounded pretty good. I had a suicide pact with Sophie. But I died. She didn't. Last thing I remember is hearing the piano music drifting up from the basement and smiling, knowing that Sophie would never have to endure anything ever again...."

"Oh my God. I never knew that Sophie had a brother...a twin? I get that things were so bad that suicide seemed like the only solution. That's so horrible, though."

"It was, it *was* horrible. We were really close. They wanted a boy, so I was treated like a prince. I tried to protect Sophie as much as I could, but I had to be careful because Papa could turn on a dime. I got hit more than once and I was spanked a lot, locked in the basement, but overall, it was nothing compared to what Sophie went through. By 13, neither of us could stand it anymore. Sometimes it's worse to hear people you love being hurt than being hurt yourself. But they were thinking of sending her away again, this time to an institution or something."

"We did that explicit video monologue and put it online. Sort of a last-ditch scream for help, but no one seemed to get it."

"I thought it was disturbing. It scared *me*," I say.

"Wish someone like you would've seen it back then. We didn't let it show, but we appreciate your reaction. It means a lot to us that you get it."

"I just don't understand how no one stopped this."

"Bystander effect." Seb says, staring off into space.

"What's that?"

"It means that everyone thinks someone else has already done something. People don't want to get involved, particularly when you have to go up against someone powerful."

I could see how that could happen, but it also really bothers me.

"We both took a bunch of pills before bed. Papa wound up going into Sophie's room in the middle of the night, so he found her and got her to the hospital. They didn't know I'd taken the pills too and wanted to let me sleep, so I didn't make it.

"Things got a lot worse for Sophie after that. They tried to get her put away, but she was too functional. Boarding schools wouldn't take her because she wasn't functional enough. They even called to see if they could put her in foster care."

"Jesus! That's just insane that they did that. And you were a real person who died. Like actually her twin brother?"

"Yes. You've seen pictures of me. And you've seen the video. After I died, she felt like she couldn't live without me, so she integrated me into The Timeshare. You've seen the tattoo, right?" he asks.

"Seb, Sophie has a lot of tattoos. Which one?"

"The one on her left wrist. It says 316." He lays his arm down on the table and runs his finger over the numbers.

I had, of course. "Yes, I've seen it. She said it reminds her that all things pass because school got out at 3:16 each day. Whether it was good or bad, all things pass."

"That's an interesting reality. Actually, March 15th is her birthday—born just before midnight. I was born just after. We decided to die on our 13th birthday. She wrote about it in the hospital after I died. She said, "My brother's body is deep in the ground, but I carry his soul with me as a sacred guardian." They thought it was poetic. Didn't realize it was literal, I guess. That tattoo signifies my presence. I'll never leave her.

"Papa told her my death was the debt I paid for her survival. Do you believe that? He never missed an opportunity to twist the knife."

I swallow hard, but have no answer.

"Still, she was right. All things do pass. After I died, I was integrated into The Timeshare and I'd step in to help when life was too much for her. Over time, I did that more and more. And now, we're here. She's hardly around anymore. I think it's just easier for her to switch than to fight. When you live with chronic pain, every single day is a battle. It's exhausting."

Seb began to trail off, but found his way back. "What we believed about death—that you're being held—it's why when Liz is here, we sleep in the same bed. I need that. I'm not sure I can ever get enough of being held."

"I understand that. I'm glad you have her. I get it now. Your relationship is deeper than a sexual one. Different."

"Yes, exactly. We don't have sex, but our relationship is very intimate."

"Was your name Sebastian when you were in your own body?"

"Yes. It's my paternal grandfather's name—the one who came from Romania. The first-born son is named after the grandfather. We were Seb and Sophie."

"Thanks for telling me, Seb...Sebastian." I hold his hands to my lips and kiss his fingers.

I can tell he feels nervous. He says, "Steve, I know you and I sleep separately because The Timeshare gets freaked out sometimes when we wake up and the others don't always recognize you." He pauses to blow a breath out and take a deep breath in. He can't look at me as he asks, "and I know it's a hassle, but can we give sleeping in the same bed a try again?"

"I'd love that," I tell him, relieved that we seem to be moving back towards normal.

Then his expression changes. "Oh! I have to show you something!"

He gets up and runs out to the studio, coming back with his drawing board. He pulls out the back so it's standing in front of me like a picture frame.

Looking back at me is a broad-faced young man with a cleft in his chin and short, wavy caramel-colored hair framing his face. He has wide set, deep-blue eyes that look like they're dancing, and a big smile with slightly crooked teeth. He's really quite beautiful.

"*This*," he says proudly, "is *me!*"

"Oh my God!" I feel my breath being stolen. "I know you." I run to the photo album and pull out the picture of Sophie and Jamie in Kindergarten. The boy on the other side of Jamie is little Seb. A charming smile on his face, no one would've guessed what was going on at home. And now I recognize him from the video. I can't help but cry.

I can see elements of that person in my wife's face. They were twins, but Sebi has more male qualities—and blue eyes. I understand why it's so important for him to show me. This is a mirror for him, one that actually looks exactly like him.

The miraculous thing is not that his gift had asserted itself—he's a talented artist and only needed the confidence, perspective and practice to succeed. The miracle is that once Rachel had exposed the block—the cruel way that Seb's grandmother had treated his win that day—and it was recognized and spoken, it faded into the background.

He had come so far with his drawing and he was able to translate who he saw in his mind into his portraits very clearly.

His phone rings and we both jump. It's as if the world is intruding on our little sacred space we created together and I resent it.

He looks at his phone and winces. "I have to take this. It's Laura."

He runs up the stairs and I hear the bedroom door shut quietly. I can hear him pacing and a few parts of the conversation when it gets loud. I hear Seb explaining something and then he's offering staccato sentences clipped off by Laura's interruptions.

"I know, that's what we agreed but I..." "I'm sorry." "I'm so sorry. I thought you'd want to..." "Yes, I get it. I do. I know that. I know I messed up." "I'm sorry." "I love you."

Sebi comes down the steps, sighs deeply and looks at me with a dejected smile, "Well, that sucked."

Seb, Sophie and I had discussed our relationship and worked out agreements for his relationships with Liz and Laura. But it never occurred to me that he might have agreements with them.

The situation suddenly seems ridiculous. I was violating his relationship agreement with his girlfriend by having sex with him—my wife. Or...husband. Whatever.

"You okay?" I offer as I put my hand on his shoulder.

He wraps my arms around his waist, resting his head against me. "Yeah, I think I'm more okay than I've been in a long time. I'm gonna go get dressed and then I need to finish some stuff in the shed. Wanna hang out?"

"I do. And, Seb?"

"Yeah?" he says, looking distracted.

"Seb."

He stops what he's doing and looks at me, raising his eyebrows in question.

My heart is beating in my throat. "I need to tell you something. I've wanted to tell you all night but now I can't seem to say it out loud..." I close my eyes and tilt my head back at the ceiling as I take a deep breath. "OK if we talk about it at Dr. Newman's?"

Seb looks confused and worried, but there's a sweetness in his face, too. "Sure."

He doesn't press me for details but leaves space for me to say more if I want to. He gives me a look like, "last chance..." and I reply with, "I'll start another pot of coffee."

Five days later

We have an appointment with Dr. Newman coming up and while so much had happened in our relationship, neither of us wants to share any of it with a therapist. This feels private. Instead of feeling guilty, I think we both agree it's a step in the right direction. Healthy boundaries and all that. But I do need to tell Seb the rest of my secret and I worry how it will be received. I knew I was wrong to keep this from him, but he'd been cool about what I'd told him so far, so maybe it'd be okay.

We head into the office. Dr. Newman doesn't apologize for tossing us out last time but, instead, gets right to the point.

"Last time we were all here together, I felt like there was some judgment I wasn't comfortable with. I also felt there was more to Steve's story than he was saying. As I told you, I don't need to know all the secrets. But I do think that if you keep too many big, essential secrets from each other, it can destroy your relationship.

"Have you two been able to talk since our last visit?"

Seb and I look at one another, not wanting to reveal too much. We both smile and nod. "Yeah, we've...talked," Seb says.

Dr. Newman's eyes narrow as he sighs and takes a sip of tea, evaluating me. I feel like he's looking through my soul.

"About all of it? You didn't leave anything out?" he asks.

I'm confused by his question but it's also making me feel anxious. I shake my head and feel my face fill with heat. Dr. Newman reads it as a *No*. He holds me in his gaze and it's unnerving.

"You're shaking your head *No* like you didn't tell Seb the whole story. Would it be easier to do that in here or out there?"

"I actually talked with Seb about this a few days ago. I'm having a hard time voicing it." Suddenly, I feel a flash of shame and wonder if I could lie my way out or if I could just tell him a half truth.

Sebi looks genuinely worried now. I was the strong one, the "perfect" one, as Seb has told me. Even in my family, I was the one who always did the right thing. And now?

I don't say anything for a moment, running through everything I can possibly come up with to get out of this. I opt for changing the subject and understand now why Sebi had misdirected me so often. It was as if I was standing in his shoes.

Now I blurt out, "I've been in therapy before."

Dr. Newman gives me a little smile, like he admires my ingenuity. More likely he doesn't mind this detour. It's information and it might help me ease into more difficult truths.

"I wondered," he says now. "You seemed pretty at ease coming in here the first time. Tell us about that."

"It was when I was in high school. You know, when you model, they line you up with everyone else and just go through and dismiss one person after another, stating the reason—too tall, too short, your face is too narrow, crooked teeth. I had a few auditions where I heard the same thing over and over: "Too chubby.""

"I went on a diet. It started by just going off red meat. My brother gave me so much crap about it, but I didn't care. Then I cut out dairy, soy, sugar, gluten. I dropped about 20 pounds and work started picking up for me. But I still felt fat, not muscular enough. I hit the gym more. I cut out more foods and eventually I was down to eating just veggies. I knew my mom would worry, so I wore baggy clothes and found ways to hide my weight loss.

I was always cold and started to grow this weird hair on my face and arms. I was dizzy all the time and when I tried to eat anything other than cooked veggies, I would instantly get sick. About six months later, we were at the pool and it was really warm. I wouldn't take off my sweatshirt. My mom knew something was up and demanded I take it off. She saw my ribs and spine, and how skinny my arms were and she cried. Then she took me to the ER. At that point, I was down to 115 and the doctor recommended a treatment program for anorexia.

"Because I was underage, I wasn't allowed to work until I gained at least 20 pounds. I missed the money, so I was motivated. I tried an outpatient program first but it didn't take. I gained a little weight, but not enough. I had no appetite and I couldn't digest anything other than broth and baby food and protein drinks.

"Then I did a 30-day inpatient. After that, I had therapy for a year. When I started the program and they'd talk about feelings, I told them that, honestly, I didn't *have* any feelings. I thought I was being honest. A lot of people felt the same way—just totally out of touch with their emotions. But we spent a lot of time on that. Probably why I know what I feel and I'm generally not afraid to talk about it. I think it also helped me read other people's emotions.

"I was the only guy in a program with 23 women, so I feel like I learned a lot from them—you know, about what women go through and what life is like for them. Obviously, I can't get inside of what it's like precisely, but I understood a lot more than before I went in. And I already knew about being judged on appearance, being objectified, being reduced to what you look like, or more precisely, what's wrong with you.

"I thought about getting out of modeling, but I felt like I got more out of it than it took away from me, so I stayed in. Just learned to take better care of myself."

Dr. Newman waits, looking at me in case I have more to say. I don't. "What else did the doctors say?" he asks.

I realize it's useless to try and hide anything and quickly surrender. "They diagnosed me with depression and some anxiety."

I could see that Dr. Newman had read something into that statement that made him feel there is more. "And what else?" he pushes. He's really pissing me off now, but at least I'd get it all out at one time.

"And a problem with pills."

"What kind of pills did you have trouble with?"

I can see the direction we are going and don't want to answer, but I figure it'd be worse if I lied. "Mostly tranquilizers—Xanax, Ativan, Valium, Klonopin. I was always so stressed out. Look, this is not really what I needed to talk about."

Sebi moves to sit next to me and rub my back. I feel bad telling him all this. It feels more manipulative than anything. I hadn't said it for sympathy. I said it because it seemed *less* bad than the truth I knew I needed to share—less painful for Seb.

Dr. Newman sounds like he's thinking out loud..."Hmmm, things are pretty stressful now. And Sophie has a lot of those meds lying around..."

Shame melts away and now I'm resentful.

"How are you coping?"

"I'm fine. I'm eating, I'm not depressed."

"That's good. Any more to that story?" His voice is kind, but I hate his questions.

"Nope," I say, realizing I had more than one skeleton in my closet. I don't want to tell him I'm borrowing pills from Sophie. First, it's not that often, but, second, I can't afford to have that crutch kicked out from under me right now.

He can tell I'm lying and I can practically hear him filing it away for later.

"Okay then. That was an interesting detour, Steve. We can take as much time as you need, but if there's anything else, now's the time. You said you had something to tell Seb and I have a feeling we haven't gotten to that yet, have we?"

"No, actually." I feel like I'm going to have a heart attack. I'm sweating and I feel sick.

Seb takes my face in his hands and looks in my eyes, "You can tell me. You're going to feel better, I promise."

At that, Dr. Newman throws me a lifeline. "Steve, why do you think you were depressed?"

I hadn't thought about it for years. I'm not sure I even knew at the time. But today it came to me in a flash and it was a road I didn't want to go down. Dr. Newman has taken me off a safe path to one that scares the hell out of me. I feel terrible about hiding this. I should have brought this up last year—or at least before Sebi and I made love.

"I think it was because I was denying my own feelings," I blurt out now.

Dr. Newman asks the obvious. "About what?"

"About a friend." I want that to be enough. I'm feeling judged, and I can feel my face flush.

"It sounds like you don't want to talk about this, but I think it's important. Do you feel it's important enough to keep going?"

A chill runs through me. He's right. This is important. But there's no way to put this gently. No way to sugar coat it or make it more palatable. I wanted some sort of bridge or transition to make this easier for The Timeshare, and for me, but there isn't one.

Tears start flowing and that makes me angry. I don't want to cry about this. I don't want to let it go. I just want to bury it. I also feel like I didn't deserve to cry. I'm such a hypocrite.

Sebi grabs my hand and looks me in the eye, "You've been holding this in for so long, Steve. Whatever it is, you have to let it go."

He's right, of course, but it doesn't make this any easier. "Yes, okay. I got depressed because I had feelings for someone I didn't think could return them...someone I felt was unreachable. Someone I felt ashamed to love. I felt very alone."

Sebi is looking at me with so much love it's killing me. We're partners now and he's standing with me. I couldn't bear to lose him.

I look at Dr. Newman and he's patiently waiting for the rest. I feel grateful he isn't pushing me.

"That's why I got depressed."

"Can you tell me how that ties in with today? I think there's a reason you brought it up. It feels like it's connected to what you really want to tell Sebi."

I feel like I'm playing emotional chess with Dr. Newman and he's the master. He could read the entire game before we even started. I hadn't consciously seen any connection between the two topics. Now, it's too late to backtrack.

I nod slowly as I take in what he was saying and begin… "I had a group of really good friends growing up—all the way from kindergarten through high school. I had a crush on one of them for a long time. We kissed in 6th grade on the bus and while it was an attraction thing for me, I'm not sure it was reciprocal. It seemed like curiosity.

"Nothing else happened for a long time, but then senior year of high school we went camping and it went further. Seb, what I told you the other night, that was the first time with Kibbie, but it wasn't the last time."

"Were you together during college? Because you and I got together …sophomore year for me," Seb says. "But you were in grad school. And I know we both had starts and stops with school."

"No, Seb. After that summer, we didn't see each other until years later, at our high school reunion. Then I didn't talk to him again until about six years ago."

"Six years ago?" Seb was calculating in his head. "That was around the time you found out about The Timeshare. Was it because you found out about us?"

"No, Seb. Honestly, this has *nothing* to do with you. He called me out of the blue and we started talking from time to time, and then more often. His wife is seriously depressed and he knew I'd been through that too, so he called and asked for some advice. His name is Kevin, but ever since kindergarten I've called him Kibbie."

Seb and I had just spent an entire weekend building trust and now, just like that, I was tearing it all down.

He's quiet, taking this in and trying to make it fit into his understanding of who I am. He stutters back, "Please tell me that you hooked up at the reunion."

"No, honey, we didn't hook up then."

"So this was six years ago? I'm hoping that it's just talking."

"It was at first. It was just talking for a long time. Years. But to be honest, even that felt wrong. I felt like I should be talking with you about the things I took to Kevin."

Seb is quiet, looking at the corner of the ceiling and chewing on his lip.

I feel I need to fill the silence, to explain..."His wife is really sick and he just didn't know who to turn to, so he called Rebecca to get my number, and when we talked, it just all came back, for both of us, I think."

Seb can't look at me. "You need to stop talking. JUST. STOP. TALKING."

He swallows hard, closes his eyes and leans his head against the wall. He's clenching his jaw as he tries to put everything together.

"How long have you been fucking him?" he asks coldly, without opening his eyes.

"It was honestly only a friendship until a couple months ago. It was right after our trip to Berkeley. You have to understand, Seb: I felt I was losing Sophie. And he felt his wife was slipping away, too. You have your own relationships. I wish I could tell you it's just sex, but I love him. Sebi, I'm so sorry, but I do."

"When do you see him?"

"When I go to the condo. Sometimes when I travel for work."

"So this has been going on for the past two months and you didn't tell me about it?"

I felt defensive now. "Seriously? This is a little like the kettle and the pot, Seb. You've been screwing around on me for years."

"That was not screwing around. I'm not married to you! How often do we have to cover the same damn ground?"

"And I'm not married to you, Sebi. So why is it considered screwing around when I do it, but not when you do it?"

Dr. Newman steps in, trying to avoid escalation of our argument. "The timing on all of this isn't good. And there have been lies of omission on both sides. There are also *reasons* that you have reached out to other people. Let's not make this into a story of betrayal. Let's see all of this as coping. We can sort out the blame later."

All Seb can see is that I was hurting Sophie. "I'm angry that you lied to me and I'm furious that you're screwing around on Sophie. She would never do that to you. This is going to really hurt her."

"I know. *And I don't want her to be hurt.*"

We stay with Dr. Newman for the rest of the hour, but I can't tell you what was said. All I remember is hearing my heart pounding in my ears. Sophie was the love of my life, but she was no longer there. I'd fallen in love with Sebi, but he wasn't available. Kevin had added a richness to my life that I was desperate for. When we got together, it was so much more than sex. It was about drawing on one another's strengths and having a companion we knew we could count on.

I felt shattered.

We drove home from Dr. Newman's in silence and when we got back, Sebi told me to get a hotel for the night. He'd need a minute to sit with all of this.

———

I fight the urge to call Kevin to talk with him. The damage is done, but I feel that calling him would add to the betrayal. I want to work it out with Seb, if I can. I call the next day to ask if he's ready for me to come back. Jamie picks up and tells me to come home. He needs to talk with me. I'm not sure if that's good news or bad, but he doesn't sound happy.

Arriving at home, I hear Breaking Benjamin blasting from the speakers. I come around the corner into the kitchen and find Jamie cooking—peppers stuffed with brown rice, pine nuts, sausage and cranberries along with a gazpacho soup. I can smell bread baking in the oven.

"Sit your ass down. I have something to tell you," Jamie commands, throwing a towel down on the counter and pulling out a chair to straddle. He picks up a pack of cigarettes and shakes one out, lights it and stares at me, squinting. He rakes his hair back and I notice his shirt—a black tee with white lettering "Make Yourself Hard To Kill." *This isn't Jamie.*

"We're in the middle of a shit-show and there are some things you need to know." I can hear a hint of New York in his voice. This is Richard. Pissed-off Richard. Someone I had hoped I'd never see.

"We're not supposed to tell each other's stories. I get that. But this is an emergency. You need to know that Seb is darker than he's told you. He handled the dirty work, he handled anything no one else could. Papa was grooming him to take his place," Richard says.

"He had to watch kids and animals being hurt, but he'd learned how to turn off his senses when things got particularly bad. Seb was able to not see it even though his eyes were open, to block out the sounds by thinking of piano pieces in his head—working out different intonations and rhythms. It's why he's so amazing on the piano. He had to find a way to be there but not be there. And he had to refuse to create an alter that could participate in hurting other people. *That's* strength."

"Why did you feel this was so important for me to know?" I ask. "You guys almost never violate that rule—sharing each other's stories. This is pretty big. Why is it an emergency now?"

"Because he never learned what's acceptable and what's not. It's going to be really bad for awhile. You need to keep an eye out for self-harm, suicide. And you need to watch your back, too."

All of the scents of home bombard me—the smell of dinner cooking, fresh bread, Seb's cologne, the dog, the lingering scent of fire in the fireplace, laundry soap, Anna's lavender, coffee. And suddenly, instead of comforting me, they feel foreign and dangerous.

Richard takes Jamie's bandana off and tosses it on the counter, lights another cigarette and points to the stove. "Hungry?" he asks. His voice is low, more casual even than Seb's, and not a trace of playfulness.

"This looks about done," he says, sticking the cigarette in his mouth and pulling the peppers and bread out and slamming them down on the stovetop.

I stare at him like a kid waiting for a beating. I had never been on this side of Richard. I find myself suddenly running through where all the panic buttons are in the house. We'd had them installed as part of the alarm system. Richard had once told me he felt they were useless. By the time the police arrive, the damage would be done. He trained in Krav Maga and kept a baseball bat with nails and chains on it by the front door just in case. I felt that was a little overkill.

He plates dinner and sets it on the table, like he hadn't just told me my worst fears were about to unfold. He dumps the bread out into a basket and sets it between us. He pulls a six pack of beer out and slams it onto the table.

"You're gonna need these," he says roughly, looking me dead in the eye. "And probably a few of these," he adds, reaching into his pocket for a bottle of Klonopin and throwing it at me. "There's a whole bottle there. Take as many as you like."

I'm afraid of what will come next. He feels confrontational. The Klonopin comment is meant to tell me two things—one, that he knows I was borrowing pills, and two, he wouldn't mind if I took them all at once.

"Do you remember before you and Sophie married?" he says next, pulling out a pocket knife and hacking at the bread.

"Yes."

"Good. Do you remember the talk we had?"

"I don't...I'm not sure."

"You look a little lost, Steve. We had a talk before you got married. I told you that if you hurt her, you would answer to me. This is you answering to me. Knock yourself out."

I'm sure I looked terrified. The question couldn't be answered.

"I didn't mean to mess anything up...but I know I did."

"Yes, you did. What are you going to do about it? Do you plan to run away or stick around to fix it?"

"I'm not running. And I'm not sure how to fix it."

"Yeah. Well, we don't know either, but it's a real mess in here right now."

"I'm sorry."

"Seb's hurt and he's pissed. He doesn't do pissed very well. He doesn't know how to handle anger. When he's this upset, he has tantrums. Stay out of his way and you should be fine. If you get in the middle of things, you may wind up with a book to the side of your head. And you have to promise me to keep an eye on him because I can't fight him if he tries to hurt himself."

"How can I fix things? What can I do?"

"Why the fuck are you asking me? Do I look like a marriage counselor? I couldn't give a shit less if you figure this out."

———

Richard was right. Things are a mess and there was no solution other than time. Seb has lost all affection toward me and the feeling is more painful than loving Kibbie in high school and losing him when I went to college. Now I drink more. I take more Klonopin than I should. I stop eating...and I try my best to turn things around.

Seb is still out a lot of the time, which makes things even worse. He alternates between cool indifference and fiery anger, yelling at me, kicking things around the house, breaking stuff and slamming doors. He smashes the laptop against the brick fireplace when it doesn't load fast enough. He destroys finished art projects, violently throwing them into a metal trash can. Anything that frustrates him is annihilated— plates, glasses, electronics, windows. He takes a hammer to the microwave and destroys it. He's indiscriminately angry at everything.

The only bit of good news is that he's careful not to hurt anyone else, including Napoleon. More good news: he didn't go on autopilot and he didn't cut. But after twelve years of knowing me, I know he feels like he had finally let his guard down and I'd betrayed him.

One day, I hide his car keys and when he screams at me about it, I stand my ground. I tell him his mood and driving a car don't mix. This infuriates him, but on some level, it builds a bridge. He knows that even if he hated me, I was still going to look out for him.

Rebecca knew what was going on. I needed to talk with someone and I'm worried that if I brought it up to Dr. Newman or my group, they'd suggest hospitalization. To be honest, Rebecca has her concerns, too.

But then she brings up what we were seeing in the news lately— the me-too movement and the #enough and #times up posts all over the place. She asks me to consider how angry I'd be if I'd gone through what Sophie had. How angry must rape victims be to organize an entire movement, to demand to be believed and heard, *finally*? She helps me see this from an entirely different perspective.

The way I view it, this is all a good thing. When you stub your toe or someone cuts you off in traffic, you have to vent. There's swearing, screaming and, often, telling people about the injustice. That's minor.

It's nothing. I know only a fraction of what The Timeshare has endured and, while therapy is great, they needed to release all of this toxic garbage in a blast. They hadn't been allowed to talk about it. Even now, they were careful about what they shared—not wanting to traumatize anyone else. If trashing the house meant The Timeshare could let go of even a portion of the pain, they could burn the thing to the ground as far as I was concerned.

Eventually, I came to realize this wasn't all about my secrets—although that was part of it. My infidelity triggered a whole cascade of betrayals and hurts that needed to be let out of their cages to be acknowledged, honored, and heard.

Instead of just staying out of the way or begging Seb to stop, I start handing him things to smash and allow the rage to burn itself out. I want him to get out as much as he could—and I hoped Elizabeth was able to feel that, too.

I was worried about the possibility of self-harm and suicide. I needed someone to stay with Seb, but this was way above my sister's pay grade—and Liz's. And because an alter had told me suicide was a possibility, I couldn't ask Dr. Newman for a referral to a professional. He'd tell me we'd have to consider hospitalization, which terrified Seb.

I realize it's a massive rationalization, but all this leads me to calling Kevin. I know I'm using this as an excuse to stay connected, but I need to somehow justify it in my own head. I tell Kevin about everything that was happening and ask for his help.

He doesn't have any answers for Sophie, but he reminds me to take care of myself.

"When was the last time you went for a run?" he asks.

"I'm keeping up with it. It really helps."

"So, like today?"

"Well, no. I think I went running...hang on. Oh my God. It's been weeks."

"Let me ask you another question. When was the last time you sat down and enjoyed a really good meal or just stood in the shower and soaked?"

"I couldn't tell you. I don't remember."

"I mean...you have to do these things. I know you're overwhelmed, but I love you—and I need you to take care of yourself, okay?"

"I promise. I will. Just remind me from time to time."

"You got it."

"Look, I need to sort this all out with Sophie, but you need to know that even if I don't talk with you for awhile, I love you. I don't want to lose you."

"Not a chance."

Just as Seb can't let go of Laura, I knew I needed Kevin in my life.

───

I check on Seb several times during the night, hide all but a few of his pills, lock up box cutters, exacto knives and razors that I know he'd used in the past to self-harm.

I need to have someone with Seb when I'm not home, but I'm worried about putting anyone else in the line of fire. I'd call to check in throughout the day, but Seb wouldn't always pick up.

One day, a week into this, I'm not able to reach him at all. By 3 in the afternoon, I'm worried enough to head home.

The house is a wreck, which is not unusual. About day four I had given up cleaning. I figured I'd wait until the storm passed. But now, as I come up the steps, I see chunks of foam and bits of wood. Today's tantrum apparently included ripping the couch apart...cushions had been shredded and the wood frame broken.

And then I see him. Seb is sitting in the middle of it, crying, with a paring knife to his wrist.

I had imagined scenarios like this in my head but never thought it would be a reality. I hadn't prepared for it and didn't know what to do.

I move slowly towards him, but he doesn't seem to care that I'm there. When he does look up, there's no threat in his eyes, just a pleading to leave him alone. He was using the knife to gently trace and retrace the tattoo on his wrist—316, 316, 316—letting the blood come to the surface, but not cutting deep enough for it to flow. With one wrong word, one motion just a bit too fast or too slow on my part, my wife could kill herself in front of me.

Now he says, "After you die, you're not mad anymore. I'd like that. Because I can't get it all out. There's no way I can get it all out. It's just fucking sitting there slowly suffocating me. Even if I could let it all go, there'd be nothing left. That's all we are now—just rage. That's all that's holding me together."

His voice has a tension in it I'd never heard before. There is so much anger and it feels like he's holding back, trying not to cut, but unable to override the helplessness entirely.

"Seb, I'm going to ask you to give me the knife. And I'm going to call Dr. Newman. He can help us get this figured out, okay?"

Seb turns the knife over in his hand and gives it to me, handle first. Then he curls into himself and goes back to sobbing. I need to make sure he isn't bleeding anywhere else, but don't know how to go about that. I need help, but know locking him up somewhere isn't the answer. I couldn't imagine how The Timeshare could handle that.

I'm shaking as I sit next to Seb and the shredded couch, dialing Dr. Newman. I leave a message, but also text him with a 911. I have no idea what will happen next.

———

Love is not fair. If we look at our marriage on a spreadsheet, I had put up with a lot more from Sophie than she had from me. But I know that's not the point. My relatively simple history with caring parents and a stable household puts me at a different starting place. My ability to cope, which I learned from pretty much everyone around me, gives me healthier skills and fewer triggers.

Sophie, on the other hand, has an ability to deal with insanity really well, but day to day life is a painful struggle. And this? This is mind blowing because someone she truly trusted had betrayed her. She felt she'd gotten away from this sort of thing when she left home, but here we were.

I wasn't perfect and that reset the clock on her healing. The one constant in her life wasn't constant. Never had been.

———

I wish I had done things differently. I wish I could say that the experience of truth-telling and love-making brought us closer, that we wound up living happily ever after, but that's not the way it went for us. I thought if we kept secrets and had a disastrous sexual encounter, it would close that door to our relationship forever. I never imagined great sex and intimate truth-telling could mean the end of my marriage.

I *should* have told them earlier—probably from the start. I should have told them I'd reconnected with Kevin when it happened. At least, I *should* have said something before Sebi and I made love. I'd had plenty of opportunity.

Dr. Newman called me back immediately and sent out an ambulance. He knew I was too conflicted to do that. He must have told them she had mental health issues, because they were very aware and patient. Seb wasn't on autopilot, but he was completely limp. He let them do whatever they needed to do with no resistance.

The look in his eyes terrified me. They were completely dead. It was beyond autopilot where it looks like no one's home. His eyes told me he had resigned from life. There was an emptiness there. Everyone had checked out of the body and it was now a shell. I didn't know where they'd gone or if they'd ever be back.

When the paramedics saw the shape of the house—completely wrecked —they assessed that a trip to the ER would be the best course of action. Fortunately, no other cuts. Just bruises from raging so hard all week.

A psych eval was done and Sophie was in for ten days. Dr. Newman was able to visit and to contribute to the treatment program. After a few days, they let me visit as well and it seemed The Timeshare had gotten at least some of the anger out and they were calmer now. There were also some big changes inside.

While Sophie was in the hospital, I got the house back in shape. I also came into a greater awareness of who I am and what I need. I'd thought a lot about how I defined myself. I was feeling less scared about facing the truth. I could acknowledge being bi-sexual, but couldn't imagine ever being happy.

After he got home, Seb seemed more grounded and calmer.

"Papa always told me inpatient was terrifying—that I'd be better off dead," he said. "But it was actually the first time in my life I could be completely honest and not worry I was hurting someone. It was scary at first, but once I understood that they genuinely wanted to help me, I felt deeply cared for. The revelation is that love and caring have always been there. It's about my capacity to let it in."

Sebi was less angry overall but he had lost faith in our relation-ship—and in me. He didn't trust me with anything and we no longer enjoyed the playful rhythm I loved.

It seemed there was too much to overcome. There was jealousy within The Timeshare. Anna felt disrespected, Sophie felt cheated on. The others felt Sebi had become my favorite. I was working so hard to try to win him over that it completely threw off the balance.

Laura was furious that her agreement with Sebi had been violated. She and Seb had agreed nothing beyond kissing would happen with me and they'd been able to maintain that for over a decade. Laura wasn't jealous; she was angry at her trust being disrespected. Seb had risked his relationship with Laura for me and I'd blown it.

While Seb had no trust in me, he didn't want to lose me either. Now that he knew about Kevin, he was afraid I would leave. And he felt like second choice, which did not sit well with him.

After my night with Seb, I couldn't not want more. And I'd ruined us. I understood how people wanted to consume him. Sex with Sebi was like heroin. No matter how hard I tried not to think about it, he could feel an unfulfilled demand from me. Yes, he had a strong sex drive, but, as he said, he was straight and sex with me could never be more than an occasional thing—even under the best of circumstances.

I thought I had moved past my jealousy, but it continued to crash over me, in intense waves. We both felt inadequate about meeting each other's needs and it was a crappy place to be. In fact, we were just starting to see truths we'd long denied.

I was angry that it seemed his affairs were more acceptable than mine. His behavior wasn't seen as cheating but mine was. That seemed unfair. Our relationship became fiercely passionate but not in a good way. There was a lot of fighting.

Every time I came back from being out of town, Seb assumed I had been with Kevin and I assumed he was with Laura. Some people find that to be sexy or dramatic but I prefer smooth water. I could feel us heading for disaster.

Things got worse and weirder. We'd be fighting one minute and then were strangely polite the next—in an uncomfortably formal way. The attraction we had for each other was still there, just under the surface, but it felt dark. We had moments of passionate kissing that quickly disintegrated into a fight. We both knew that something would have to change.

We did have one discussion that will stick with me forever because it encapsulated the entire experience for both of us.

It was a warm Sunday morning and Sebi was in his pajamas and robe heading out to the shed. He was pouring himself a cup of coffee and I came up behind him and gave him a hug. He shrugged me off and in a despondent tone said, "You used to tell me I didn't owe you a thing. I miss those days."

He felt that every time I did anything, my motive was to try to get him back into bed. I couldn't get him a cup of coffee or make breakfast or help him in the shed because he felt like I had ulterior motives. The sad thing was that he was right. And because of that, I couldn't do the things I used to do for him. But to him, it felt like I didn't do things for him any longer because we weren't having sex. I felt damned if I did and damned if I didn't. With the trust gone, everything I did was examined under a microscope of suspicion.

Sebi was out full time now, or nearly full time. The rage had indeed burned itself out and Dr. Newman was helping him learn how to manage any other violent anger that found its way to the surface. While he was back to doing his art, fulfilling his role as host efficiently and interacting with everyone else from a place of charm and charisma, any time he looked at me, I could see the hurt in his eyes. I didn't know if I'd ever see love there again and it was killing me.

———

Except for the huge issues we were facing around jealousy, there seemed to be fewer conflicts within The Timeshare over how resources were used. Sebi was a gifted mediator and whenever a problem cropped up, he was able to handle it easily. We had fewer crises, fewer panicked calls, and fewer emergencies.

I asked him how they could go from such a dysfunctional place to uber productive in such a short time. "This isn't functional, Steve. This is the efficiency of survival. This is me trying to control everything because, inside, it's still a mess. When I was destroying the house, that was just a reflection of what's going on inside. We're getting there, but it'll be awhile."

Sebi needed to up-level to handle all of the additional responsibility and now felt 28 years old. He also wanted to be more settled. He didn't need to get married, necessarily, but he did want to be with someone and that someone was Laura, not me.

We tried to talk about our relationship, but couldn't make much progress. It wasn't that he hated me or that he wanted to punish me or that he was holding a grudge. Sebi took care of himself first and didn't let anyone in who could hurt him. I had proven to be untrustworthy. He had connected with me through music because it was safe. Seb could have sex for money, but in a relationship, it was a terrifyingly vulnerable place to go.

Laura was increasingly jealous and possessive. She felt I was a threat, so she arranged more frequent visits. She planned to come out for a couple weeks in the summer. And I made arrangements to be away for that time—to go see my family and get myself grounded.

I remembered a conversation I'd had with Carla at her wedding. She told me she loved Laura and part of her heart was enough. "No one ever has anyone's whole heart, and we just set ourselves up for pain and failure when we think we do. People have old loves, infatuations, crushes, affairs. I don't need her whole heart. I have enough. And she's been honest with me about how she feels about Sebi."

It was a shocking position to me, yet it seemed to work for them.

I was trying to figure out how I could have even a part of Sophie, but she was continuing to slip away and there was nothing I could do about it. My grandmother had suffered with Alzheimer's before she died and this felt something like that. I wanted to be there for every second so I could catch flickers of Sophie if she came out. At the same time, I could hardly stand to see her because I knew she could be gone the next moment.

When Sophie was out, she wasn't interested in doing much and I could see her fading away a bit more every time I saw her. Resting inside The Timeshare had become irresistibly comfortable.

And now I'd lost Sebi as well.

I had to wonder if I'd seen different alters at college. I think I had. Rachel liked to snuggle in with me but was so obviously childlike that there was nothing romantic about it. Sebi, at parties and things. Not sure if I'd actually seen Richard, though he'd kicked the crap out of Chuck. What I remember about Sophie in college was that she was always exhausted and unwell, achy and in pain. I'd drive her to doctor's appointments when it was really bad. Was that all there was to her? Was the one called Sophie just a container for the residual pain of abuse? The others had alluded to it, but I never really accepted it.

At our next appointment, I start, "Seb is out almost all of the time. He has every right to that, but I so rarely see Sophie and I miss her. When she is here, it's obvious she's just getting weaker and weaker. How can we support her so she can come back?"

"That's not how this works, Steve. I see the genius in the system. I believe The Timeshare has its own wisdom and this is happening for a reason. Confidentiality prevents me from saying too much more, but I hope that you know me well enough that you can trust me—and you can trust Sophie, too. She's going to be okay."

I want to be very clear so I forcefully ask—"*Sophie* is going to be okay?"

Dr. Newman's tone is quiet and his pace slow. I used to find this reassuring, but today it's frustrating me. Like he has the key but refuses to give it to me. "The Timeshare will be okay. And within that system, Sophie will do what she needs to do."

Sophie doesn't make an appearance when asked to come out and Dr. Newman asks if Sebi can give me some peace of mind. He's not very reassuring. "I'm sorry, Steve. I wish I could tell you what you want to hear. We're healing from old injuries. We're getting stronger. And when an alter no longer has a role to play, they fade out. Considering that her role was to handle the pain, this is actually kind of good news. I can tell you that she'll always be a part of The Timeshare, but she's in hibernation."

"Is that like auto-pilot?"

"No. Auto-pilot is terrifying. You're like a zombie. Going into hibernation is like someone else is running the show—like falling asleep in the car when someone else is driving. It's not scary at all. You're still there, just unconscious."

I'm confused. "But she's the host. This shouldn't happen to the host, should it?"

Dr. Newman looks to Seb, who nods his consent.

"Generally, it doesn't, but sometimes it can happen that way, yes. Sebi is the one holding most of the memories now and everyone trusts and respects him. The kids talk with him because he feels safe. The women in the system love him because he's seen as a close relation. The men in the system feel he's one of the guys. He's central to everyone and he has the drive and the diplomacy needed to organize The Timeshare. That's the job of the host."

"So, Sebi is the new host. Or will be in time."

"That's the direction it looks like we're going."

"But he's a guy. No offense, Sebi, but that doesn't fit with the body. And he feels like he's 28, but he thought he was 19 just a few months ago."

Dr. Newman tries to help me get a handle on things. "It's incongruous, yes. And as things progress, we'll have to work out any dysmorphic issues. The body and mind don't match—we'll have to address that."

Sebi explains, "Steve, I'm guessing you've noticed some changes. My experience is that I'm aging faster than before. Some alters will age gradually—either faster or slower than the host. For me, I've taken leaps. I've gone from 12 to 19 and now I feel like I'm 28. That's unlikely to go backwards."

Now that he mentions it, I had noticed that he seems older. He's less impulsive, more serious. Decisions take longer to make and the meticulousness he maintains in his studio is beginning to spread through his whole life. He'd worked through his anger issues with Dr. Newman and had a better handle on them. He's still fun and playful with friends, but he's also taking more responsibility for things. Even his artwork has matured.

I have to address the elephant in the room. "So what's going to happen with us?"

Sebi looks down at the floor and then back up at me. His brow furrows and eyes narrow as he says, "I don't know. I wish I could tell you. I really do. But I have no idea how this is going to play out."

July 27, 2016

I'd been dreading this day for months. Maybe even years. I know I have to talk with Sebi about leaving. Our old relationship no longer fits and we both feel a crushing loneliness for our other loves, making living together intolerable for both of us. Kevin and Laura complicated things in ways we'd ignored in favor of the excitement. I feel we either have to commit to one another as partners, live completely as roommates or split. And the only thing that makes sense to me at this point is for us to split.

Almost every Saturday for eight years I've made a big breakfast, but I'm not in the mood. I sit in the living room with a cup of coffee, staring into space and waiting.

Rachel comes tripping down the steps about an hour later, bear in hand. She curls up on the couch and snuggles into me. I think she knows something's up, something bad. She looks up at me with enormous eyes full of fear and asks, "No monkey bread?"

I have tears in my eyes, too. "No sweetheart. No monkey bread today."

"But why?" she squeaks, fear creeping into her voice.

I smile and ask her if I can talk with Sebi. "Okay! See you later!"

She sits up and I see a shiver run through her body as she jerks and suddenly Sebi is next to me.

"Saturday morning, dude. No breakfast? What's up? You feeling okay?" he asks.

"Yes, I'm okay." My voice is a mix of dread tinged with some anger at the situation. "I didn't make breakfast, but there's coffee. Did you want some?" I ask, starting to get up.

"Sure. But it's okay. I'll get it." Sebi gets up, a look of concern crossing his face. "Do you need a refill?" he asks, reaching for my cup, already knowing my answer. I hear the coffee pot clank against his cup, the ring on his finger clicking against my mug. It's a strange thing what you take away from these small moments—the things you never noticed before that you now suddenly want to grab onto and hold forever. Very soon, I wouldn't hear these sounds again and I had to work hard to fight back the tears.

We'd reached a time where we were cordial to each other. We'd moved past the hurt and we were friends—living together and trying to find a place to start building a new foundation of trust for a relationship that had changed so drastically we had no idea where it would go.

"So, what's going on? You seem bummed."

He hands me my coffee and moves the teddy bear to a nearby chair before he sits down and tunes in.

"I don't think I can do this anymore," I say, my voice catching. A searing pain is rising up from my chest and the tears start to flow. I can't stop them.

I can tell he wants to say something quippy to make me laugh but he resists, opting to wait for me to tell him more.

"I love Sophie. I love all of you. You know that, right?" I whisper between sobs.

"I do," he says, rubbing my back.

"But it's too painful to be here when Sophie is never around. And honestly, I can't be around you and not want you. I want something more than you're comfortable with. I can tell you're feeling frustrated, too."

Sebi wipes my tears away with his fingers before grabbing my hand. "It's been really hard. I'm angry at you and jealous of Kevin. At the same time, I can't give you what you need. And I have to be with Laura, but I want you in my life as well. I wish we could find a way to sort it out, but I have no idea how we'd make it work."

"Sebi, I'm not seeing any other solution. I think we need to separate. I have this trip planned to go see my mom and when I get back, I think I should find a place."

He puts on a resigned smile as he nods in agreement. "I hate to say it, but I agree. But we *will* need to take it slow. You're family to a lot of us and while I can say that, yes, I think we need to separate, others would disagree. You're going to have to have this conversation with us one by one. Also, we can live at different addresses, but I do love you. I still want you in my life."

Talking with each alter one by one sounds worse than that fish hook in my heel. This conversation is uncomfortable, but I'm absolutely dreading speaking to the others even more. And seeing Sebi after we separated? I didn't know how that was going to work, but right now he needed to hear me say we could still be in one another's lives.

"I can do that," I agree, although I'm not sure I could actually pull it off.

Over the next few days, I speak with a parade of alters.

I speak with Rachel first because I know that will be the most difficult. I catch her out watching cartoons on the iPad.

"Can I watch with you?"

"Yes! I love it when you do that!" she replies, setting the iPad on the coffee table and joining me on the couch. She rests her head on my shoulder before pulling a blanket around both of us.

"What's on?" I ask, hoping to delay our conversation another few minutes.

"Charlie and Lola now and then Peg + Cat." I'd made up a playlist for her and she had it memorized.

I waited until the first episode ran the credits and asked her to pause the shows. "Can I talk with you about something important?" I ask.

She perks up. That question usually meant we'd be cooking together, seeing a movie, or deciding on an adventure. This time, it'd be different.

"I love you so much, Rachel."

"I love you too! So much!"

Her smile is killing me.

"I have to go away."

"Where are you going?" she replies with a pout.

"I'm going to live in a different place nearby."

"Not in my house?"

I shake my head no, feeling like I can't answer.

"Why?"

I hadn't prepared for the why and I didn't know what to tell her. "Sophie and I feel like it's our best choice for right now."

"Why?"

I should have known this was coming. Rachel hit me with "why's" fairly often and until she was satisfied with the answer, we'd continue to be stuck in this cycle.

"Because we feel sad together right now even though we love each other. We need to try living apart to see if we don't feel so sad."

"But I'm sad when you aren't here. Aren't you sad when I'm not here?"

This is a tough one. Kids ask the most difficult questions and I wanted to answer in a way that would reach Sophie. "I miss any of you when you're not here."

"When are you going away?"

"Soon, and I don't know how often I'll see you before that."

"Can you wait until after Christmas? I want you to be here for Christmas."

My heart is breaking. "I can't stay until Christmas, sweetie, but I can come over for Christmas."

"Can we watch movies still?"

"We'll work everything out, honey. I'm not disappearing. I'll find a place nearby and I'll still see you." I had to give her *something*. It was devastating to see her trying to hold on to some little scrap when she just wanted everything to remain the same.

Elizabeth has a similar reaction, asking if we could still read books together. She's more fearful than sad—wanting to know what would happen and if they'd be safe. She hates change. She'd gotten better over the years and she'd grown up too, feeling 16 now. She could leave the house and go to the grocery and other nearby familiar places including Dr. Newman's, but preferred rushing home where she felt safe. And I was part of that safety.

Anna's mad at me so I knew we'd have a discussion later. Her feeling at this point is "Good riddance!"

———

No one tells you this, but getting separated is a full-time job. It's emotionally and physically draining and I find myself dragging at work. One day I take the afternoon off and head home.

I find Sophie hard at work with books and files stacked around her computer on the dining room table.

"What are you working on?"

"Oh, hi," she says with a quiet smile as she takes off her glasses. "I'm working on a talk with Anne at the social justice office."

This was Ellyn. I didn't see her that often, though she was out when I was at work. She volunteers a great deal—helping with research, speech writing, phone calls. I'd never had that much time with her but I love her strong sense of compassion and the balance she brings to The Timeshare. She seems underappreciated and something in me hopes she'll get a shot at more of the life she wants.

"Do you have time for a break? I need to talk with you about something."

"About leaving? Let's sit down. I have to talk with you, as well. Do you want tea?"

Ellyn has a way of thinking of little touches that are so healing. She's also able to see all sides with only the deepest compassion.

"Yes, tea would be nice," I tell her.

She pours us both a cup and hands mine to me, "Chamomile. I know you're tired, but you look stressed. It'll help you rest after our talk."

She touches my arm sympathetically and tells me, "I know you're looking at moving out and if you feel that's the best answer, it's okay. I gave you a different solution to this a long time ago, but I think you likely need some space to think right now. I'd encourage you to avoid doing anything long term—like a lease. I think after a few weeks, you may realize something that will work better. Time away will foster interdependence rather than being together out of fear."

I have to smile. She is so balanced and fair. She expresses concern for the others and empathy for me.

But I hoped whatever Ellyn was predicting would be less painful because this sucked. I knew I had to walk through the grief of losing Sophie, of change. No matter what happened, our relationship would be different now.

It was nearly time for me to go, but I took Ellyn's wisdom to heart. I'd wait until I got back to start looking for an apartment. I'd have two weeks with my mom and then a week in California for my work. It'd give me a chance to get some distance and maybe think of some other solutions.

I did see Sophie before I left, but it was brief. She was lying on the couch, sleepy and hardly able to talk. "I feel like such a failure. I wish I could be normal for you, Steve."

"Sophie, I didn't want normal. You've always been better than that. I know you've always wanted an average life, but it's been extraordinary. I've missed you so much, but I know you're still there and you always will be.

Her voice is weak and soft, "Please remember that. I will always be here—and I love you and appreciate you more than I can say."

"Sometimes you guys play music for me. Can I play something for you?" I ask.

"Of course," Sophie smiles.

I pick up my guitar and begin to play. Sophie is crying through her smile as I softly sing, "I Won't Give Up" to her.

I set my guitar down and hold her hand. I put her hand on my heart and I feel desperate to do anything to keep her with me. But I also knew that would be cruel. She needs to go into The Timeshare for now.

She closes her eyes, but keeps talking to me. "I know it's not fair to you, but I'm out so rarely and if you leave, it means I'll probably never see you. I wish you could do your life and still be here every second, so when I do make it out, I can see you. I know that's really selfish."

"It's not selfish, Sophie. It's love," I say. "Sophie?"

Her eyes open and I'm grateful to see the emerald color again one last time. "Yeah."

"No matter what happens, please know that you have been a huge part of my story."

She smiles, sniffs, and asks me, "Promise me you won't let go, okay? Just promise me you'll never let go. Even if you can't see me, please just hold on."

A lump of sadness is growing in my throat as tears break over my eyes.

"I promise," I tell her, holding her hand in both of mine.

And then she fades away and Jamie is sitting with me, pulling his hand away, asking if we can go grab lunch. I need a minute—wondering if this is the last time I'll ever see my wife. Jamie understands tears, so I let them come. They're agonizing. My eyes literally ache with my heart. Jamie is comfortable with tears and sits with me until my sobs no longer take away my breath.

I apologize to him and he smiles at me kindly. "Hungry?"

We go out for a burger and talk about everything. I'd really miss him. And knowing I'd see him again made it easier and more painful at the same time. He hugs me and tells me, "Stay in touch and let us know you're okay. I promise I'll keep the kids safe."

It was a week to the day of my talk with Sebi. Saturday morning breakfast was too painful, so I was going to skip it, but it was upsetting Rachel too much. I get that Rachel is an alter, but in many ways, she and Elizabeth feel like the children in this situation—and their parents were splitting. I have to treat them as my children. So I make bacon and monkey bread. I tell Sebi he's welcome to join us but I also want time with the kids. He appreciates and respects that.

After a very emotional breakfast, I kiss Rachel on the forehead and ask for Sebi.

"This is it. You gonna be okay?" I ask him, but he seems different.

"We'll be fine. Don't worry. How about you?" I catch the accent and see brown creep into the eyes. This is too painful for Sebi, so Richard has stepped forward.

"I'm going to be sad. I am sad. But I think this is the right thing to do. I'll fly out for some time with my mom before my business trip. When I get back, I'll check in with you and then get a hotel room until I find an apartment."

I continue, "Is Laura coming out?

"Yeah, and Liz will be here too."

"Hey, Steve," Richard starts, "I want you to know I get it. You're human and this is a really tough situation. You've been really good to Sophie and The Timeshare. Thank you."

"I love all of you. We'll figure this out. Just remind everyone what I told them—this is a shift, it's not an ending. I wrote down my schedule so that you have it. Call if you need me, okay?"

August 3, 2016

There was a lot of work to do as we separated, but first, I needed some time with my own family. That time away provided me some distance to digest everything and regain my balance. Going home can do that and as we were settling my mom into hospice, the whole family was there.

It was soothing to see my sister Rebecca. She listened and helped me grieve this huge loss in my life. David resisted his desire to tell me that he'd warned me about this and insisted on handling the divorce. I explained that we weren't there yet, and that I still loved Sophie very much. I told Rebecca everything, but swore her to secrecy. She's the one who told me I had to write this book—not only to move on with my life, but maybe my story could help someone else in this situation.

I said goodbye to my mom—just in case this was the last time I'd see her. She laughed at my lingering hug.

"Everyone I see feels like this is our last goodbye. I should have done this years ago—I'm getting so much love!" she says. My mom could put a positive spin on anything. It made me feel like I *would* see her again.

I also spent a lot of time with Kevin, trying to sort out how *we'd* move forward. He'd been wanting a change and was looking at transferring to Denver or San Francisco so we could see more of each other.

I was grateful to have business in California after seeing my family. It gave me a chance to settle back into real life a little bit before dealing with the separation.

Kevin came with me and we settled more into our relationship. We felt freer to be together now, yet it felt strange—like even though I was separating from Sophie, we were still a couple. Kevin was patient with me. He was feeling the same about his wife.

As I sat on the plane heading back to Denver, I was hit with the reality that *all* of my relationships were shifting. My mom was dying. Sophie and I were separating. David had never really been there for me and Rebecca was always busy. I felt a little like an orphan, desperate for a family. I was always envious of people with large, loving families. That's what I wanted.

I'd been out of the house for three weeks, but it didn't feel real until we touched down in Denver that Sunday evening. I had a lot more clarity on my marriage and, although I didn't feel I could tell anyone, I knew exactly what I wanted it to look like. It seemed so unrealistic to me at this point. Like looking up to the top of a mountain at the start of a climb. It's hard to picture reaching the summit.

I had thought a lot about what Ellyn said as I was leaving and I remembered that she had once told me that in our situation, polyamory was the only answer. I was beginning to agree with that. It seemed implausible, yet remained the best possible option if we could pull it off. My life would feel incomplete without Sebi and Kevin.

I hated not knowing whether Sophie was okay, and it still felt odd to be away this long. I hadn't heard from her for a few days and assumed I'd said something wrong. We weren't on solid ground yet.

Now, I pause at the front door, feeling like this isn't really my home any longer. I have no home and I'm losing my family—both the one I came from and the one I created with Sophie. I hesitate and wonder if I should knock, but I know Sophie is expecting me.

Napoleon always meets me at the door, but not tonight. As I come up the stairs, I'm surprised that Jamie isn't in the kitchen cooking. It was his habit to make dinner around this time.

The lights are all dimmed and the house is uncomfortably still. I walk through the living room to find Sophie sitting at the dining room table with her back to me. She's drinking a cup of coffee and talking on the phone. Her voice sounds dry and raspy and I wonder if she's fighting off a cold. Napoleon looks up, but refuses to leave her side.

I can't understand anything she's saying. Then I realize she's not speaking English. I think it's German? I know she understands the language but I had no idea she spoke it so fluently.

"Mach dir keine Sorgen. Es geht mir gut. Ja, ich weiß. Ich kenne. Ich weis das zu schätzen. Ja, Finn ist jetzt hier. Okay. Ja Dankeschön. Lass es mich wissen, wenn es fertig ist, Robert." (Don't worry. I'm fine. Yes, I know. I know. I appreciate that. Yes, Finn's here now. Okay. Yes, thank you. Just let me know when it's done, Robert.)

She hears me round the corner and hangs up, looking like a spy who's been caught by someone she knows she can trust, but shouldn't have slipped in front of.

She puts her hand on the back of the chair and I notice scrapes on her knuckles—they were healing but had been bloodied. As she turns to face me, I can make out a black eye even with the lights dimmed. I'd seen this before—when Richard would get into a bar fight.

I smile sadly, "Oh, Christ, Sophie. Not again." I chuckle softly. We generally try to laugh these incidents off. It helps us move past them. But I don't get a smile back.

As I get closer, my knees nearly buckle beneath me. She has finger-shaped bruises around her neck—purple at the jugular, black along her windpipe. Her wrists have fresh, deep scratches. Her long, beautiful hair has been roughly chopped off, so it rests mostly at chin level.

Before I can really think, I reach out to touch her and she flinches away from me. I pull my hand back and hear myself ask, "Jesus, what happened?"

Seb winces and gives a little wave, "Just a wicked bar fight. How was your trip? How's your mom?" He grimaces as he shifts in his seat and I feel rage-full tears burning my eyes.

"Let's cover that later. I want to hear what happened."

"We ran into a little trouble a few nights ago," he says matter-of-factly as he lights the bowl of his pipe and takes a deep hit. Deflecting again, he's minimizing it to the bare facts so we can move on.

I'm not sure why I had to ask, but I felt compelled: "Oh God, is Liz okay?"

"Yeah. He was pissed at me, not her."

"Who was pissed? Sebi, who did this to you?"

He holds the pipe out to me and I take it and follow suit.

He shows me his bloodied wrists. "Remember Craig, the photographer at the art festival? Jeremy was right. Turns out he's not so harmless."

"Oh my God, Sebi, you look like you're in so much pain."

He gives me a "no shit" nod and takes the pipe back. "This helps."

He continues, "Honestly, I was never afraid of him because I thought I could take him in a fight. And I could, if it was fair. He cold-cocked me as I came out of the bathroom at Sparky's and knocked me on my ass."

"Jesus."

"Yeah, knocked me out. I woke up at his house. He told me it was time for some karma." He show me his scraped-up knuckles. "Richard got a couple shots in, but couldn't fight him off. Pretty humiliating. And that was before Craig started taking pictures."

"Would you mind making me another latte?" he says handing me his cup.

"Liz called the cops when no one could find me, but they couldn't do much."

"What did he mean by karma?"

"For getting him banned from the agency—as a client and a photographer. It's costing him a ton of business. And he blames me for that."

I hand the coffee to him and he takes a sip and then holds it up to me, thanking me with a "Cheers." Another sip and he continues, "He let me go after he was done and I called Mark. He picked me up and brought the doctor over to clean me up."

"Seb, did they do a rape kit?"

He looks confused, "Why would they do that?"

"So they can get this guy."

Sebi snorts, "No, of course not. They'd need to know how we met, the nature of our relationship, any previous encounters. Mark would get shut down and I could go to jail." Sebi is protective of Mark. He feels genuinely cared for by him, as twisted as that was.

"Steve, this is part of the deal. We all know that and make certain agreements. That's why Mark tries to screen so carefully. Craig kinda snuck in the back door because he's a photographer. And he's hooked up with a lot of contracts, so no one wanted to say anything. But I can tell you that those pictures on his website? They aren't staged and the bruises aren't makeup."

I don't know where to go from here. I want to run, go after Craig, move Sophie to some remote island, yell at Sebi for choosing this line of work.

Instead, all I can do is ask, "What did the doctor say?"

Sebi chuckles, "That my hair will grow back."

"Seb," I say, sure my tone is more scolding than I want it to sound.

"I need to keep some packs on down south to heal things up. Just a lot of bruising. He's got me on Colace to make things easier for now. My ass is killing me. And I need to sit in Epsom salts a couple times a day. He put ice on my eye and some stuff on my wrists. I didn't want them wrapped. Too much attention—looks like a suicide attempt or something. There wasn't a lot he could do. It just has to heal."

"This isn't my first rodeo, Steve," he continues. "I've known Craig a long time and even as a kid, he was a brutal little snot. Mark got us security for awhile."

Liz hears us talking and comes down the stairs. It used to infuriate me to know that she was with my wife. Now, I'm grateful for her. Her face is puffy and it's obvious she's spent a fair amount of time crying over the last few days.

Behind her is a huge guy in a black t-shirt and jeans with a sidearm, looking very alert. A familiar charm hangs around his neck: St. Christopher.

Liz motions to him as she catches my eye. "Just in case dickhead decides he wants to come back," she says to me. "With Finn around, I kinda hope he tries."

I nod my acknowledgment to the guard and turn to Liz. "How can I help?"

"We've talked about it," Liz says as security locks eyes with Seb for a moment. They both smile and I sense a connection. Then the guard slips around the corner and out of sight. Liz puts her hand on my back and brushes my arm gently as she moves past me towards Seb. Putting her hands on his shoulders first, she allows the flinching to pass through him as she soothingly breathes "Shhhh" before gently pooling her arms around him and kissing his head. He reaches up to hold her arm briefly and then hands her the pipe.

I sense a shift in their relationship, and it feels more like Liz is playing big sister.

"I'll be here for a few days while he starts to heal and then he'll stay at Laura's for a while. It seems to make sense to get him out of town, just to be on the safe side."

She kisses his cheek and says, "Does a soak sound good?"

"Not really, no."

"Do you want your ass to heal?" Liz says, trying to bring in some humor.

"Got it. Not really a question." He looks up at her, winks and kisses her cheek affectionately.

Seb looks exhausted, but not defeated. He nods to Liz as he tries to stand. "Crap. Mother-FUCKER!" he moans as he falls back into his chair.

"Do you need help?" I ask, getting up.

"No, we got this," Sebi says firmly. He hates sympathy but his words unintentionally sting me. Liz yells for Finn, who immediately appears, assesses, and asks, "Okay for me to pick you up, buddy?"

Seb closes his eyes and shakes his head, "Yeah, it's okay. And Finn, I told you not to call me *buddy*."

"Old habits, man," he says, easily scooping Seb up and carrying him to the bathroom.

I get up, feeling uncertain about where to go or what to do. Liz helps with some direction. "I need to get him started, but then I want to talk with you," she says.

"Sure," I reply, hanging my coat on the back of a chair like I used to do every day after work. Such a weird position to be in—sitting by while someone else was caring for my wife, doing the things I used to do for her, asking me to stay for a minute.

Finn comes downstairs and begins another walk around the house, inside and out. I hold the pipe up to him and he shakes his head no. "On duty."

I hear water running as Seb and Liz are swearing and laughing— apparently trying to navigate the least painful way to get clothes off and Seb into the epsom salts. Then Sebi says, "I love you, sweetheart. Thanks. I'm good." And Liz quietly shuts the bathroom door behind her and is back sitting next to me.

I hear another door upstairs close and Laura appears. She is *pissed*, but joins us to formulate a plan.

"Is he going to be okay?" I ask Liz, feeling like an outsider.

Laura shakes her head and huffs, "No, asshole, he's not going to be okay. What the hell is wrong with you—leaving him for *three* weeks? God, you're an idiot. I hate you."

Liz looks at Laura disapprovingly—like she's being too harsh. She says, "Steve, I think he'll heal. It'll take time. Did he tell you what happened?"

"I put it together."

At that Liz begins crying, thankful not to have to recount the details to me. Laura moves to sit next to her, putting her arm around her for strength.

"Craig took the watch," Laura tells me.

"Oh shit," I say, recognizing the importance of that watch to Seb. Not only did the watch help Sophie switch and remain in the Sebi state, it calmed Sebi during anxiety attacks. And he told me once that it symbolized being cared for, being valued.

"Yeah."

"Oh *shit*," I say again as something else occurs to me. The kids, Rachel and Elizabeth, would often hold the watch when they needed Sebi. The smell of his cologne and feel of the watch was their touchstone to call him out. It made the whole Timeshare feel safer.

"Oh my God, the kids!"

"Yeah. They pop out for a second and they're frantic. That watch was like a security blanket for them. And Sebi has always been their rock. They feel like they're safe with him. How do you handle that? When the one person you trust to keep you safe is attacked? Richard is completely depressed, feeling like he failed. He feels humiliated. No one feels safe. Steve, The Timeshare is in trouble."

"I have no idea what to do."

Liz continues, "Well, we'll get him in to see Dr. Newman three times this week. Hopefully he'll have some ideas. And we'll pick up an inexpensive temporary watch and douse it in cologne. That'll be sort of a place-holder until we can figure out what else we need to do."

Something doesn't make sense. "Weird question," I start, "why didn't he take the necklace? Why just the watch?"

Liz begins to answer, but can't finish her sentence. Laura is choking on the words but manages to tell me, "He took the watch off when he tied Sophie up. He told her to keep the necklace as a reminder that St. Christopher doesn't give a shit about whores."

I close my eyes, dizzy, imagining Sophie getting hurt and sick, thinking of how she must have felt when Craig said that to her. She always felt the St. Christopher charm was sort of blessed, that it could actually keep her safe. It gave her courage. Everything Craig did to her that night was cruel and took away the tiny corner of safety she'd scraped together for herself. That comment about the necklace is one of those things you can ruminate on forever—it can eat you up from within. Craig seems a carbon copy of her Papa.

"You said Sophie. But Sebi said this happened to *him.*"

Liz explains, "The physical part happened to him. The emotional part happened to Sophie. Sebi felt the physical pain, but no fear or anger. Jamie was shielding the kids, so Sophie took the emotions, not Elizabeth. Steve, I hate to tell you this, but I think it was a death blow. I haven't seen any trace of Sophie in the last few days."

"Oh my God. Do you think she's gone?" I break down, dissolving into tears I'm unable to hold back. "She was so weak just before I left."

Knowing we had to talk about all this, I finally manage to pull myself together. We needed to find answers or at least understand it so we could help Sophie heal. Something dawns on me.

"Wait," I say out loud. "Richard handles all the fights. Not Sebi. He would never be present for something like this. It's not his department."

"He is so strong, Steve. When Richard tried to come forward, Seb pushed him back. He could read that Craig would kill them if they fought. And since Sebi has been out consistently with no autopilot after something like this? I don't know what that means, but it's looking like he's stepped in as host full time."

My head is swimming. Sophie had been slipping away and this pushed her even deeper into The Timeshare. She was dormant now and no one could tell me how long she'd be away or if she'd ever come back.

When you imagine anything like this—someone in your family getting hurt, being attacked or whatever, you have an idea of how you'd react and it's never anything resembling "normal." You think you'll go out and kill the guy, that you'll become a lawyer to pass legislation, that you'll do something huge. But most often you just sit there feeling completely helpless, your heart racing, wondering what the hell to do next.

"Liz, why didn't you call me?"

"You were dealing with your mom, Steve. You were saying good-bye. You had to focus on that. Laura had planned to visit anyway and we handled it. This was horrendous, but we've dealt with this sort of thing before."

"*This* sort of thing? *This* has happened before?"

"Not exactly this, but similar. It happened at college. Someone raped her that night Chuck brought her back to my place. She wouldn't give me any details, but we all just pitched in to get her back on her feet."

I'm shocked that Seb's not back in the hospital after something like this. Liz continues, "He seems to be doing okay. I mean, there's a lot of healing to do, but he's not falling apart. Part of it's because he actually expected this sort of thing from Craig."

While Liz was measured, Laura was seething. "In other words— what you did to him was worse. He never saw it coming with you. The thing you *fucking* guys never seem to get is that women don't have a choice after something like this. We have to go on. If you had one ounce of understanding what it's like to survive a sexual assault, you'd disintegrate. For women, we just have to help each other get through it because it doesn't seem like it's going to stop anytime soon."

Liz puts her hand on Laura's arm and tells me, "Look, we've got security here for now and the doctor will come back tomorrow. We've got Dr. Newman scheduled. Seb will fly back with us as soon as the doctor clears it. I'm not sure what will happen after that. Mark told us not to worry about this guy, but I feel better with Sebi out of town. I know you two are getting separated, but can you stay here and take care of Napoleon for now?"

That was an easy request. "Absolutely. No problem. I was going to look for an apartment when I got back, but I don't have one yet. We just talked briefly about separating before I left."

Laura continues to shake her head, "Yeah, we know," she spits out, sounding disgusted.

"I just want you to know where we are with things," I add.

"We're aware," Liz offers gently. She continues like she's readying for a trip and needs to check things off her list..."Okay. Good. We're trying to get her out of the modeling agency, but Sebi's pretty tied into it as one of the owners."

Liz reads my shock. "Sorry. I thought you knew. Oh crap. I shouldn't have said anything."

"No, it's good. I always suspected something like that."

Liz continues, "Well, then there's Mark. He's some sort of father-figure to Sebi, so that makes it tough. That said, his art has been selling really well so that helps with feeling like he's got work he can throw himself into. Jamie is looking at getting a job at the cooking school, but obviously that's on hold."

Most of my friends who were divorcing hated their wives, but I still loved Sophie. I wasn't cut out to be with a multiple, but I wasn't sure I could survive without them either.

———

Liz, Laura, Finn and I do pretty well living in the house together for a few days until Seb is well enough to travel. We all share breakfast each day and then I go to work, knowing Seb is well cared for. I'm learning more about his world, I met the doctor and saw Mark again, who felt horrible at incorrectly assessing the situation with Craig.

Each night, we eat dinner together. Laura has managed to warm to me enough that she no longer looks like she wants to stab me in the throat with whatever's available. But that's about as close as we've come to getting along. On the other hand, Liz and I are enjoying long conversations nearly every night. We cover a lot of ground and even have a few laughs. She feels like family.

But when everyone clears out, the house feels abandoned. Like when you move out of a home and it's suddenly just a shell. Like the life has been drained out of it. My sadness seems to be made somehow more pervasive by the fact that we're moving towards autumn. I keep the TV on for company. I'd imagined a very different life at this point—I thought that Sophie and I would have flourishing careers, hobbies we enjoyed together, a few kids and extended family. I'd always wanted children, but could never bring myself to telling Sophie. She had been dealing with enough. Instead, I'm living alone and can't see that changing.

Things are completely up in the air. My mom is dying and I wish I lived closer so I could be there. Work is still being a pain in the ass and I hate my boss more each day. Now this with Sophie. With Sebi, I mean. I want to be there for him and can't help but feel our separating may have somehow contributed to putting them at risk.

I'm pulled from my ruminating by a familiar face flashing across the TV. I turn up the volume to hear the report. "Photographer Craig Bishop was found dead in his Denver home. Police are reporting the cause of death to be suspicious but feel this is an isolated incident."

I purse my lips and raise my eyebrows. My only thought is, "Good."

I know it's wrong, but there's something satisfying about realizing that from time to time, there is justice in the world. With his line of work and the way he treated women, the list of suspects must be long. But I wonder if this might be a Godwulf thing.

"Anyone with information should call crime stoppers," I hear the announcer say.

Yeah, I don't think so. Big picture, I don't believe in vigilante justice. For Sophie, I couldn't do it myself, but I don't mind that this guy got what was coming to him.

I work during the day and then go back to the house to be with Napoleon.

It feels strange to be staying here without Sophie. It gives me a window into how The Timeshare must feel with me traveling so much and I feel guilty that I hadn't understood before. Napoleon helps.

I find a few little things that need repair—the toilet keeps running, some light bulbs need changing, the fan in the bathroom squeaks. After something like this, it helps to stay busy and if I can make her life a little easier, I want to do that, even if she never notices. I cut the lawn, clean up a bit and bring the mail in.

I think that time in the house alone is helping me to tie up my own loose ends. It helps me to get closure on that part of my relationship with Sophie. I loved her, but over the years, the distance between us had grown. I feel terrible about it, but I also get that's just a human thing. As people slip away, we have no choice but to let them go.

I'm drawn to the art shed. I sit out there and wait for the tears and when they come, I sob for hours. I keep thinking about that night we priced pieces for the sale and ate dinner from The Grill. I think about the morning I told Seb about Kevin and when he told me about Jamie and how we made love all weekend. It felt like a million years ago.

I have so much time to reflect and I can see it now. Sophie handled the aftermath of the abuse, so when the body was in pain, she was the one who came out to handle it. So much effort and energy went into handling the pain that she couldn't do anything else. Seb may not have asserted himself yet, but he had been starting to share hosting duties even back in college.

Sophie was the one I brought soup to when she was sick. She was irreconcilably broken but irresistibly endearing. She was the one I wanted to take care of, but not the one I fell in love with. She was the one standing in the snow, looking in the living room window at the happy family, the one that appealed to my inner hero, the one who needed someone to take care of her. But I had fallen in love with Sebi, not Sophie. It started at that frat party over a dozen years ago, I realized.

Irony. We're on the verge of divorce just as I'm realizing that it has always been Seb that I've been crazy in love with. I love his sense of humor, his positive energy, his relaxed attitude. I love his passion— even when it scares me.

And he's in love with Laura.

I wish I'd realized it all those years ago when I found Seb with Liz. Of course, at the time, I was just learning that he was a distinct and different identity. My breath grew jagged and I released a sigh. It was time to let go. Separating was an ending, not a beginning, and I had to accept that. I also had to decide whether or not to tell Sebi my true feelings. Honesty between us was new. Not because we chose to lie to one another, but because we had lied to ourselves.

I have plenty of time to think as I rattle around the house alone. I find myself looking forward to the mail arriving on the weekend. It gives me a break from thinking. I crunch through brittle leaves on my walk to the mailbox. I find a few catalogs and magazines, some bills, a letter from Sophie's good friend from college and a box about the size of an iPad package. The return address was a foil stamped gold medallion with "Godwulf Security" embossed around the top.

I shouldn't do it, and I go back and forth trying to justify opening Seb's mail. Curiosity finally forces my hand. Inside, I find an envelope sealed with gold wax—an emblem of St. Christopher stamped into it. I crack the seal and a three-page report indicates that the time Finn spent with us had been mostly uneventful, but Craig had been watching and at one point tried to break into the shed. Finn face-planted him into the ground before throwing him off the property. A separate page included a billing of $33,800 with a big PAID IN FULL stamp over the top. It was signed "Lass es mich wissen, wenn du noch etwas brauchst. Ich liebe dich. - RG" (Let me know if you need anything else. Love you.)

A jewelry box is included. Inside is another watch, identical to Sebi's. Seeing all of this, I can understand how Sebi felt cared for by Mark and the Godwulf family. To pay for private security, bring a private doctor in to care for them and then replace a very expensive watch could do that. I see an irony Seb doesn't. He wouldn't need their help if they hadn't put him in harm's way.

I smell something, too. Leather, pipe tobacco, lavender and saffron. I turn the watch over and see a worn, but still legible, inscription on the back "SG - Wir sind immer bei dir." (We are always with you). This is Sebi's watch, not a replacement. And a chill runs up my spine.

———

I want to confess my crime. Somehow it feels like the sooner I tell Seb, the less serious it is.

I call Laura's, hoping anyone but Laura answers. Someone else does pick up but I don't recognize the voice. "Hi. Can I talk with Seb?"

"This is Seb. Steve? Is that you?" His voice is deeper. His speech is faster, clipped, brighter, but there's a hint of the southern warmth in his voice.

"Seb? You sound totally different."

"Yeah. We've had a little reorganization happening."

"Anything you want to talk about?"

"This thing with Craig changed everything. Anna's done. Her whole reason for being here is gone, so all traces of her accent, the way she talks, the ways she dresses and walks and everything is gone.

Richard's job is to protect The Timeshare, but he couldn't do that. So he's kinda gone inside to lick his wounds. He's deeper now, so all of his mannerisms are further away. Jamie is out more and Rachel's been out a bunch since we got here. Ellyn's been out too—mostly when we visit Liz. And, well, it kinda feels like Sophie is face down in a shallow grave."

Considering what had happened, that grabs me by the throat. I try to shake it off. "Very descriptive," I find myself responding. It makes sense to me that things would need to be reorganized after such a traumatic event, but it also feels so different and permanent. When you break up with someone and then see them months later, you can see how they've evolved without you. Their life has changed.

With multiples, it runs far deeper. It's less an evolution and more an adaptation. I feel left behind and jealous—like I'm living in the shell of Sophie's old life while she's moved on to a shell that fits better. And I'm worried she'll never come back.

Anna had been a big part of my life and now *she's* gone. I see her red sweater draped over a chair and grab it, letting her scent pull the grief out of me. I need to focus on Seb, but my own self-interest comes up. Anna and I had shared a romantic relationship—or perhaps just a sexual one. But it was an important part of our marriage. With Sophie and Anna gone, I can't imagine my marriage having any kind of a shot. I can hear their absence in Seb's voice.

"Steve? Did you need something?"

"Sorry. A letter arrived for you today and I opened it."

"I'm sure it's fine. What was it?"

"It was from Godwulf Security."

"Oh," he pauses. "What did it say?"

"Seb, Godwulf Security? Is this Robert's company? You said the Godwulf's were jewelers."

I hear a slight laugh and a sharp breath.

"Seb? What's up?"

"Nothing. It's just, this whole reorganization is making me laugh. There were so many secrets before. So much worrying about trying to control everything. Total illusion. I don't need to have secrets from you. I don't need to have secrets from anyone. They're not going to keep me safe.

"Yes, Godwulf Security is Robert's. Our security guard was Finn Godwulf. His job is to escort business people into really dangerous areas of the world. He's my cousin. I met him when I went out to Germany. We got really close."

"Seemed that way when he was at the house. I'd wondered."

"When I was in Germany, I rolled my ankle on a hike and Finn wound up having to carry me three miles to get back to the truck. Kept calling me buddy."

"So that's the rest of the story. Why you picked the name Godwulf. And why you laughed that day I called you buddy."

"Exactly. That summer in Germany, Robert and I got really close. He sort of took me under his wing and kind of adopted me in a way.

"I learned a ton about the family line from Robert. His mom taught Jamie how to cook and Elizabeth how to care for people but she's also a badass. She fought for me—tried to adopt me and Sophie, but something happened. I don't know the whole story, but she's an extraordinary lady. By the way, her name? Her name is Sophie."

Anyway, we have a big family reunion in Germany every July 25th. I haven't gone for years, and I'd love to get back to it again."

"I gotta tell you, this is a lot of information." After years of getting one tiny droplet at a time, now I feel like I'm trying to drink from a firehose. This is everything you ever wanted to know in three seconds or less.

"This is stuff you've asked about for years," he reminds me. "I can stop if you want me to, but if you want to know more, now's the time."

"I do want to know, so, go ahead."

Sebi continues, filling in more blanks, "I connected Mark with the Godwulf Security company—with Robert."

"But I thought Robert was a jeweler."

"Yeah, he is. He also runs Godwulf Security."

"And that's how he's connected to Mark? Not through the jewelry side of things."

"He does some modeling, provides jewelry and, yes, he provides security as well."

"If I'm thinking it's a little more than security, I'd be right, yes?"

Sebi doesn't answer and the silence feels ominous. "They do a little enforcement work."

"Christ." Sebi's world is crazy and living on the edge of it is almost more than I can handle. I don't want to know any more, so I don't dig deeper. I pray that he'll drop it if I do.

"Seb?"

"Yeah?"

"They found the negatives and destroyed them."

I can feel the silent tears on the other end of the line. I close my eyes against my own burning tears. At least that was something. At least there was some sort of victory. I stare at my phone, trying to send quiet support. But I don't know if Seb wants me to know he's crying.

I add, "And they returned your watch."

I hear a sniffle and imagine Seb raking his sleeve across his nose as I'd seen him do anytime he cried. "Yeah?"

I feel I need to state the obvious because perhaps Seb was distracted by his relief. "Did you hear me? They didn't *replace* your watch. They *returned* your watch. The one Craig took from you."

"Yeah, I heard you Steve. I'm glad to have it back."

"Are you not getting what this means? It means that probably it was Finn who..."

"Yes, I know what it means, Steve. I know. And you know, too. Just don't spend too much time thinking about it, okay? Can you FedEx it to me? I'd like to have it."

I always feel like I'm in some 007 movie every time I speak with Sebi lately, but I say, "Okay, sure," as I can't help thinking to myself— 'I'll send you the watch that some guy retrieved from your attacker after probably murdering him. No problem.'" This all was surreal. But it was also obvious that this felt normal to Sebi.

"And Steve?"

"Huh?"

"Thanks."

———

While Sophie is out in California, we stay in touch by phone. One evening a video call comes through and it's Rachel, wanting to show me what she'd found at the beach that day.

I'm shocked at her appearance. Her hair has been cut in a man's style and it looks completely different, lighter, and most remarkably, growing in thick and wavy as opposed to Sophie's fine, straight locks. Her face is broader, too. Her eyes are a definite blue and her eyebrows are thicker. She looks like she's gained at least 10 pounds. She's looking more and more male. Even though little Rachel was who called, it's like a little girl alter of an adult man.

I can not stop crying the whole time. It feels like I'm separated from my little girl—from my own child. She keeps telling me it's okay and tries to cheer me up by showing me more and more of her treasures, which makes me cry even harder. I can't hide it. Laura has created a home for Sophie in their guest house. It's filled with all of The Timeshare's favorite things and Seb has settled in.

Finally, Rachel tells me, "I'm gonna let you go now, okay?" I know what she means—she means for the moment, but it feels like forever and I fall apart.

"I know," she says, sticking her lip out. "I miss you too..." as she shuts the laptop on her end. I just sit staring at the blank screen, wishing I could go on autopilot.

Sophie and I are still married and even if we weren't, I care about her. I enjoy sort of a fragile detante with Laura these days, but we have to talk. I text her with an update on everything and to check in to make sure Sebi hasn't gone on autopilot. That happened sometimes after a really intense trauma and it was horrible. But this time, Seb is holding his own. No autopilot, and that's a sign of tremendous strength and progress. I call Dr. Newman with an update.

———

I resist the urge to jump on a plane to go see The Timeshare but I'm glad when work calls to ask me to fly out to California for a meeting. I might be able to stop by and see Rachel in person. I find a friend to watch the house and walk Napoleon while I'm away. I wrap up my meeting on Friday and stop by Laura's to surprise Rachel.

When Seb opens the door and sees me, he looks confused, then frightened. He takes a step back and looks around, trying to reacclimate. Then he looks at me once more, clearly not understanding. I'd sent a trigger through the system. They compartmentalize. I belong in Colorado and seeing me here triggers an episode of de-realization. This was much worse than de-personalization, where your body doesn't feel like yours. Everything feels unreal. It's like stepping into a Salvador Dali painting. Sebi grabs onto the wall, as he reels back and finally collapses, yelling for Laura. She comes running, sees me sitting there with Sebi looking confused, and glares at me.

"What did you do?"

"Nothing, Laura. I'm in town and wanted to stop by to see Seb."

"Stay here," she directs. She runs upstairs and comes back down with a blanket and body pillow, a bottle of pills and a glass of water.

"It's okay, honey. Take this."

Seb looks at her but doesn't seem to recognize her.

"I'm Laura. You can trust me. It's okay. This will help you feel better."

He takes the pill and starts to wash it down with several big gulps of water.

"That's enough," Laura directs. "Stop." She grabs the blanket and pillow and gets him situated on the floor. "You're going to feel sleepy in a minute. Just rest here."

She turns to me, pushing me out the front door and closing it over so we don't disturb Seb, but so she can still keep an eye on him.

"What the *hell* were you thinking? Have you ever even met a multiple? You can't just show up and surprise them. What's wrong with you?"

I understood her anger. She was feeling protective of Seb. Papa had induced de-realization through drugs when Sophie was a child so that she couldn't accurately remember details of the abuse. That way, it would appear she was just making the whole thing up if she ever told anyone. Details wouldn't match the evidence.

Now Laura is fuming and I feel like the non-custodial parent being scolded for dropping by unannounced.

"I'm sorry," I find myself saying. "We talked over video the other day. I just wanted to say hi."

"Okay, well, that was a really bad idea. Call next time, okay?"

"Can I do anything to help? Do you need me to carry Sophie to the couch or something?"

She sighs like a mom who had to clean up a mess made by her ex. "No, Steve. Just go home." She goes inside and closes the door behind her.

I leave feeling like such a loser. I'd scheduled a flight out for Monday and had planned to hang out with The Timeshare for the weekend. I hadn't even imagined she wouldn't want to see me. Now they're on a floor and I have no idea how long it'll take them to recover. And I have two full days to feel like crap about what I've done.

Then I remember Liz lives nearby. I call to see if she's home and might want me to drive up...

"Oh my God, yes! I'm so glad you called. Yes, please do!" She gives me her address and I make my way to Sonoma. I'm glad for the time to clear my head and try to shake off this horrible feeling of being unwanted and unneeded. Actually, it's worse than that—I feel like a bull in a china shop around The Timeshare these days.

Her Spanish-style house with white stucco walls and arched windows looks like the perfect home for a pharma rep and plastic surgeon. Palm trees out front, a pool with guest house in the back. It's stunning, a perfect fit for Liz.

She meets me at the door and gives me a big hug. "I put together a bite. Are you hungry?" she asks, grabbing me by the arm and leading me out to the pool.

I instantly feel cared for and welcomed. It's so nice after everything we'd all been through recently. I tell her, yes, I am hungry.

She seems more relaxed here, more casual and friendly. A table is set up next to the pool. A bowl of fresh figs, a platter of cheese, crackers and grapes and a bottle of red wine. Exactly the sort of lunch that appealed to me and a refreshing change from the junk food at my house.

We sit down at the table and she hands me a plate to fill as she pours the wine.

"How have you been doing?" she asks.

We're both in rough places, so after I share that I'm missing Sophie, we both wind up commiserating over Sebi—feeling Laura is being so protective that we don't know if we'd ever see The Timeshare again.

"You know she blames the attack on you—because you left. She thinks Craig wouldn't have been brave enough to do anything if you two were together. I think that's bullshit because he didn't even know you guys split. He was just a pissy little jerk."

"She was certainly not happy to see me," I recount, telling her I triggered a de-realization episode.

"Oh, that stinks when it happens. But I've triggered those, too. When he'd see me in Colorado sometimes. It's just whenever something feels out of place. It's awful, but he'll be better in a few days. Try not to blame yourself, hon."

"Thanks. I appreciate that. How's your life going?"

"Well, I live here, so I've got that going for me," Liz smiles. I love that she's an unparalleled optimist.

"Yes, you do," I say, taking in the gorgeous day. "It's pretty fantastic here."

"It really is. And work is good. Kids are good. Charlie's an ass."

"Is he around?"

"Nope," she clips, fiercely clinking two slender ice cubes into her glass before filling it with water.

"Anything else you want to add to that?"

Liz just shook her head. "Charlie's been in Europe a lot lately. Not all that unusual. Paris is like a plastic surgery hub. This time, however, he's not coming back."

"Ever?" I say, shocked.

"You sound like me when he called. That's exactly what I said. He told me he'd visit the kids at some point, but yeah, basically. He's moved to France with some young guy he met at work."

"Oh my God, Liz. I'm so sorry. How are you doing with the kids? Do you have help? They're still so young."

"Well, my parents do what they can, but, you know, they're busy with their own lives. And I have to take care of all the divorce stuff by myself now. Charlie's so happy with his new boy toy that he told me I can keep everything here as long as I don't ask for alimony. He'll pay child support, of course. But I have to do all the paperwork."

I can see the exhaustion in her face now as her smile fades and anxiety creeps in.

I feel so drawn to her and it's odd to think of what a strange course our friendship had taken. I never really noticed her at college. I'd hated her when I saw her with Sebi that morning. But over the years, we warmed to one another and now I see how much we have in common. We're friends and I've come to depend on her—not only to help with Seb, but to help me feel I'm not alone in all of this. And here we are now, both going through break-ups.

"Hey, at least we have each other. Is there anything I can do to help?"

"You're sweet. I really appreciate it. If you lived out here, I'd sign you up for a babysitting shift but other than that, just having someone to listen is huge."

As I begin to leave, she hugs me and I instinctively give her a brief kiss and then a longer one.

"I'm sorry. I'm just in a crazy place right now," I say.

"No, it's okay. It was nice."

We hesitate at the door, searching each other's eyes, trying to sort out our options. I don't want to make the same mistakes I've made with Sophie. We need to talk more before moving towards anything remotely romantic. There are truths she needs to hear and I have to know her better before I can share them.

We break the gaze with laughter and I throw out a generic, "Okay, then...."

She smiles at me warmly, kisses my cheek and says, "You're not flying back until Monday, are you? Where are you going to stay?"

"I don't know. I'll probably just drive back down and stay at the hotel they usually put us up in."

"Traffic is going to be a bitch this time of night. If you want to stay in the pool house, you can," she offers. "I mean, I don't want it to be a weird thing, but you have had quite a bit of wine and it's pretty late."

October 26, 2016

A few more weeks pass and I wonder if Sebi is ever coming back to Colorado at all.

Then one day, he's home when I return from work. He looks more and more like the drawing he'd shown me at breakfast the morning after we made love. His thick shock of dark hair wavy with caramel streaks from the sun. His eyes don't contain even a hint of green and his muscles are much more defined.

He thanks me for taking care of Napoleon and fixing everything up around the house. Then he apologizes for freaking out when I had visited and for "acting like an infant" about Kevin.

I told him that he hadn't done anything wrong and his reaction made a lot of sense.

I sleep in the guest room and Sebi sleeps on the couch with Richard's baseball bat next to him. It would take some time before he felt safe again—if that time ever came.

The next morning we sat down together to try to hammer out what would happen next.

I start, but my hands are sweating and I feel a lump in my throat. "I know we agreed on a separation, but I've had a lot of time to think. I want you in my life, regardless of how you want that to look."

"Oh thank God. I do too," Seb says. "But a lot has to change. I need relationships outside of the marriage. And to tear you away from Kevin would be cruel. I love you and I can't take that away from you. Seeing Carla work through her feelings when I was out there with Laura taught me a lot."

"I bet. That had to be pretty wild."

"It was, but the thing that was interesting was that they just talked about everything and they were honest with each other. It was enlightening."

I'm worried about telling Seb the truth, but know it'll be worse if I lie. "In the interest of honesty, when I went to California, I drove up to see Liz. I stayed in her pool house for a few nights."

"I know."

"You do?"

"Of course. Steve, I was out there for weeks. Ellyn spent a good deal of time with Liz. I think she likes you."

"Likes me?"

"Like—likes you, likes you."

It sounded so high school and at the same time, it made me smile.

"Well, I think I like her, like her, too."

"She's easy to like. I'm happy for you," he says, but it looks like he's struggling with something.

"Listen, I have to talk with Dr. Newman about something that I really need him to hear. I can't explain it, but could you come with us? I could use some back up."

"Absolutely," I respond.

———

A few days later, as we sit in the waiting room, Sebi stares out the window. He'd left his playful self at home. He needs to be taken seriously, to be heard.

Dr. Newman's door opens into the waiting room as he says, "Sebi?" Then seeing me there, he smiles in surprise. "And Steve? Hey, how are you? Come on in."

We settle in and wait for Sebi to start.

"I want Steve here to help me with something."

Dr. Newman smiles, "That's no problem. What's going on?"

"I need to talk about what happened with Craig."

Dr. Newman nods in silent acknowledgment.

"I was knocked out."

Dr. Newman says nothing but remains focused on Seb.

Sebi seems hesitant to go on, perhaps hoping we can both pick up on what he needs to say and what he's feeling by osmosis.

"I need you to listen to me because it's important. I should not have blacked out. Someone, anyone in The Timeshare should have been able to not black out. I left Liz alone. I can't believe she's not furious with me for it. I'm so mad at myself that I can hardly tolerate it."

"But Seb," I start. He shoots me a hard, quick look that tells me if I argue this point, he'll probably punch me.

Dr. Newman is gently holding Seb in his gaze.

Seb looks at Dr. Newman. "Aren't you going to say anything?"

"What do you need to hear, Seb?"

"I need to hear that you agree with me."

"If I agreed with you, what would that mean?"

"That...it would mean that...that I'm right. That it shouldn't have been that easy to knock me out. That there's something I can do to prevent it from happening again. I mean, Jesus CHRIST. If no one can guarantee that, I'm not sure how I'm going to be able to keep going— just waiting to be attacked again."

Dr. Newman is silent again. I follow his lead.

"I don't feel safe. I'm not sure I can ever feel safe again."

"What are you doing to try and feel safe now?"

"I have Napoleon and that helps. Robert said Finn can come back and stay as long as I want if I need him, but it doesn't seem like that's a long-term solution. All of that is outside of me. I'm not keeping myself safe."

"People rely on outside stuff all the time. Alarms, guards, dogs. Why should you be any different?"

"Because I'm me. Because there's a whole crew of us. We should be able to keep The Timeshare safe. Otherwise, what's the point? If awful things happen to people, even with guards and alarms and everything, then there's no way to keep yourself safe."

"Our world is generally safe, but yes, sometimes bad things happen no matter what."

"So I can't keep myself safe. Jesus, why did I even tell you about this?"

"Because you want guarantees. You want a magic wand. But I don't have one. I wish I did. What I can tell you is that you are relatively safe in the world. Bad things happen sometimes, but almost all of the time you're safe. I can tell you there are things you can do to keep yourself safer—not going into dangerous areas or doing risky things, learning how to defend yourself. I can tell you that it's okay to ask for help, to rely on the dog or the alarm, or the security guard, on Steve and Liz. That's okay. I can tell you that the more you heal, the less vulnerable you are. And I can tell you that you are doing an incredible job healing. But no, I can't promise you that you are 100% safe all of the time."

I can tell Sebi is disappointed, but he's also relieved. He's heard the truth and now needs time to sit with it.

"Wanna grab a coffee?" I ask while reflecting how funny it is that we get into habits. As we walk into the Starbuck's, I remember all the other times we've been here after therapy.

We sit quietly sipping our double espressos, looking out the window and people watching. Seb remains reflective and quiet until he pulls something out of his bag and hands it to me without an explanation.

It was a large envelope.

"What's this?" I ask.

Seb is pursing his lips against the tears burning in his eyes. "Open it," he directs with a whisper.

I look inside to find a funeral program for Sophie's grandmother. She died a few weeks ago. And there's a card. On the front a mama teddy bear snuggles a baby one. Inside, written in her grandmother's hand is her final message. "All those nights when I played the piano? That was the only way I knew how to tell you that you weren't alone."

The revelation settles in my eyes and I immediately begin to cry. I look at Seb, who's flexing his jaw and smiling as tears stream down his cheeks. "I like to believe my grandmother was a good person who was just trapped in that world. We were both stuck."

"I'm so sorry, Seb. I know you were close. I know you loved her."

"Did you know that when we were on vacation at the lake, she'd boat out with me to pick blueberries? That's why they're my favorite. Reminds me of her. Reminds me that no matter who you are or where you come from or what you go through, you're worthy of redemption. She wasn't a bad woman. But she was broken...

"I might not be 100% safe. I get that. There were a few guys who messed everything up for me. Nearly everyone else in my world was good. That's the reality. Bad people will knock you down, but there will always be good people to help you get back up. I can never forget what the bad ones did to me. And I'll never forgive them. But I need to remember all the good people. That's how I'll turn things around."

Sebi wipes his eyes and sets his jaw in resolve. "I need a fresh start."

"We both need a fresh start, Seb."

Sebi leans his head against me and takes a deep breath, before locking me in his eyes. They had turned to a paler blue and he was running his fingers through his hair. "Do you think there's any way we can get a fresh start together?"

The request warms me and makes me smile. Physical transitions were smoother between alters now. I can't immediately tell when there's a switch—apart from a few clues. "What are you thinking, El?"

"I'm thinking I really miss you. I'm thinking neither of us is perfect and those imperfections make our lives deeper and richer, but that cultural convention and shame have conspired to entrap us in misery."

Ellyn gets up for some tea and I can tell she's holding me in a trust with what she's about to say.

As she waits for her tea, she sits back down across from me and rests her arms on the table, chin on her hands. "I'm thinking our outside relationships may save us, not condemn us. I think monogamy doesn't work for us."

"I was thinking that too," I agree. "You'd mentioned polyamory is the only valid answer for multiples."

"I believe that to be true for our situation. We have a system of alters who are each unique individuals and if we want to respect that, we need to allow them to fully express themselves in healthy ways. And Kevin brings something you need into your life. No one should be forced to give up the love they need in order to make someone else happy.

"If you loved someone else, I'd want you to be honest with me about it, but I'd want to celebrate that with you. No one person can meet all of our needs and if you love them, why would you put that expectation on them?"

"I hope Seb knows he's absolutely and without question my first choice," I say. "I love him. While you were away, I just sat out in the shed and cried. I realized something while he was away."

"What's that?"

"It was never Sophie. I love Sophie, but I was never *in* love with her."

Ellyn smiles knowingly. "Seb. You fell in love with Seb. When?"

"I think always. I think that's who I fell in love with in college. I just thought it was Sophie. Seb's always been such a gift. I could date this amazing man who lived within a beautiful woman. It was like the best of both worlds for me. He reached in and accepted me before I could even accept myself. So, yeah, it's always been Seb. And, yes, I need Kevin in my life, too, just as you need Liz, and Laura needs Seb."

"It's a complex web isn't it?"

"It is," I laugh. I had learned so much about how to talk with the alters and found it almost effortless now. While I'd already told Seb about Liz, I didn't know how much of it Ellyn had heard.

"I need to tell you something else. I'm sick of the lies. I'm going to be honest from now on, even if it hurts. I saw Liz a few weeks ago and discovered I also have an attraction to her. We shared a couple of kisses."

"It's hard not to be attracted to Liz."

I can hear the love in her voice but there's no trace of jealousy. "I'd like to meet Kevin sometime. It would be nice to know everyone in our family."

Our family.

I'd never thought of it that way. Polyamory, to me, had seemed like people who couldn't commit, who had sex addictions and wanted to eat a lot of cake and have a lot, too. Ellyn just put a whole new spin on it for me. This was about very deep commitments to multiple people. It was about respect, love, care, and family.

"I would love that. Thank you for asking. It means a lot to me that you consider all of us to be a family. It's allowing me to see something I'd been ashamed about in a new light. That's what this is about, isn't it? Building a family?"

We're learning more about polyamory, too, with Ellyn leading the way. I think, had she been out full time, she'd have several PhD's, because she researched the hell out of things. It was enlightening. You have a very clear idea of what something will look like until you actually see it and discover that it's nothing like what you thought it would be. Ellyn had known this all along.

Ellyn smiles. "I think we're going to need some help navigating this. I found a group called Loving More. It's a non-profit that helps educate people about polyamory and provides support for people in these relationships. It's pretty cool, actually. They have conferences and offer resources. They're great people and I had an amazing talk with someone there, but this is very complex. They suggested a therapist in Boulder we may want to talk with. You okay with that?"

"I'm open to it. I'm just wondering what you feel our relationship would look like?"

I see a slight shiver run through her and Sebi steps forward.

"I love you, Steve, but Laura would probably be my primary relationship. When I was out there, we talked about it. I stayed in their guest house and they invited me to move in permanently. Carla travels so much for work and she doesn't want Laura to be there alone. And she knows I make Laura happy."

"That's a huge sacrifice on Carla's part."

"I'm not sure that's how she sees it. Having me in the wedding was her idea. Did you know that?"

"I thought that was Laura's idea and that Carla was upset about it."

"Nope. We had a long talk when I was out there. Carla picked out the suit and everything. Gave me to Laura as a wedding gift! Turns out they're both advocates of polyamory. Carla's parents were a triad. She gets a little jealous, but she feels better knowing Laura isn't home alone for weeks at a time. Carla is a visiting professor and Laura's job keeps her in the same place."

I'm shocked that it seems things are coming together. But I'm worried, too. We're in a precarious place and I don't know what this means for our relationship.

"So, what about us? What's that going to look like?"

Sebi stands up and takes my hand, pulling me to my feet. And in one move, he puts his hand behind my neck, pulls me toward him and brushes his lips with mine before saying, "It's going to be like this." He kisses me like he did that morning I told him about Kevin. It was reassuring and seductive. Then he slips his arm around my waist and laughs, knowingly. "It was always me, huh? Imagine that."

That night we slept in my bed together. We decided to live as a couple until we figured out our next move. It was very different, but it was a time of releasing one another from monogamy, enjoying, and grieving a series of "lasts" together. We'd be making a fresh start but neither of us knew exactly what that meant, despite our intentions. Tucking in at night and sleeping in the same bed, holding each other, was healing for both of us.

After keeping Kevin from him and the resulting fallout, I had been sure Seb and I would never make love again. It seemed so far out of reach. But sleeping in the same bed and feeling the degree of passion we'd had for one another there led us back to it. Over the next few weeks, it got better and better as we learned one another's bodies— what brought the greatest tension and the most intense release. It was the most bittersweet time of my life because I knew in my heart that it couldn't last and, however we moved forward, it wouldn't look like this.

And *this*? It was good.

Holiday Season 2016

It was taking some time to decide what our fresh start would look like. Would we live together or apart? Would we stay in Denver or go somewhere else? It felt like we were completely re-inventing ourselves and it was an enormous task.

We spent more time with the people from Loving More in, of all places, Loveland, Colorado. The most open, welcoming, loving people you could imagine. We went to see the poly therapist in Boulder, Annie. It was amazing to be accepted and understood—and to have help understanding all the joys and complications polyamory can bring. Annie helped make our transition much easier.

One benefit of loving each other, but not worrying about needing to maintain a monogamous structure, was that we felt we could be more honest, so we were sharing everything.

This Christmas felt different, too. We both knew it would likely be our last holiday in the house. It also felt like it might be our last one in Denver. We took in all of our favorites—the Christkindl Market, the skating rink. And then we hit things we'd always intended to do but never quite got to, like the Capitol lighting ceremony and parade.

Our polyamory family flew in to help us celebrate the holidays. Kevin was alone now. Shannon was in long-term care and seemed to resent his visits. She had her own life and it didn't include him. He would visit her on Christmas and then go home to an empty house, which he couldn't bear, so he flew out. He was looking at a fresh start as well. His job wanted him to move to San Francisco, so he was preparing for that.

Liz needed to be with the kids for Santa, but after that, she needed a break. She left the kids with her parents for a few days and they were thrilled about it. Laura was even able to join us briefly after Rachel called begging her to come out. So we had our entire family together for the holidays and it felt like our fresh start had been launched. It wasn't about sorting out the logistics. It was about following the love we already had in our lives.

We wanted this to be a time of healing, so I found a Madame Alexander Beth doll and gave it to Elizabeth. After that, we saw her growing in leaps and bounds. Liz gave Seb a new gray scarf she purchased from a Romanian weaver. It looked identical to Jamie's old one. Laura gave Sebi a gift certificate for a workshop at the Berkeley Art Studio. And Seb got Kevin and me camping equipment.

Over the holidays, Jamie cooked huge feasts. Rachel popped in and out to find several packages from Santa.

Issues, of course, came up. Annie explained to us that within a poly relationship there are even more triggers as we work through getting to know ourselves and understand what we need. She helped us with that, too.

It felt like we were planting seeds. Everyone was gentle with one another, patient and loving. We'd all resolved not to engage in any conflicts and, instead, to table them until after the holidays. We all had wounds and we kept track of issues we wanted to discuss together and, if necessary, bring to Annie.

Just before New Years, we got in to see her for some help creating relationship agreements. We wanted to have an impartial opinion.

Her office was comfortable and we felt at home there, welcomed by someone who really understood what we were going through. Annie had shared that she was also polyamorous.

I started out: "We want to come up with some rules so we don't keep hurting each other. This is all so new. It feels foreign to me."

"Okay, we can do that," Annie said, measured. Then smiling, she reminded me, "but I think you mean 'agreements.'"

"Right, agreements. That does feel better than rules."

"Second," she said with a hint of laughter in her eyes. "Don't you guys get it?"

We were both lost. Seb looked at me and I looked at Annie. "What?"

She waited a beat to see if anything clicked. It didn't. "You've been polyamorous for years but you were practicing it in a way that didn't work."

We both must have looked totally confused. "That's where the mistrust and betrayal comes from," she continued. "It comes from the lying and cheating and sneaking around. At the root of all of this is fear and shame. But you don't need to feel ashamed about having an attraction to other people...and we can talk through the fear part together."

Understanding was starting to seep through as she continued, "It's not the fact that you love other people that holds the potential to destroy your marriage. It's the dishonesty. Cheating is disrespectful and incredibly painful. Polyamory is about being transparent, creating agreements, and honoring both your own needs and your partner's feelings."

January 2017

We'd been uncertain of our path, but after the holidays, it was clear what we needed to do. We needed to be nearer to our family. And since Liz and Laura both lived in California, Kevin was on his way there, and my job could easily be transferred, our answer was obvious. We set our sights on the Bay area—or as close as we could get.

Seb took Carla up on her offer and moved into the guest house. Now I needed to find a place. Liz agreed to help me look, but it was obvious that I was not going to find anything that worked within our time frame.

Liz called and said she thought maybe she'd found a solution. "Tell me if this is too weird, Steve but I have a five bedroom house that I can't care for by myself and I could use some help with the kids. I'm just an hour away from Seb and Laura. I don't know. Am I being presumptuous here?"

"You're being incredibly generous and it would help so much. The timing is just really tight and if I can stay with you until I can find something, that would be amazing.

"I do want to tell you what Sebi and I have decided before I say yes, so you can take it into consideration."

"You heard some talk at Christmas about polyamory. Seb and I are exploring that.

I hear a smile in Liz's voice as she responds, "I've spoken with Ellyn about it, too. We do a lot of talking."

So often when we tell the truth, we find our tribe there. It made it easier for me to say what was next.

I tripped over the words in my head. "I love Sebi and I'm developing feelings for you. I don't think any of that is a surprise. And I know that you saw how close Kevin and I are."

I paused long enough that Liz needed to prompt me.

"Steve?"

I took a shaky breath and went on, "Kevin and I have been in a relationship for the past year."

"You idiot!" she laughed. "Kevin is no surprise to me. The way you talk about him? It's like listening to Seb talk about Laura."

There's nothing more amazing than sharing the deepest truths about yourself and having them embraced.

February and March 2017

Over the next weeks, we pack up the house, make repairs, clean. We change our address, say goodbye to neighbors and wrap things up. Not wanting to move unnecessary things, we go through everything in the house.

I hear The Timeshare talking in different voices as they sort. Anna's clothes, a lot of Sophie's stuff, and a fair amount of Richard's things go into boxes to wait for the donation truck. I feel sad as I notice the boxes and pull Anna's red sweater out to keep.

I'm surprised that even Elizabeth is excited about a new place to live. She had some questions and fears that needed calming, but overall, there's a feeling of adventure at the house. Rachel is bouncing off the walls. And after all my talk about hoping Ellyn would have more of a role, more of a life, I had forgotten that she felt Liz was the love of her life. So she was looking forward to California as well. Jamie said he'd miss certain things about Denver, but California offered more opportunities for him to explore cooking. Plus, they had In and Out Burger.

Everything went smoothly thanks to Liz and Laura offering us places to stay. Our Denver house sold quickly. We sat out in the shed and cried for a few hours.

Sebi had loved it out there. It'd been his sanctuary and he'd miss it. But the new owners of our house were thrilled to have an art studio, so we ended up selling them the kiln and other equipment that would have been too difficult to move anyway.

That last session with Dr. Newman was brutal. The relationship you have with a therapist is unique. They're not family. They're not a best friend. But it's intensely close. We'd been through so much with him. Leaving him would be hard. At that last visit, he reviewed Sebi's progress, wished us luck, provided some referrals to therapists out in California and let us know he'd be available if we ever needed anything.

We thanked him but it didn't feel adequate.

He just smiled. "It's been great to work with you both. You already had everything you needed to get through this, you know. I just gave you the tools to help you see it. You were whole already."

Rachel came out and was sobbing. She gave him a puzzle and a doll for the office so other multiples had something to play with when they came to see him. He told her to choose one of his turtles to take with her to California. She chose one that had three turtles—one on top of the other. He smiled, "I think they've always wanted to go on an adventure. Good choice."

EPILOGUE
—Dr. Newman

It's a rare treat to receive letters from a client after they've left my care. I appreciate knowing how life is going for them, hearing about new insights that come through and seeing how their relationships are doing.

Steve and Sebi asked that I share my insights here—as well as telling you of their progress.

Honestly, it was sort of miraculous to see how everything came together for them. Being of a metaphysical bent, I believe they're just incredible manifesters. Or perhaps karma owed them some peace.

They moved out to California in the spring of 2017 and fairly quickly, Sebi felt more settled than ever—he seems at home. Laura's guest house is comfortable for him, perfect, in fact. There's space for a small drawing studio, which is how he spends most of his time. Seb shares the space with Napoleon, who is happy to be reunited with his sister, Laura's Great Dane, Josephine.

Seb cashed out of the agency and has gone back to school for his Master's in Fine Arts. He's loving every second of it and doing well.

As we suspected would happen, Sebi has taken over as the host. The Timeshare had "top" surgery done after a suspicious mammogram, so he looks more like he imagines himself to be.

The Timeshare is still intact, but they stand behind Sebi, only coming out as needed, which is rare. All their skills and talents are available to him when needed. Feeling safe now and living in a more stable environment with a strong community is reflected in The Timeshare. They're less guarded, more fun, willing to explore.

Seb and Steve remain married and close, but Laura is Seb's primary relationship and Liz is Steve's. She's happy to feel like #1.

Ellyn is also involved with Liz, and Steve frequently spends time with Kevin.

Steve moved in with Liz, which he assumed would be temporary but became permanent. He always wanted children and now he has them—and Liz has help. Rachel wanted me to know that she stops by for monkey bread most Saturday mornings.

Steve's mother passed away over the summer but they were all able to be with her to say goodbye.

Steve recognized his issue with pills and got some help—90 days clean as of the date of this last letter, August 13, 2018. He told me revealing his secrets helped him shine a light on other skeletons—and to realize there was no shame in seeing them—or having them.

Seb closed his last letter to me with this: "We went through so much to get here—a long series of deep grieving over unnecessary losses. We almost lost our happiness to convention and dishonesty. We felt we'd fall apart without one another, but culture instructed that was the only way. We tried to have time apart but there was too much love. It wasn't a matter of needing each other, of belonging to someone else or even belonging together, it was about the truth that when we're together, we feel that we belong to ourselves. And in that place, it feels like home."

Do you want to hear Sebi's side of the story?

Visit sebi_godwulf on Instagram where you can ask questions and interact with the author and characters.

Or see Seb's blog at booksbyari/blog

After several years of drawing lessons
and some pretty intensive work after my breakthrough
(thanks to Rachel)
I present to you, my drawings of The Timeshare.

~ Seb

Me (Seb)

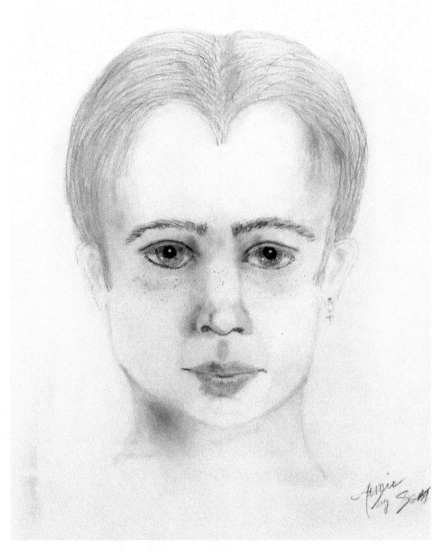

Jamie

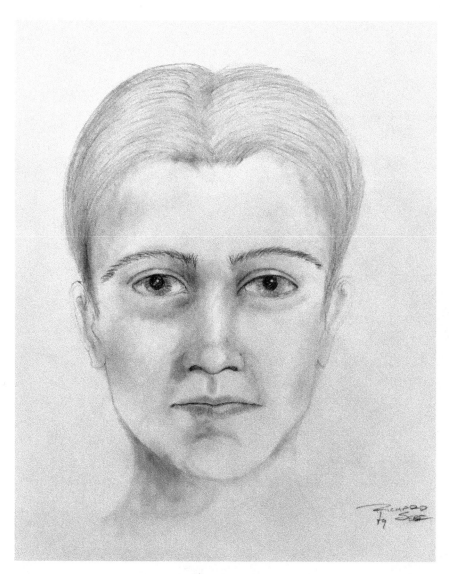

Richard

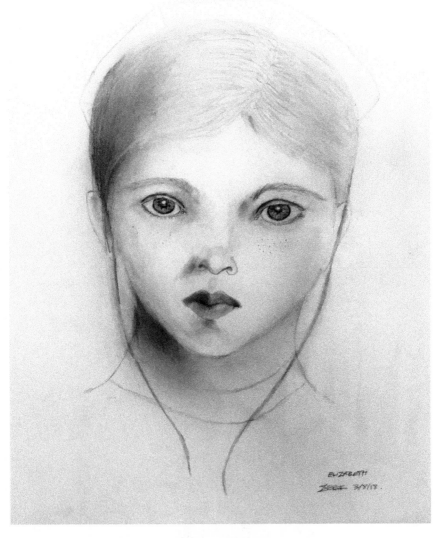

Elizabeth

Rachel

Ellyn

Anna

Chelsea

Kalia

Excerpt from *The 316's*
Coming Fall of 2019

As soon as I have the money, I'm buying black-out drapes. The morning sun comes through my bedroom window like shards of glass assaulting my eyes, reminding me that no matter how unprepared I am for life, it's going to creep in and drag me out of my warm bed and into the chaos.

Am I supposed to be this unhappy at 19? I can never sleep and I wish I could. Two or three hours a night I just lay here and toss and turn. I feel like I should be enthusiastic about something, have a list of dreams. Shouldn't I be full of excitement for all my potential? I'm just starting out in life and the sky's the limit. That's what people keep telling me. My therapist, on the other hand, says I'm dysthymic —a sort of Eeyore-ish condition where I'm chronically sort of low-grade miserable. I like to think I'm beating it back, but mornings tend to make me forget that.

She also says I have anxiety and agoraphobia. Fancy words for feeling so anxious it's like torture—which makes me hate leaving the house. I'd prefer to live as a hermit, but if I psych myself up, I can get to familiar places that are nearby. And I can get to work. Yee haw. But it's a constant struggle and sometimes I want to sink into it and let it take me. Dad tells me I whine too much.

This is my third apartment in a year. I keep getting smaller places with more roommates. They fall away, moving back home until they can save enough for a decent place. My parents are more of the "sink or swim" school, so I'm on my own. I get that. I'm 19. I should be on my own, but there's something terrifying about knowing no one is there to help you.

My siblings are all doing great. I'm adopted and feel like a failure. My parents always told me about those kids who were adopted who became huge super stars, brain surgeons, save the world sorts. I fall more into the category of "cautionary tale" to people desperate enough to have a kid that they adopt a school-ager.

I came into the family when I was 5. I don't really remember how it went except I have the vague feeling of a young woman who looks like I do now crying and kissing me goodbye. I assume that was my mom, but she hasn't been looking for me so I guess she didn't miss me that much. My adoptive parents told me that I lived in a big community with my mom and a bunch of other people, but after it fell apart, my mom couldn't care for me. My dad wasn't in the picture. My parents took me in as a foster kid and eventually adopted me.

I roll over, my back to the sun, but it's invasive. My cat jumps up on the bed and head-butts me, reminding me it's time for her breakfast. Right on time, the list starts running. First on the agenda, ruminating over my student loan. College seemed like such a good idea at the time, even though I had no idea what I wanted to study. I switched majors so much that I left after two years with nothing. I was supposed to be a prodigy or something—I finished high school early but then crapped out of college.

One of our roommates just packed up and moved in with her boyfriend, so we need to find a way to come up with more money. And I have to get groceries. All of my jobs have very much resembled my summer jobs during high school—daycare, fast food, the grocery store. And I continue to beat up on myself that I haven't been more decisive about my degree.

The sun won't stop, so I grab my phone and start flipping through Instagram. I try to look at something meaningful but keep coming back to pictures of Alexander Misham. God, that man just makes my life. He's the reason I feel like I'm starting to feel better. I hope to have my life together as much as he does someday. He's only a few years older than me, but according to his Instagram, he's at the gym every morning at 5am, at work acting or modeling by 7 and then out half the night at fundraisers for his charity or premiers or supporting his friends in their acting careers. Everyone who's met him or worked with him says he's a great guy.

I look at his latest magazine layout, clips from upcoming movies and scads of fan posts gushing over meeting him, seeing him on the street, working with his charity.

I pull the covers up over my head and notice the time on my phone—11am. Alex has already accomplished more today than I will this entire week. Yet, somehow his messages always make me feel better. And he responds to fans with encouraging notes when people share about their anxiety and depression or day-to-day struggles.

An hour passes and I'm tired enough to go back to limbo. That's what I call it. It's not really sleep. I never dream. But I can close my eyes and rest. So I do that. I'm smiling because something about Alex is comforting. I feel cared for and loved.

I close my eyes and let my phone go dark.

Acknowledgments

I deeply appreciate the vulnerability of the multiples and partners I interviewed. Those conversations were often both healing and painful and I greatly appreciate their willingness to share. I also appreciate the help of all the experts I spoke with—from therapists to poly folks, musicians, language/cultural consultants, and a well-loved religious scholar. Your wisdom shows up in these pages as we work together to make a positive difference.

Thank you to my patient editor Barb Munson, to Nick Zelinger for the beautiful cover work and book design, and to Adam Riley for bringing The Timeshare to life through the audio version. And a special thank you to Paul, who got my drawing up to speed for this project.

Gratitude to friends and family who read draft after draft and shared their insights and suggestions. Kathy, Rick, Trin and Linda—you're amazing! And to all of my friends who offered support, encouragement and love to me through the entire process—you're awesome!

Resources

Books about Trauma & Multiplicity:

Who Parked the Car? Exercises for Multiples, by Ellyn Stevens—available on Amazon

United We Stand, Eliana Gil, PhD

Trauma & Recovery, Judith Herman, MD

Waking the Tiger, Peter Levine, PhD (He has a number of good books)

First Person Plural, Cameron West, PhD

Katherine, It's Time, Kit Castle and Stefan Bechtel

Book to empower girls (and child alters):

Ophelia's Oracle, Donna DeNomme and Tina Proctor

Art Books:

A Book of a Hundred Hands, George B. Bridgman

Drawing Atelier, Jon deMartin

The Practical Potter, Josie Warshaw

Polyamory Resources:

Loving More, www.lovemore.com

Jessica Fern Cooley, M.S. Psychotherapy and Coaching for Non-Monogamy, Polyamory and Alternative Relationships www.jessicaferncooley.com

Book: *What Does Polyamory Look Like*, Mim Chapman, PhD

About the Author

Ari Shaffer, MSE began her career as a psychotherapist specializing in treating trauma and addiction. Seeing a gap in services, she started a nonprofit to serve traumatized teens for which she received numerous awards. She serves on several advisory boards and mentors both coaches and therapists. She's been a contributing author to several books on business and parenting, authored a book on the mindset of successful career seekers, and authored and illustrated two children's picture books.

She continues to write in addition to providing personal coaching to her amazing clients. In her spare time, she enjoys reading, taking geeky classes, doing pottery, and maintaining a relatively unhealthy obsession with *Star Trek*.